MW01620476

Anytime Korean

Beginning 2

Sangbok Kim, Ph.D.
Jaemin Roh, Ed.D.
Danielle O. Pyun, Ph.D.

Anytime Korean Beginning 2
애니타임 한국어 초급 2

Written by Sangbok Kim, Jaemin Roh & Danielle O. Pyun
Edited by Yejoo Lee
Designed by Eun Jeong Lim
Illustrations by Jae Young Lee

Published by KONG & PARK USA, INC.
1480 Renaissance Drive, Suite 412
Park Ridge, IL 60068 USA
Tel +1 (847) 241 4845
Fax +1 (312) 757 5553
usaoffice@kongnpark.com
www.kongnpark.com

1st published March 1, 2020
2nd printing, October 25, 2021

ISBN 978-1-63519-016-8

Library of Congress Control Number: 2019954015

DISTRIBUTORS

United States: KONG & PARK USA, INC.
1480 Renaissance Drive, Suite 412
Park Ridge, IL 60068
Tel +1 (847) 241 4845
Fax +1 (312) 757 5553
usaoffice@kongnpark.com

South America: KONG & PARK CHILE SPA.
Presidente Riesco 5435, Of. 1601, Las Condes
Santiago, 7561127 Chile
Tel: +56 22 833 9055
chileoffice@kongnpark.com

Other countries: KONG & PARK, INC.
85, Gwangnaru-ro 56-gil, Prime center 1518
Gwangjin-gu, Seoul, 05116 Korea
Tel +82 (0)2 565 1537
Fax +82 (0)2 3445 1080
info@kongnpark.com

Printed in Korea

Table of Contents

Preface

The Anytime Korean Textbook Series is an interactive and engaging learning material. The series provides powerful practices for acquiring conversation skills in Korean easily through carefully designed systematic learning steps grounded in pedagogic research that is proven most effective. In our program, learners can practice Korean via various platforms including print, web resources, and mobile app devices. The series and the accompanying audios, videos, and online resources help learners build hands-on communication skills in Korean through an integrated practice of listening, speaking, reading, and writing.

Anytime Korean Beginning 2 aims to provide a solid foundation in Korean, high-frequency vocabulary, common sentence patterns, and phrases for daily communication continuing from Anytime Korean Beginning 1. An emphasis is placed on the ability to apply the target expressions and associated functions in various encounters in life.

Each lesson of the book consists of two major parts. The first part includes model conversation, vocabulary, expressions, sentence patterns, practice and culture. These serve as the building blocks for the next sequence, a conversation-oriented language application practice set.
The second part includes three-part application exercises: listen & discuss, guided conversation, and spontaneous conversation, reflecting the theories of Scaffolding, Zone of Proximal Development, and Comprehensible Input.

The content, procedures, and layout presented in this book are a result of the collaboration of the three authors' experiences in teaching Korean for many years. Dialogues and examples in this book are based on and informed by conversational analysis research. The authors made attempts to use authentic language and include culture in the book. The model conversations in this edition best reflect contemporary Korean used by Korean native speakers in their 20s and 30s. They include contemporary and colloquial expressions, such as shortened forms of words, with explanations of formal or unabbreviated and full expressions as needed.

Intended users

Anytime Korean Beginning 2 is for learners who studied Anytime Korean Beginning 1. The book can be used for classroom instruction, online courses, or self-study. The book series is accompanied by Anytime Korean learning website which provides interactive self-study materials. (See AnytimeKorean.com for more information.)

Acknowledgements

The three authors contributed equally to this book. The authors would like to express their gratitude to the individuals who have helped improving the manuscript of this book at different stages: Nhi Do, Jennie Oh, Alexis Bauer, Caitriona Techman, and Jiwon Kim, who reviewed and proofread the manuscript closely from a learner's perspective and offered feedback and suggestions; and Dr. Hee Seung Suh, who reviewed the manuscript from a teacher's perspective. The authors also give their thanks to the students who appear as the main characters in the conversations: Jiwon Kim (as Amy Lee), Hoon Park (as Minjoon Kim), Mia Cheatle (as Jessica Jones), Jianhao Wang (as Xiaoming Huang) and Shana Williams (as Shana Williams).

How to use this book

Use the following chart to find the best sequence of study. The Conversation, New Words & Expressions, Patterns, Expressions & Practice, Culture, Listen & Discuss, Guided Conversation, and Spontaneous Conversation sections are included in the textbook. Pronunciation Practice, Interpretation Practice, and Performance Practice are available online at AnytimeKorean.com or with the mobile application.

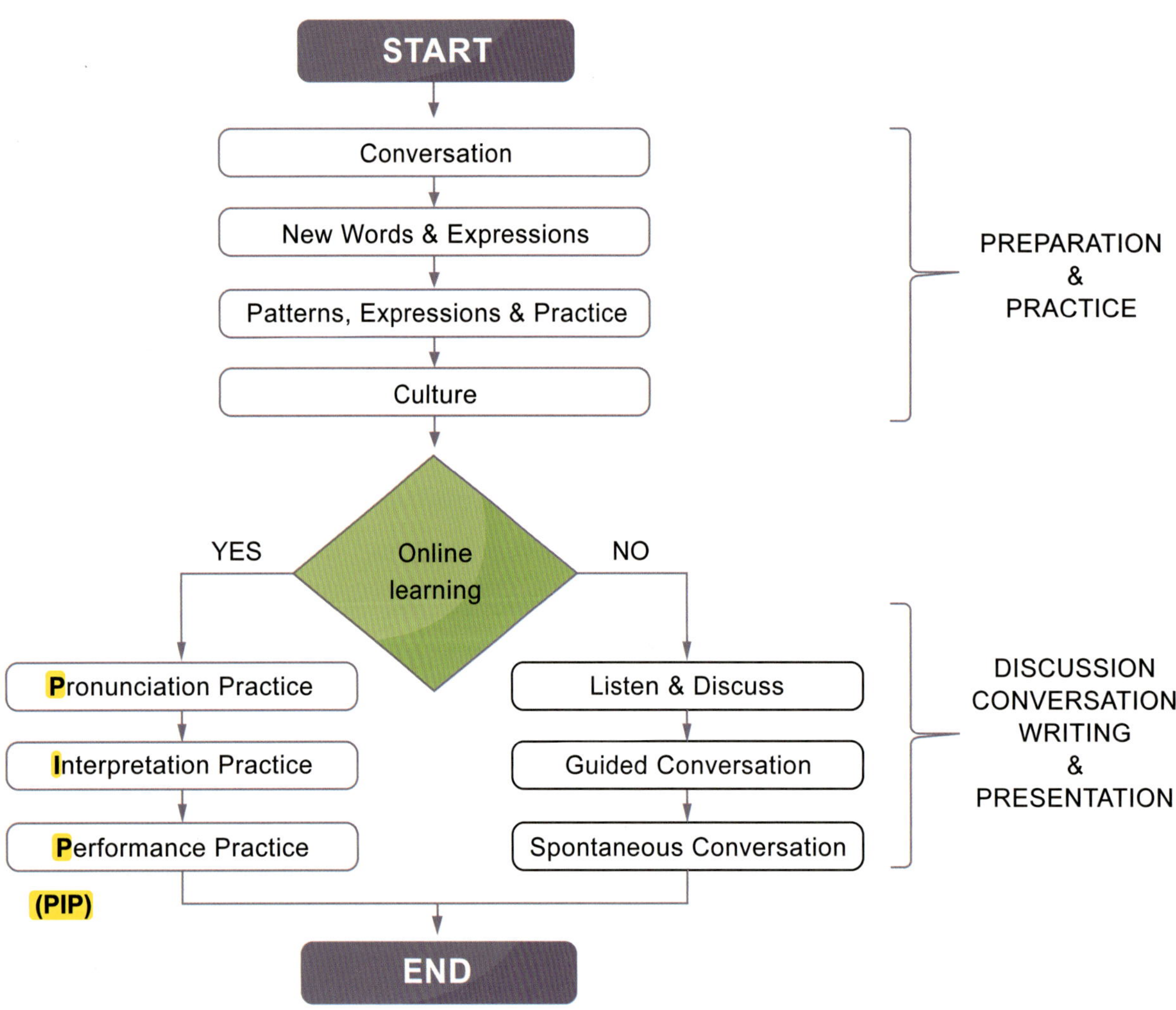

• Title Page

The title page of each lesson gives you an overview of the content, including the learning objectives, key expressions, culture notes, and conversation activities. It also features a comic that shows the context of the lesson's model conversation. A video dramatization of the model conversation is also available at AnytimeKorean.com.

• New Words & Expressions

This section includes vocabulary and expressions from the model conversation. Audio is available at AnytimeKorean.com to aid in your practice of the pronunciation of new words and expressions. The exercises that follow test your knowledge of not only the new words and expressions, but also the words and expressions you learned in previous lessons.

• Patterns, Expressions & Practice

Here you will find explanations of the key grammar patterns and expressions introduced in the model conversation and practice their usage through examples and exercises. This section will help you get ready for the following sections of Listen & Discuss, Guided Conversation, and Spontaneous Conversation. Audio is available at AnytimeKorean.com.

• Culture

The culture section offers insight into Korean culture. The information in this section provides additional vocabulary and expressions which will help you expand your Korean usage. They will be used in the next sections, Guided Conversation and Spontaneous Conversation.

• Listen & Discuss

This section checks your comprehension of the model conversation and provides space for discussion. While you discuss your understanding of the conversation with your classmates, you can practice writing in Korean simultaneously. Audio is available at AnytimeKorean.com.

• Guided Conversation

Following specific guidance, you will engage in conversation activity by taking turns with a partner and responding appropriately to the given options for further conversation practice and application. Complete your version of conversation and act it out without looking at the written script. Through this activity, you can learn and use additional expressions related to the topic, while utilizing the target grammar points actively in a different context and improve your fluency.

• Spontaneous Conversation

This is the last stage of the conversation activities. This section may involve several kinds of speaking activities. You may (1) interview your classmates (or people) and (2) create a modified version of the model conversation. For the interview, you will write down the information you collected from the people you interviewed and present it orally. Alternatively, you may also create a conversation that reflects your own situations using the model conversation or the guided conversation as an example. Present the conversation in class without looking at any written script. Through this activity, you will improve all four language dimensions: speaking, listening, writing, and reading fluency.

Main characters in this book

1. Kim Minjoon: A Korean man who works as an intern at a company in New York. He is 24 years old.

2. Amy Lee: A Korean-American woman who is working as an intern at a company in New York. She is a junior in college.

3. Jessica Jones: An American woman who is a junior in college. She is taking a Korean language class. She cooks Korean food and is interested in Korean culture.

4. Huang Xiaoming: A Chinese student who is a sophomore at an American university. He is taking a Korean class with Jessica. He is interested in Korean culture and food.

5. Shana Williams: An Indian-American who is Minjoon's colleague at a company in New York. She is a member of the Korean Conversation Club.

Kim Minjoon　Jessica Jones　Huang Xiaoming　Amy Lee　Shana Williams

Scope and Sequence

Lesson	11	12	13	14	15
Topics	지금 몇 시예요? What time is it now?	김밥 좀 드세요. Please have some *gimbap*.	저는 이제 스물 다섯이 돼요. I am now becoming 25 years old.	오늘 정말 춥네요. It is really cold today.	우리 점심 먹으러 가요. Let's go to eat lunch.
Objectives	Talking about one's daily agenda and arranging a meeting	Talking about Korean food and recipes	1. Talking about one's age 2. Reading and saying months, dates, and days of the week on a calendar	1. Talking about weather conditions 2. Talking about temperature	Talking about what to eat for lunch
Preparation & Practices	Conversation I. New Words & Expressions II. Patterns, Expressions & Practice 1. Telling time in Korean (Korean numerals) 2. Verb/Adjective base + 아서요/어서요 "It is because ..." 3. NOUN + 에 vs. NOUN + 에서 "at/on/in/to ~ " III. Culture Times of the day	Conversation I. New Words & Expressions II. Patterns, Expressions & Practice 1. Past tense: Verb/Adjective base + 았어요/었어요 2. Object marker: -을/-를 3. Who ... What ... Verb/Adjective. 4. ~네요: Expressing the speaker's spontaneous reaction or realization III. Culture Korean food made with *jang*	Conversation I. New Words & Expressions II. Patterns, Expressions & Practice 1. Talking about one's age (Korean numerals) 2. Expressing a date 3. Noun + 으로 보여요/로 보여요 "to look like ~" 4. Adjective + 아/어 보여요 "to look ~" III. Culture Meeting new people and asking about their age	Conversation I. New Words & Expressions II. Patterns, Expressions & Practice 1. ~이면/~면, ~으면/~면 "if ...; when ..." 2. Weather expressions 3. ~아지다/ ~어지다 "to become ~" 4. ~아 죽다/~어 죽다 "~ to death" III. Culture Weather conditions in Korea	Conversation I. New Words & Expressions II. Patterns, Expressions & Practice 1. Responding to a negative question 2. ~으러 가다/~러 가다 "to go for the purpose of ~" 3. ~아 봤다/~어 봤다 "to have done ~" 4. ~는데, ~은/~ㄴ데, ~인데 "... and/so/but" III. Culture Everyday Korean meals
Discussion Conversation Writing & Presentation	IV. Listen & Discuss V. Guided Conversation VI. Spontaneous Conversation	IV. Listen & Discuss V. Guided Conversation VI. Spontaneous Conversation	IV. Listen & Discuss V. Guided Conversation VI. Spontaneous Conversation	IV. Listen & Discuss V. Guided Conversation VI. Spontaneous Conversation	IV. Listen & Discuss V. Guided Conversation VI. Spontaneous Conversation

16	17	18	19	20
생일 축하해요! Happy birthday!	한국말 정말 잘하시네요! You speak Korean very well!	소개팅 하실래요? Would you like to go on a blind date?	시간 있으면 보통 뭐하세요? What do you usually do when you have time?	지난번 소개팅은 어땠어요? How was the blind date last time?
Celebrating a birthday and giving a gift	Complimenting one's ability and talking about one's future plans	Introducing a person and setting up an appointment	Talking about hobbies	Explaining the situation and making an offer
Conversation I. New Words & Expressions II. Patterns, Expressions & Practice 1. -한테; -한테서 "to [person]; from [person]" 2. ~지만 "... but; although ..." 3. -아 보세요/~어 보세요. "Please try (doing)" 4. ~아봐도 돼요?/~어봐도 돼요? "Is it okay to try to ~?; May I try to ~?" 5. Non-honorific speech level : The "~아" speech style III. Culture Counting age, birthday food, and important birthdays	Conversation I. New Words & Expressions II. Patterns, Expressions & Practice 1. ~을 거예요/~ㄹ 거예요 "will ~" [prediction; volition] 2. Sentence ending ~지요?/~죠? : Seeking the listener's agreement 3. -으로/-로 "by~; in ~; with ~" [Instrument/means] 4. 잘해요; 못해요; 잘 못 해요 : Expressing one's ability 5. ~으려고 하다/~려고 하다 "intend to ~" ~으려고/~려고 "intending to ~; in order to ~" 6. ~는데도, ~은/~ㄴ데도, ~인데도 "even though... ; even if ..." III. Culture Courteous responses to compliments	Conversation I. New Words & Expressions II. Patterns, Expressions & Practice 1. NOUN + 동안; Verb base + 는 동안 "during/for ~; while ~ing" 2. Noun-modifying forms of verbs 3. Noun-modifying forms of adjectives 4. Describing people's appearances 5. 이; 그; 저 "this; that; that over there" 6. ~거든요 "It is because ... ; ..., you see." III. Culture Culture of blind dating in Korea	Conversation I. New Words & Expressions II. Patterns, Expressions & Practice 1. ~다가 : Depicting transition from one event to another 2. 어떤 + NOUN "which ~/what kind of ~; some/any ~" 3. Honorific speech level : The ~습니다 speech style 4. -겠- "must" 5. Frequency expressions 6. -도 하고 -도 하고 "to do NOUN 1 and to do NOUN 2 as well" III. Culture Popular hobbies in Korea	Conversation I. New Words & Expressions II. Patterns, Expressions & Practice 1. 주다, 주시다, 드리다 "to give" 2. ~아 주다/~어 주다 "to do (something) for (someone)" ~아 주시다/~어 주시다 ~아 드리다/~어 드리다 3. ~기로 하다 "to decide to ~" 4. -을/-를 하다 "(for someone) to do (something)" -이/-가 되다 "(for something) to be done" 5. 지난/이번/다음+NOUN "last/this/next ~" III. Culture Popular dating places and activities in Korea
IV. Listen & Discuss V. Guided Conversation VI. Spontaneous Conversation	IV. Listen & Discuss V. Guided Conversation VI. Spontaneous Conversation	IV. Listen & Discuss V. Guided Conversation VI. Spontaneous Conversation	IV. Listen & Discuss V. Guided Conversation VI. Spontaneous Conversation	IV. Listen & Discuss V. Guided Conversation VI. Spontaneous Conversation

11 지금 몇 시예요?

What time is it now?

Talking about one's daily agenda and arranging a meeting

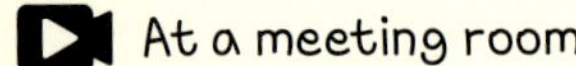

08 네, 그래요. 그럼, 제가 나중에 문자할게요.

09 네~그럼 이따가 봐요.

Preparation & Practice	I. New Words & Expressions II. Patterns, Expressions & Practice 1. Telling time in Korean (Korean numerals) 2. Verb/Adjective base + 아서요/어서요 It is because ... 3. NOUN + 에서 vs. NOUN + 에 at/on/in/from/to ~ III. Culture Times of the day
Conversation Activities	IV. Listen & Discuss V. Guided Conversation VI. Spontaneous Conversation

I. New Words & Expressions

 **Study the words and expressions with the audio.**  01

NOUN

수업	class
저녁	(1) evening; (2) dinner

VERB

끝나다	(for something) to end
문자하다	to text
보다	to see

ADVERB

이따(가)	later
인제	now; from now on

EXPRESSION

· 나중에	later
· 1시 45분	one o'clock forty-five minutes
· 어떡하지?	What should I/we do?; What do I/we do?
· 여기서	at here [a shortened form of 여기에서]
· (만날)까요?	Shall I/we (meet)?
· 저녁에	in the evening

Form

Dictionary form (Word base + 다)		~아요/~어요 form	~으세요/~세요 form
문자하다	to text	문자해요	문자하세요
보다	to see	봐요	보세요
끝나다	(for something) to end; to be over	끝나요	--

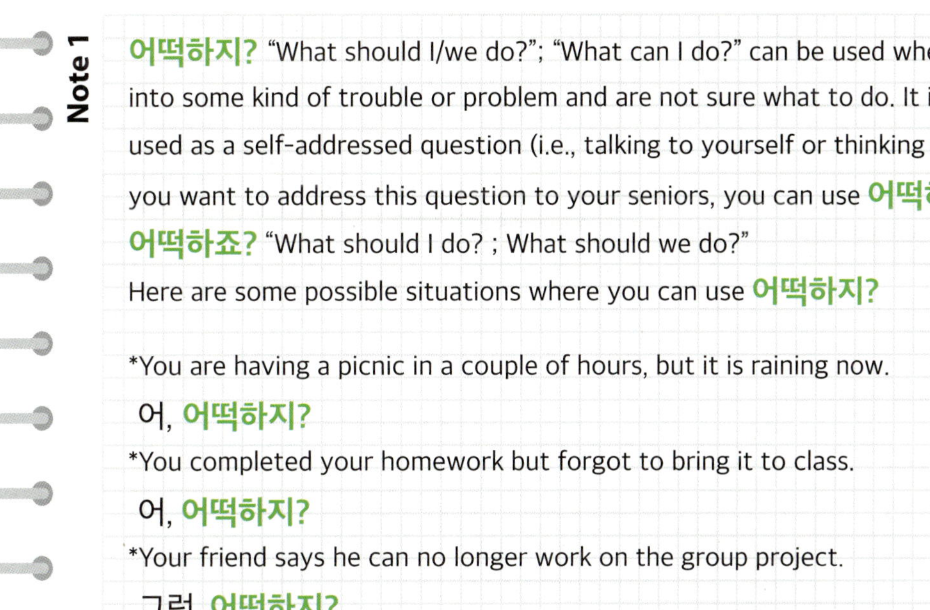

Note 1

어떡하지? "What should I/we do?"; "What can I do?" can be used when you run into some kind of trouble or problem and are not sure what to do. It is often used as a self-addressed question (i.e., talking to yourself or thinking aloud). If you want to address this question to your seniors, you can use **어떡하지요?** or **어떡하죠?** "What should I do? ; What should we do?"

Here are some possible situations where you can use **어떡하지?**

*You are having a picnic in a couple of hours, but it is raining now.
어, **어떡하지?**

*You completed your homework but forgot to bring it to class.
어, **어떡하지?**

*Your friend says he can no longer work on the group project.
그럼, **어떡하지?**

*You are on your way to an important meeting, but your car gets a flat tire.
어, **어떡하지?**

Note 2

Both **나중에** and **이따가** mean "later." **이따가** often means "a short time later," whereas **나중에** can refer to both "a short time later" or "some longer time later."

Note 3

이따가 봐요 means "See you later." There are several expressions you can use that are equivalent to "See you later." in English.

그럼, **이따가 봐요**.	See you later, then.
그럼, **이따 봐요**.	See you later, then. [이따 is a shortened form of 이따가]
그럼, **곧 봐요**.	See you soon, then.
그럼, **나중에 봐요**.	See you later, then.
그럼, **또 봐요**.	See you again, then.
그럼, **다음에 또 봐요**.	See you again next time, then.
그럼, **다음에 다시 봐요**.	See you again next time, then.
그럼, **내일 봐요**.	See you tomorrow, then.

Exercise 1

Listen to the audio and fill in the blanks. 02

1. 저 ________________ 없어요.

2. 저는 오늘 수업이 4시에 ________________.

3. 저녁에 ________________ 봐요.

4. 제가 ________________ 문자할게요.

Exercise 2

Listen to the audio and fill in the blanks. 03

1. A: 지금 ________________?

   B: 1시 45분이요.

2. A: 4시 반쯤 여기서 만날까요?

   B: 네. 그럼 ________________.

3. A: 저는 ________________. 2시에 수업이 있어서요.

   B: 아, 그래요? ________________?

II. Patterns, Expressions & Practice

1. Telling time in Korean (Korean numerals)

Usage "What time is it?" in Korean is "몇 시예요?." To tell the hour on a clock, use "native Korean (NK) numeral + 시" (e.g., 한 시 "one o'clock"; 두 시 "two o'clock").

To tell the minute on a clock, use "Sino-Korean (SK) numeral + 분" (e.g., 오 분 "five minutes"; 십 분 "ten minutes")

Telling Time			
Hour		Minute	
NK + 시		SK + 분	
한 시	1 o'clock	일 분	1 minute
두 시	2 o'clock	이 분	2 minutes
세 시	3 o'clock	삼 분	3 minutes
네 시	4 o'clock	사 분	4 minutes
다섯 시	5 o'clock	오 분	5 minutes
여섯 시	6 o'clock	육 분	6 minutes
일곱 시	7 o'clock	칠 분	7 minutes
여덟 시	8 o'clock	팔 분	8 minutes
아홉 시	9 o'clock	구 분	9 minutes
열 시	10 o'clock	십 분	10 minutes
열한 시	11 o'clock	십일 분	11 minutes
열두 시	12 o'clock	십이 분	12 minutes
		…	…
		이십 분	20 minutes
		삼십 분	30 minutes
		사십 분	40 minutes
		오십 분	50 minutes

Look at the following examples and see how the hour and minute on a clock are told.

1. A: 몇 시예요?
   B: 네 시예요.

2. A: 지금 몇 시예요?
   B: 아홉 시 사십이 분이에요.

Note 1

To tell 30 minutes on a clock, you may also use the word **반** "half" instead of 삼십 분, such as 한 시 **반** "half past one," 두 시 **반** "half past two." Do not say "**반** 분" to mean "30 minutes."

A: 지금 몇 시예요?
B: 아홉 시 **삼십** 분이에요. — It's 9:30. OR
아홉 시 **반**이에요. — It's half past nine.

Note 2

To indicate "am" or "pm," you can use **오전** "am" and **오후** "pm" before you say the hour and the minutes. Remember that in Korean, the biggest concept comes first and the smallest comes last. (The order of the time expressions: am/pm → hour → minute → second.)

9: 10: 23 am -	**오전**	아홉 시	십 분	이십삼 초
	am	hour	minute	second
5: 30: 46 pm -	**오후**	다섯 시	삼십 분	사십육 초
	pm	hour	minute	second

Note 3

As in 두 시**에** 수업이 있어요 "I have a class at 2:00," the time marker **-에** is used after a time expression (e.g., time on a clock, morning/afternoon, day, weekend). **-에** is equivalent to the English **at; on; in** according to the context.

1. 한 시**에** — at one o'clock
   두 시 삼십 분**에** — at two (o'clock) thirty (minutes)
   몇 시**에** — at what time

2. 오전**에** — in the morning
   오후**에** — in the afternoon

3. 월요일**에** — on Monday

4. 주말**에** — on the weekends

5. A: 몇 시**에** 만날래요? — At what time shall we meet?
   B: 일곱 시**에** 만나요. — Let's meet at 7:00.

6. A: 언제 만날래요? — When shall we meet?
   B: 다음 월요일**에** 만나요. — Let's meet on next Monday.

Answer the following questions in Korean.

1.

A: 몇 시예요?

B: ______________

2.

A: 몇 시예요?

B: ______________

3.

A: 몇 시예요?

B: ______________

4.

A: 몇 시예요?

B: ______________

Read the following time on a clock in a full Korean sentence.

1. 8:26 am　오전 여덟 시 이십육 분이에요.
2. 9:30 am ______________
3. 12:10 pm ______________
4. 2:15 pm ______________

Listen to the dialogue between the two people and answer the questions in Korean. 04

1. What time is it now?

____

2. At what time does the man have a meeting?

____

3. At what time does the meeting end?

____

4. At what time does the woman go home?

____

Useful expressions

끝나다　to end

Patterns, Expressions & Practice

2. Verb/adjective base + 아서요/어서요 "It is because... ."

Usage Use ~아서요/~어서요 (It is because...) when you provide just a reason or cause for the result without repeating the result (which has already been said) in your sentence. For example,

1. A: 왜 파티에 안 가세요? (RESULT) — Why aren't you going to the party?

   B1: 좀 바빠서 (REASON) (파티에 안 가)요. (RESULT) — Because I am a little busy. (I am not going to the party.)

   B2: 좀 바빠서요. (REASON) — It is because I am a little busy.

Note 1 In B1, the speaker had better not repeat "파티에 안 가"(i.e., what has already been said in A's question), which is more natural in the context. Thus B2 is preferred to B1.

Note 2 As in B2, "바빠서요" is the combination of the adjective base 바쁘 (irregular "바쁘다"), the clausal connector ~아서 "because ~," and the sentence ender ~요.
For the irregular conjugation of 바쁘다, see Appendix V, #7.

2. A: 어, 그럼 저는 인제 갈게요. (RESULT) 2시에 수업이 있어서요. (REASON)

   Um, then I will go now. Because I have class at 2 o'clock.

   B: 네. 나중에 봐요.

   Sure. See you later.

Note 3 In A, switching the order between RESULT and REASON, you may also say something like
2시에 수업이 있어서 (REASON) 그럼 저는 인제 갈게요. (RESULT)

Usage Use ~아서/~어서 in “REASON/CAUSE + ~아서/~어서 .... EFFECT/RESULT” format.

1. A: 왜 한국말을 배워요?
   B: 한국 친구가 있어서 (REASON) 한국말을 배워요. (EFFECT)

   A: Why are you learning Korean?
   B: Because I have a Korean friend, I am learning Korean.

2. A: 스티브 씨는 어떻게 지내요?
   B: 일이 많아서 (CAUSE) 바빠요. (RESULT)

   A: How is Steve doing?
   B: He is busy because he has lots of work.

Form The choice between ~아서(요) and ~어서(요) depends on the last vowel of the base form of a verb or an adjective. Note that you studied this rule in Lesson 4 (Ⅱ.3).

When the last vowel of the verb/adjective base is 아 or 오, attach ~아서(요).
좋다: 좋- + 아서(요) → 좋아서(요)
[ㅗ + 아서(요)]

1. A: 왜 파티에 안 가세요? — Why are you not going to the party?
   B: 좀 바빠서요. — It is because I am a little busy.

   바쁘다: 바쁘 + 아서요 → 바빠서요

2. A: 바쁘세요? — Are you busy?
   B: 네. 일이 많아서요. — Yes. It is because I have lots of work.

   많다: 많 + 아서요 → 많아서요

Rule2

When the last vowel of the verb/adjective base is not 아 or 오, attach ~어서(요).
먹다: 먹 + 어서(요) → 먹어서(요)
[ㅓ + 어서(요)]

1. A: 왜 내일 모임에 안 가요? — Why are you not going to the gathering tomorrow?
   B: 아르바이트가 있어서요. — It is because I have a part-time job.

   있다: 있 + 어서요 → 있어서요

2. A: 왜 한국말 배우세요? — Why do you learn Korean?
   B: 한국 친구가 있**어서요**. — It is because I have a Korean friend.

3. A: 왜 조금만 사요? — Why are you buying only a little?
   B: 돈이 없**어서요**. — It is because I don't have money.

없다 : 없 + 어서요 → 없어서(요)

4. 돈이 없**어서** 조금만 사요.
   Because I don't have money, I buy only a little.

When the verb/adjective base ends in ~하다, use **해서요**.
공부하다 → 공부**해서요**.

A: 왜 피곤해요? — Why are you tired?
B: 저녁 늦게까지 공부**해서요**. — It is because I studied until late at night.

Here are more examples which are frequently used in daily conversation:

늦**어서요**.	It is because (I) am late.
아파**서요**.	It is because (I) am sick.
배가 불러**서요**.	It is because (I) am full.
재미있**어서요**.	It is because it is fun.
재미없**어서요**.	It is because it is not fun.
맛있**어서요**.	It is because it is tasty.
맛없**어서요**.	It is because it is not tasty.
매워**서요**.	It is because it is spicy.
비싸**서요**.	It is because it is expensive.
비가 와**서요**.	It is because it rains.

Useful expressions

늦다	to be late
아프다	to be sick
배가 부르다	to be full
맵다	to be spicy
비가 오다	to rain [Lit., (for rain) to come]

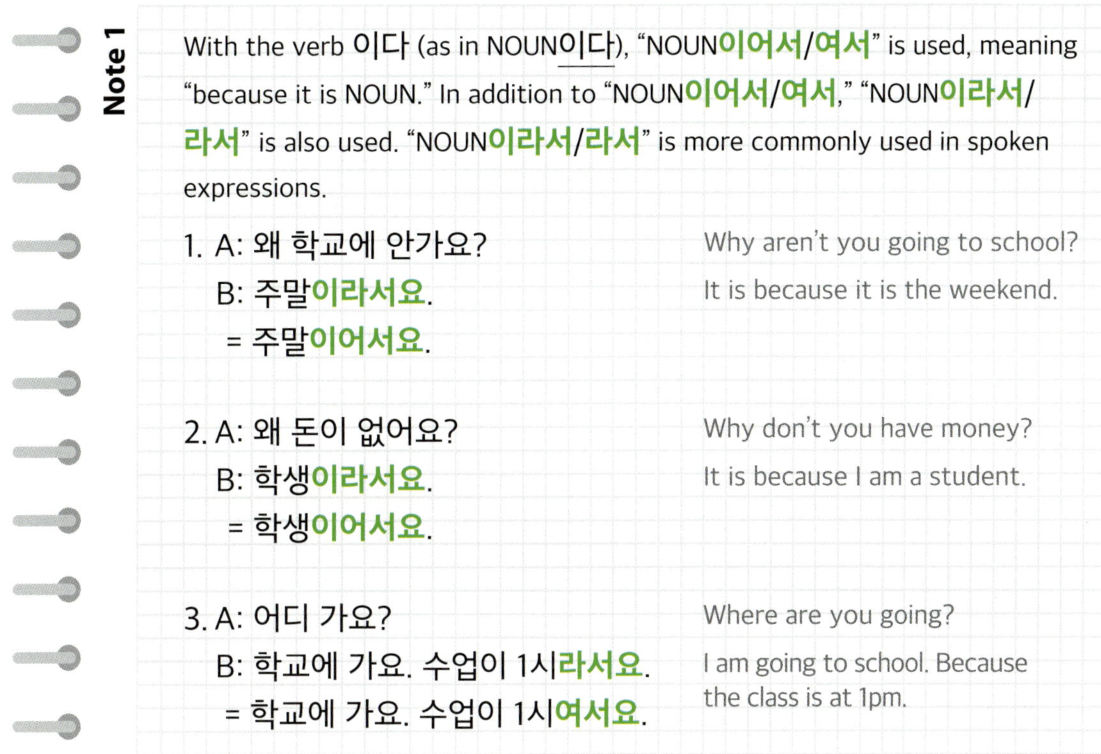

Note 1

With the verb 이다 (as in NOUN이다), "NOUN**이어서/여서**" is used, meaning "because it is NOUN." In addition to "NOUN**이어서/여서**," "NOUN**이라서/라서**" is also used. "NOUN**이라서/라서**" is more commonly used in spoken expressions.

1. A: 왜 학교에 안가요? — Why aren't you going to school?
   B: 주말**이라서요**. — It is because it is the weekend.
   = 주말**이어서요**.

2. A: 왜 돈이 없어요? — Why don't you have money?
   B: 학생**이라서요**. — It is because I am a student.
   = 학생**이어서요**.

3. A: 어디 가요? — Where are you going?
   B: 학교에 가요. 수업이 1시**라서요**. — I am going to school. Because the class is at 1pm.
   = 학교에 가요. 수업이 1시**여서요**.

Your friend is asking some questions. Respond to the questions using ~아서요/~어서요.

1. A: 왜 샐러드를 안 먹어요?
   B: (맛없다) ______________________.

2. A: 왜 이 시계 안 사요?
   B: (비싸다) ______________________.

3. A: 오늘 한국 영화 클럽 모임에 가요?
   B: 아니요. 좀 (바쁘다) ______________________.

4. A: 지금 바쁘세요?
   B: 네. 한국어하고 수학 숙제가 (있다) ______________________.

Useful expressions

샐러드	salad
시계	watch
수학	math

Complete the following sentences by choosing appropriate expressions from the box below.

늦어서	아파서	배가 불러서	비가 와서	수업이 없어서
맛있어서	숙제가 많아서			

1. A: ____________ 학교에 안 가요.
   B: 저도 감기에 걸려서 못 가요.

2. A: ____________ 등산 못 가요.
   B: 네. 요즘 날씨가 너무 안 좋아요.

3. A: ____________ 미안해요.
   B: 괜찮아요. 지금 10시 10분이에요.

4. A: ____________ 조금 바빠요.
   B: 몇 과목 들어요?

5. A: 왜 안 먹어요?
   B: ____________ 못 먹어요.

Useful expressions

감기에 걸리다	to catch a cold
등산(을)가다	to go hiking; to go mountain climbing
미안하다	to be sorry
과목	course; subject
몇 과목 들어요?	How many classes do you take?
배(가) 불러서	because (I) am full

Match the most appropriate conversation pair.

1. 백화점 세일이라서 · · a. 수업이 없어요.
2. 휴일이라서 · · b. 쇼핑하러 가요.
3. 채식주의자라서 · · c. 바쁠 거예요.
4. 다음 주가 시험이라서 · · d. 고기를 안 먹어요.
5. 집이 지하철 옆이라서 · · e. 아주 편해요.

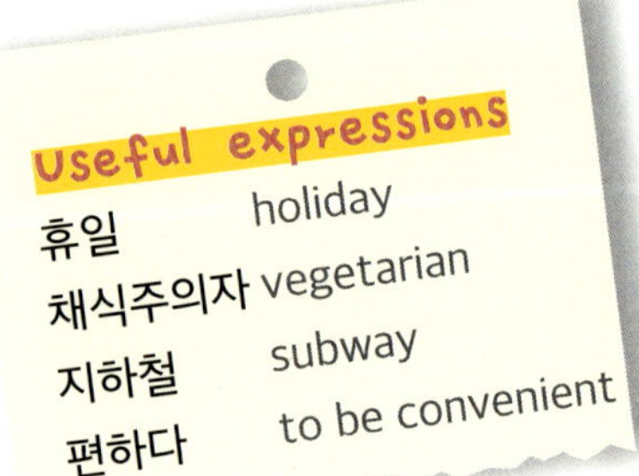

Taking turns with a partner, ask each other the reason for learning Korean. Respond by choosing from the following expressions.

1. 한국 문화를 좋아해서요.
2. 동아시아에 관심이 있어서요.
3. 북한 문제에 관심이 있어서요.
4. 한국 e-sports에 관심이 있어서요.
5. 한국 경제에 관심이 있어서요.
6. 한국 노래를 좋아해서요.
7. K-pop을 좋아해서요.
8. 한국 드라마를 좋아해서요.
9. 남자 친구/여자 친구가 한국 사람이라서요.
10. 엄마가 한국 사람이라서요.
11. 아빠가 한국 사람이라서요.
12. 할머니가 한국 사람이라서요.
13. 할아버지가 한국 사람이라서요.

1. A: 왜 한국어 배워요?
   B: 한국 문화를 좋아해서요.

2. A: 왜 한국어 배워요?
   B: ______________________________.

(Continue and practice the rest of expressions above.)

Useful expressions

한국 문화	Korean culture	동아시아	East Asia
~에 관심이 있다	to be interested in ~	북한	North Korea
북한 문제	the North Korean issue	경제	economics
노래	song	좋아하다	to like
남자 친구	boyfriend	여자 친구	girlfriend
엄마	mom	아빠	dad
할머니	grandmother	할아버지	grandfather

Listen to the conversation between Minjoon and Amy and answer the questions in Korean. 05

1. A: 한국영화클럽 미팅은 언제예요?

   B: ________________________________

2. A: 미팅은 몇 시에 있어요?

   B: ________________________________

3. A: 에이미 씨는 미팅에 가요? 못 가요? 왜요?

   B: ________________________________

4. A: 민준 씨는 미팅에 가요? 못 가요? 왜요?

   B: ________________________________

Useful expressions

이번 주 this week
아르바이트 part-time job

3. NOUN + 에서 vs. NOUN + 에 "at/on/in/from/to ~"

Usage **-에서** is a location marker. It has different functions depending on the context. The usage is similar to **at**, **on**, **in**, **from**, or **to** in English.

1. Dynamic location/Activity place + **에서** ... activity verb.

1. 저는 도서관**에서** 공부해요. I study **in** the library.
2. 집**에서** 점심 먹어요. I eat lunch **at** home.
3. 거기**서** 만날까요? Should we meet there? [Lit., Should we meet **at** there.]

Note 1 에 in "interrogative pronoun (e.g., 거기) + 에서" drops. Thus, 거기**에서** becomes 거기**서**.

2. Departing point or source + 에서

1. A: 어디서 출발해요? — Where do you depart from? [출발하다 to depart]
   B: 시카고에서 출발해요. — I depart from Chicago.

Note 2 에 in "interrogative pronoun (e.g., 어디) + 에서" drops. Thus, 어디에서 becomes 어디서.

2. A: 어디서 와요? — Where do you come from?
   B: 시카고에서 와요. — I come from Chicago.

3. 시카고에서 뉴욕까지 두 시간 걸려요. — From Chicago to New York, it takes 2 hours.

Usage The other location marker -에 was introduced in Lesson 6 (II.1). Let's review the usages of -에. -에 is used with a noun of location, destination, or time and is equivalent to **at**, **in**, **on** or **to** in English.

1. Static location + 에 ... state verb (e.g., 있다, 계시다, 많다).

1. 마크는 지금 LA에 있어요. — Mark is in LA now.
2. 에이미는 지금 집에 없어요. — Amy is not at home now.
3. 서울에 미국 사람이 많아요. — In Seoul, there are many Americans. [Lit., In Seoul, Americans are many.]

2. Destination + 에 ... coming-going/directional verb (e.g., 오다, 가다).

1. 한국영화클럽 모임에 가세요? — Are you going to the Korean movie club gathering?
2. 내일 학교에 와요? — Are you coming to school tomorrow?
3. 한국 마켓에 자주 가요? — Do you go to the Korean market often?

3. Time + 에 ...

1. 한 시에 수업이 있어요. — I have a class at one o'clock.
2. 주말에 영화 볼까요? — Should we watch a movie on the weekend?
3. 다섯 시에 만나요. — Let's meet at five o'clock.

Note 1

Sometimes you may use either **-에** or **-에서** with the same verb depending on your intention. For example,

1. 저는 뉴욕**에** 살아요. I live in New York.
2. 저는 뉴욕**에서** 살아요. I live in New York.

In 1, 살다 is used as a state verb (i.e., the state of living). However, in 2, 살다 is used as an activity verb (i.e., the activity of living).

Note 2

Both **-에** and **-에서** are location markers. Let's compare the usages of **-에** and **-에서** more thoroughly. See the different usages in the following examples:

1. 에이미는 도서관**에** 있어요.	(o)	Amy is in the library.
에이미는 도서관**에서** 공부해요.	(o)	Amy studies in the library.
에이미는 도서관**에** 공부해요.	(x)	[공부하다 is an activity verb, not a state verb.]
2. 마크는 서울**에** 있어요.	(o)	Mark is in Seoul. [Lit., Mark exists in Seoul.]
마크는 서울**에서** 영어를 가르쳐요.	(o)	Mark teaches English in Seoul.
마크는 서울**에** 영어를 가르쳐요.	(x)	[가르치다 is an activity verb, not a state verb.]

Fill in the blanks with the correct location marker by choosing 에 or 에서.

1. 저는 지금 오피스_____ 있어요.

2. 저는 지금 오피스_____ 일해요.

3. A: 보통 어디_____ 점심 먹어요?

   B: 보통 학교 카페테리아_____ 먹어요.

4. 디즈니 랜드는 LA_____ 있어요. 디즈니 월드는 플로리다_____ 있어요.

5. A: 서울_____ 맥도날드 있어요?

   B: 네, 서울_____ 맥도날드 많아요.

6. A: 마크는 서울_____ 뭐 해요?

   B: 서울_____ 한국어 배워요.

Listen to the conversation between Amy and Minjoon and fill in the blanks below in Korean. 06

1. 민준 씨 동생은 ________________ 살아요.

2. 민준 씨 동생은 ________________ 대학교에 다녀요.

3. 에이미 씨 언니도 ________________ 있어요.

4. 에이미 씨 언니는 ________________ ________________ 가르쳐요.

Useful expressions

다니다	to attend
우리 언니	my sister [Lit., our sister]
가르치다	to teach

You are at an international student meeting in Seoul. Tell people where you are from using the expression "-에서 왔어요" (came from) and tell them where your city is located. The following is a sample conversation.

싱유: 저는 광저우에서 왔어요. 광저우는 중국에 있어요.

마크: 저는 데이턴에서 왔어요. 데이턴은 미국 오하이오에 있어요.

민: 저는 하노이에서 왔어요. 하노이는 베트남에 있어요.

미셸: 저는 쿠알라룸푸르에서 왔어요. 쿠알라룸푸르는 말레이시아에 있어요.

____

____

____

III. Culture

Times of the day

Here are some useful words referring to different times of a day.

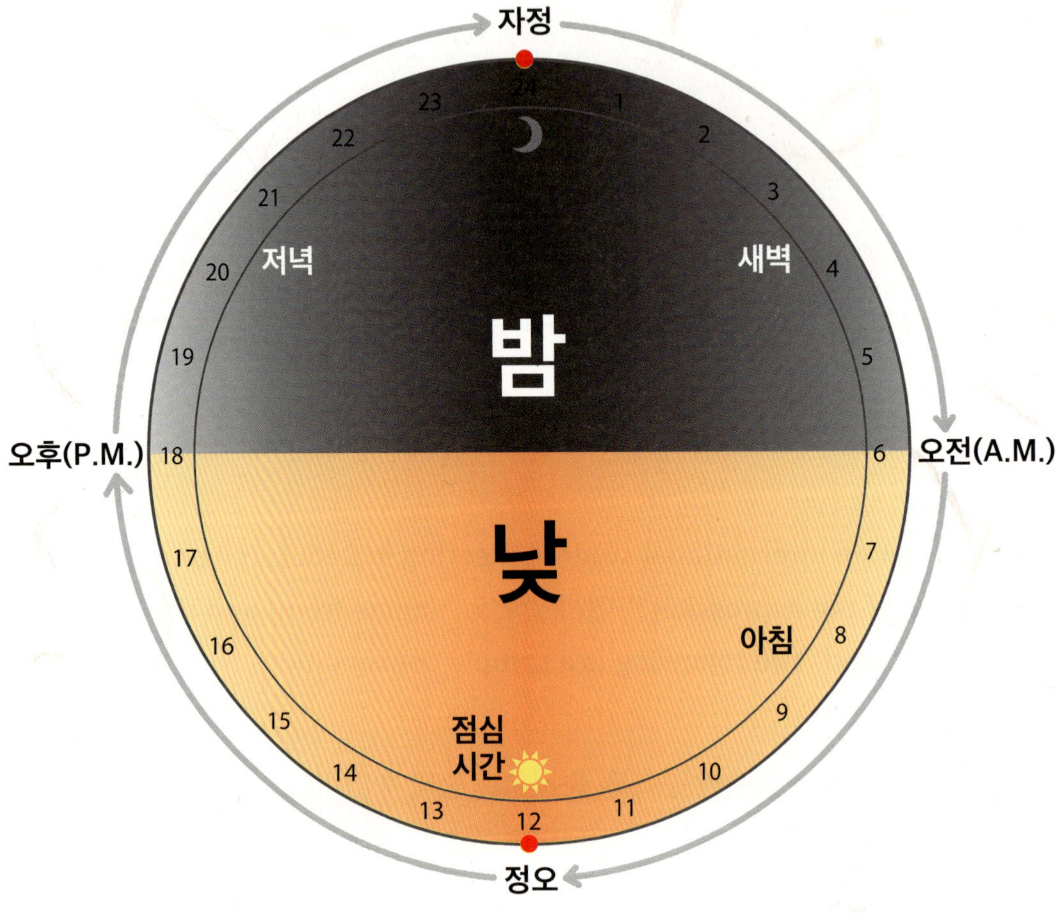

오전	A.M.	오후	P.M.
자정	midnight (12:00am)	정오	noon (12:00pm)
새벽	early morning	점심시간	lunchtime
아침	morning	저녁	evening

낮 (day) vs. 밤 (night)

Note that **아침** and **저녁** literally mean morning and evening, respectively. They are also used to refer to breakfast and dinner, respectively in another context.

IV. Listen & Discuss

☞ **Jessica and Xiaoming are talking about a group project together. Listen to the conversation carefully. Discuss the answers to the following questions with your classmates. Then write the answer in a full Korean sentence in the space provided.**

1. 지금 몇 시예요?

2. 제시카는 오늘 오후 몇 시에 수업이 있어요?

3. 제시카는 오늘 몇 시에 수업이 끝나요? [끝나다 to end]

4. 샤오밍은 오늘 수업이 있어요?

5. 제시카와 샤오밍은 오늘 몇 시에 다시 만나요?

6. 누가 누구한테 나중에 문자를 보내요?

Script

Jessica and Xiaoming are talking about a group project together.

01 제시카: 지금 몇 시예요?

02 샤오밍: 1시 45분이요.[II.1]

03 제시카: 어, 그럼 저는 인제 갈게요. 2시에 수업이 있어서요.[II.2]

04 샤오밍: 아, 그래요? 어... 그럼 어떡하지?

05 제시카: 음. 저녁에 다시 봐요.[II.3]

06 저는 수업이 4시에 끝나요. 샤오밍 씨는요?

07 샤오밍: 전 오늘 수업 없어요. 그럼, 4시 반쯤에 여기서 다시 만날까요?

08 제시카: 네, 그래요. 그럼, 제가 나중에 문자할게요.

09 샤오밍: 네~ 그럼 이따가 봐요.

01 Jessica : What time is it now?

02 Xiaoming: It's 1:45 p.m.

03 Jessica : Um, then I will go now. (Because) I have a class at 2 o'clock.

04 Xiaoming: Oh, is that so? (Talking to himself) Um, what should I do?

05 Jessica : Uh... let's see each other in the evening again.

06 My class ends at 4 o'clock. How about you, Xiaoming?

07 Xiaoming: I don't have class today. Then should we meet here again around 4:30?

08 Jessica : Yes, let's do that. Then, I will text you later.

09 Xiaoming: Yeah~ see you later, then.

V. Guided Conversation

☞ **With the organization of the model conversation in Listen & Discuss (Script) in mind, practice the modified conversation below with your partner.**

step 1 **Two classmates (A,B) are scheduling the next meeting for a class project. Practice the following conversation with your partner, choosing one of the options in (   ) to make the conversation flow naturally.**

01 A: 지금 몇 시예요?

02 B: ____________ 이요.
(10:50; 1:45; 2:23; 3:50)

03 A: 어, 그럼 저는 인제 갈게요. ____________ 에 수업이 있어서요.
(11:00; 2:00; 2:30; 4:00)

04 B: 아, 그래요? 그럼....

05 A: 음. ____________ 다시 봐요.
(점심 때; 오후에; 저녁에)

06 저는 수업이 ____________ 에 끝나요. ____________ 씨는요?
(12:30; 3:45; 3:30; 5:20) (B's name)

07 B: 전 오늘 수업 없어요. 그럼 ____________ 쯤 여기서 다시 ____________?
(12:40; 3:55; 4:00; 5:30) (만날까요; 볼까요)

08 A: 네, 그래요. 그럼, 제가 나중에 문자할게요.

09 A: 네~ 그럼 ____________ 봐요.
(이따가; 나중에)

(Switch roles and continue to practice.)

Guided Conversation

step 2 **Present the conversation from Step 1 in front of the class. Try not to read!**

VI. Spontaneous Conversation

Now is your chance to have real interactions with your classmates in Korean. You can practice speaking with your classmates, writing, and presenting in front of the class!

step 1

Using the information below, set up the next meeting for the ongoing project with your partner. Create a conversation with your partner similarly to the one that you practiced in the Guided Conversation.

	A's schedule	B's schedule
오전	Korean class (10:00 am - 10:50 am)	Korean Movie Club meeting (11:00 am - 11:50 am)
오후	Meeting another friend (12:00 pm - 12:40 pm)	Working at a Korean restaurant (1:00 pm - 3:30 pm)

step 2

Write down the conversation you had with your partner in Step 1.

Present what you wrote in Step 2 in front of the class. Try not to read it!

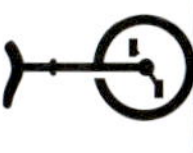

12 김밥 좀 드세요.

Please have some *gimbap*.

Talking about Korean food and recipes

Preparation & Practice	I. New Words & Expressions II. Patterns, Expressions & Practice 1. Past tense: Verb/Adjective base + 았어요/었어요 2. Object marker: -을/-를 3. Who ... What ... Verb/Adjective. 4. ~네요. Expressing the speaker's spontaneous reaction or realization III. Culture Korean food made with *jang*
Conversation Activities	IV. Listen & Discuss V. Guided Conversation VI. Spontaneous Conversation

I. New Words & Expressions

 **Study the words and expressions with the audio.** 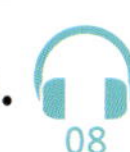 08

NOUN

고기	meat
고추장	gochujang (red pepper paste)
김밥	*gimbap* (seaweed rice roll)
당근	carrot
떡	rice cake
떡볶이	*tteokboggi* (stir-fried rice cakes)
마트	mart; supermarket
맛	taste
밥	cooked rice
설탕	sugar
시금치	spinach
양파	onion
인터넷	Internet
전	as for me [the shortened form of 저는]

VERB

드시다	(1) to eat; (2) to drink [honorific form of 들다, 먹다, 마시다]
들어가다	to go in; enter
만들다	to make
맛(을) 보다	to taste; try something's taste
배우다	to learn
사다	to buy

ADJECTIVE

대단하다	to be great; tremendous; incredible

MARKER

-에서	at ~ (e.g., 한국마트에서)

EXPRESSION

· 아침에	in the morning

Form

Dictionary form (Word base + 다)	~아요/~어요 form	~으세요/~세요 form
들어가다 to go in	들어가요	들어가세요
배우다 to learn	배워요	배우세요
사다 to buy	사요	사세요

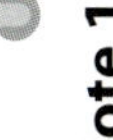

Note 1

These are photos of Korean foods and ingredients.

1. 고추장 2. 김밥 3. 떡 4. 떡볶이

Note 2

드시다 is the honorific form of 들다 "to eat; drink," 먹다 "to eat," and 마시다 "to drink."

Dictionary form (Word base + 다)		~아요 ~어요 form	~으세요/~세요 form
들다	to eat/drink	들어요	드세요
먹다	to eat	먹어요	드세요
마시다	to drink	마셔요(마시+어요)	드세요

Note 3

-에서 "from ~" vs. -한테서 "from ~"

1. Use -에서 after a place noun: [Place] + 에서

저는 서울에서 왔어요. I came from Seoul.
인터넷에서 배웠어요. (I) learned (it) from the Internet.

2. Use -한테서 after a person: [Person] + 한테서

에이미한테서 배웠어요. (I) learned (it) from Amy.
마크한테서 들었어요. (I) heard (it) from Mark.

Listen to the audio and fill in the blanks. 

1.

____

2.

____

3.

____

4.

____

Listen to the audio and fill in the blanks.

1. A: 김밥 ________________________.

   B: 어, 제시카 씨가 만들었어요?

2. A: 전 떡볶이를 만들었어요. 맛 좀 보세요.

   B: 음~ ________________________.

3. A: 여기 뭐 들어갔어요?

   B: ____________하고 ____________하고 ____________요.

4. A: ____________________ 배웠어요?

   B: 인터넷에서요.

II. Patterns, Expressions & Practice

1. Past tense: Verb/Adjective base + 았어요/었어요

Usage By adding ~았어요/~었어요 to a verb or adjective base, you can express past tense in Korean.

1. 오늘 학교에 가요.	I go to school today.
어제 학교에 **갔어요**.	I **went** to school yesterday.
2. 지금 점심 먹어요.	I eat lunch now.
1시에 점심 **먹었어요**.	I **ate** lunch at 1:00pm.

Form ~았어요/~었어요 is a combination of the past tense marker -았/-었 and the sentence ending ~어요. In Lesson 4, you learned that the choice between ~아요 and ~어요 depends on the last vowel of the base form of a verb or adjective. The same rule applies to the choice between ~았어요/~었어요.

When the last vowel of the verb/adjective base is 아 or 오, attach ~았어요.
좋다: 좋- + ~았어요 → 좋았어요
[ㅗ + 았어요]

Dictionary form (Word base + 다)	Base ending in 아/오 + ~ 았어요	Vowel contraction	~았어요/~었어요 form
가다	가- + ~았어요	가았어요 → 갔어요	갔어요
오다	오- + ~았어요	오았어요 → 왔어요	왔어요
보다	보- + ~았어요	보았어요 → 봤어요	봤어요
싸다	싸- + ~았어요	싸았어요 → 쌌어요	쌌어요
많다	많- + ~았어요	--	많았어요
좋다	좋- + ~았어요	--	좋았어요

When the last vowel of the verb/adjective base is not 아 or 오, attach ~었어요.
먹다: 먹 + 었어요 → 먹었어요
[ㅓ + 었어요]

Dictionary form (Word base + 다)	Base ending in 어/이 + ~ 었어요	Vowel contraction	~았어요/ ~었어요 form
먹다	먹- + ~었어요	--	먹었어요
마시다	마시- + ~었어요	마시었어요→ 마셨어요	마셨어요
맛있다	맛있- + ~었어요	--	맛있었어요

Rule3

When the verb/adjective ends in ~하다, use 했어요.
공부하다 → 공부했어요

Dictionary form (Word base + 다)	~았어요/~었어요 form
하다	했어요
공부하다	공부했어요
일하다	일했어요
좋아하다	좋아했어요

Not all verbs and adjectives follow the above rules. Here are some examples of irregular verbs and adjectives: (For more information, refer to Appendix V.)

Dictionary form (Word base + 다)	~았어요/~었어요 form
바쁘다 to be busy	바빴어요
예쁘다 to be pretty	예뻤어요
크다 to be big	컸어요
모르다 to not know	몰랐어요
맵다 to be spicy	매웠어요
이다 to be	이었어요/ 였어요
아니다 to be not	아니었어요

Note 2

With "이다", after a noun ending in a consonant (e.g., 선생님), attach **이었어요**. After a noun ending in a vowel (e.g., 간호사), attach **였어요**.

1. 선생님**이었어요**. (He) was a teacher.
   [ㅁ + 이었어요]
2. 간호사**였어요**. (She) was a nurse.
   [ㅏ + 였어요]

Exercise 1

Complete the following dialogues, using the past tenses of the given verbs.

1. A: 어제 뉴스 봤어요? (보다)

   B: 무슨 뉴스요?

2. A: 어제 뭐 ____________________? (하다)

   B: 백화점에서 ____________________. (쇼핑하다)

3. A: 저는 중국 사람이에요.

   B: 저는 미국에서 ____________________. (오다)

   제 고향은 시카고예요.

4. A: 어제 한국 음식을 ____________________. (먹다)

   B: 어디서요?

   A: 에이미 씨 집에서요.

5. A: 대학생이세요?

   B: 아뇨. 작년에 ____________________. [졸업하다 to graduate]

6. A: 주말에 한국 마트에 갔어요?

   B: 네. 라면을 ____________________. (사다)

7. A: 한국어 어디서 ____________________? (배우다)

   B: 대학교에서요.

Your friend is asking what you did. Tell her/him what you did using the words in the box below.

하다	가다	보다	자다	만나다	청소하다	먹다

1. A: 주말에 뭐 했어요?
   B: 집에서 영화 ____________. 그리고 숙제 ____________.

2. A: 어제 뭐 했어요?
   B: 친구하고 온라인 게임을 ____________. 그리고 친구하고 같이 점심 ____________.

3. A: 지난 주말에 뭐 했어요?
   B: LA에 ____________. LA에서 친구를 ____________.

4. A: 주말에 뭐 했어요?
   B: 피곤해서 많이 ____________. 그리고 집을 ____________.

Useful expressions

온라인 게임	online game
자다	to sleep
청소하다	to clean
피곤하다	to be tired

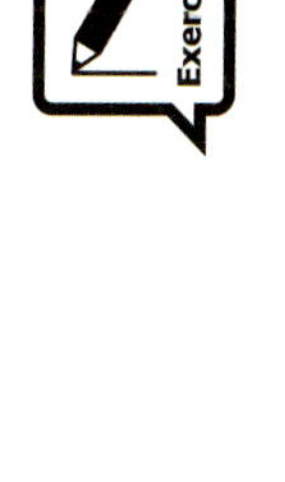

Jessica went to Korea last summer. Listen to her narration about her trip to Korea and fill in the blanks. 11

1. 제시카는 작년에 한국에 ________________.
2. 제시카는 대학교에서 한국어 수업을________________. 수업이 ________________.
3. 한국어 선생님이 아주 ________________.
4. 제시카는 서울에서 한국 음식을 많이 ________________.

Useful expressions

작년	last year	많이	a lot
수업을 듣다	to take a class	한국말로 얘기하다	to speak in Korean
친구를 사귀다	to make a friend; to make friends	한국말이 늘다	for one's Korean to improve

2. Object marker: -을/-를

When you mark someone or something as the object of your sentence, attach the object marker -을/-를 after the noun. -을/-를 does not carry any meaning but simply indicates that someone or something attached to it is the object of the sentence.

1. 저는	민준 씨를	좋아해요.	I like Minjoon.
as for me	Minjoon-object marker	like	
2. 마크는	한국 음식을	좋아해요.	Mark likes Korean food.
as for Mark	Korean food-object marker	like	

Form

- ▶ After a consonant-ending word, -을 is attached.
- ▶ After a vowel-ending word, -를 is attached.

1. 저는 떡볶이를 만들었어요. [ㅣ + 를] — I made *tteokboggi*.
2. 한국 마트에서 김밥을 샀어요. [ㅂ + 을] — (I) bought *gimbap* at the Korean supermarket.
3. 오늘 김 선생님을 만나요. — (I) meet Mr. Kim today.
4. 리아나가 매일 커피를 마셔요. — Leana drinks coffee everyday.

Note

In colloquial conversations, the object marker -을/-를 is frequently dropped.

1. 저는 떡볶이(를) 만들었어요
2. 한국 마트에서 김밥(을) 샀어요.

Underline the object of the following sentences, as in (1).

1. 드라마 봐요.
2. 주말에는 가끔 라면 먹어요.
3. 저는 한국학 전공해요.

4. 오늘은 제가 커피 살게요.

5. 사진 좀 보여주세요.

6. 떡볶이가 매워서 물 마셨어요.

7. 스티브는 지금 서울에서 한국어 배워요.

Create sentences, using the words given in the parentheses, as in (1). Make sure to include the subject marker -이/-가 and the object marker -을/-를 in your sentences.

1. 

(마크; 햄버거; 먹다)

마크가 햄버거를 먹어요.

2. 

(저; 텔레비전; 보다)

____

3. 

(민준 씨; 김밥; 아주 좋아하다)

____

4. 

(제임스; 한국에서; 영어; 가르치다)

____

Listen to the audio and write what you hear. 12

1. ____________________

2. ____________________

3. ____________________

4. ____________________

3. Who .... What .... Verb/Adjective.

Usage One common sentence structure in Korean is "who + what + do (verb)," as in 저는 (Who) 한국어를 (What) 공부해요 (verb) "I study Korean."

Note the difference in word order between English and Korean in the following examples.

1. English:	I		study		Korean.	
	who	+	verb	+	what	(subject-verb-object)
Korean:	저는		한국어를		공부해요.	
	who	+	what	+	verb	(subject-object-verb)
2. English:	Mark		like		Korean food.	
	who	+	verb	+	what	(subject-verb-object)
Korean:	마크는		한국 음식을		좋아해요.	
	who	+	what	+	verb	(subject-object-verb)

In grammatical terms, the "who" element is called the "subject" and the "what" element is called the "object." English sentences have the word order of "Subject-Verb-Object," whereas Korean sentences have the word order of "Subject-Object-Verb."

Let's look at some examples of the sentence pattern "Who ... What ... Verb/Adjective."

		공부해요.	(I) study.	(verb)
	한국어를	공부해요.	(I) study Korean.	(what-verb)
저는	한국어를	공부해요.	I study Korean.	(who-what-verb)

Attach -은/-는 after someone (who) or something (what) to mark the topic of your sentence, and -이/-가 to mark the subject, or -을/-를 to mark the object. For example,

1. 저는 — 한국어를 — 공부해요.
   I-**topic marker** — Korean-**object marker** — study
   As for me, (I) study Korean.

2. 마크는 — 한국 음식을 — 좋아해요.
   Mark-**topic marker** — Korean food-**object marker** — like
   As for Mark, (he) likes Korean food.

3. 마크가 — 한국 음식을 — 좋아해요.
   Mark-**subject marker** — 한국 음식-**object marker** — like
   Mark likes Korean food.

Note For more details about the usage of -은/-는 and -이/-가, please see Lesson 7 (II .1,2).

Describe "WHO is currently doing WHAT"or "WHO did WHAT" in Korean. Use -은/-는, -이/-가, or -을/-를 if necessary.

1. 

(지금; 제니; 한국어; 배우다)

____

2. 

(저; 어제; 백화점에서; 옷; 사다)

____

3. 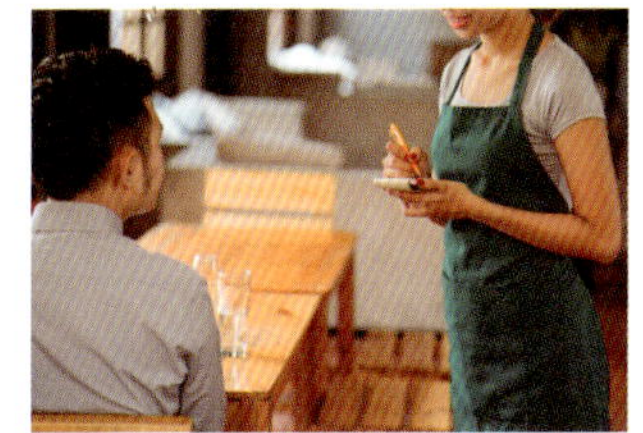

(지금; 마이클; 피자; 주문하다)

____

4. 

(저; 지난 주말에; 친구; 만나다)

____

Provide your own responses to the questions. Make sure to include the object marker -을/-를 in your sentences.

1. A: 무슨 스포츠를 좋아하세요?
   B: ______________________________.

2. A: 무슨 수업을 들었어요?
   B: ______________________________.

3. A: 뭐 전공했어요?
   B: ______________________________.

4. A: 무슨 음식을 잘하세요?
   B: ______________________________.

5. A: 어제 친구하고 뭐 했어요?
   B: ______________________________.

6. A: 오늘 아침에 뭐 드셨어요?
   B: ______________________________.

Listen to Jessica's narration about her friends and fill in the blanks. 13

1. 제시카는 오늘 오후에 ____________________ 만나요.
2. 소피아는 ____________________ 공부해요.
3. 소피아는 이번 학기에 ____________________ 들어요.
4. 린다는 ____________________ 좋아해요.
5. 린다는 이번 학기에 ____________________ 들어요.

4. ~네요. Sentence ending indicating the speaker's reaction or realization

Usage ~**네요** is a sentence ending expressing the speaker's spontaneous reaction to new information or the speaker's realization or discovery of something. It often involves the speaker's surprise, admiration, or sympathy. Read the following examples to see how ~**아요**/~**어요** and ~**네요** are used.

1. 김밥이 맛있어요.	This *gimbap* is tasty.
김밥이 맛있**네요**.	(Oh) this *gimbap* is tasty.
2. 비가 와요.	It's raining.
비가 오**네요**.	(Oh, I see that) it's raining.
3. 한국말 잘하세요.	You speak Korean well.
한국말 잘하시**네요**!	(Oh) you speak Korean well!
4. 이거 괜찮아요.	This is good.
이거 괜찮**네요**.	Oh, this is good.
5. 마크 씨가 없어요.	Mark is not (here).
마크 씨가 없**네요**.	(Oh I see that) Mark is not (here).

6. 마크 씨가 안 왔어요. Mark did not come.
   마크 씨가 안 왔**네요**. (Oh I see that) Mark did not come.

Express your spontaneous reaction or realization using the ~네요 ending.

1. 어, 방이 (크다)________________.

2. 오늘 날씨가 (좋다)________________.

3. 이거 아주 (맛있다)________________.

4. 브라이언이 오피스에 (없다)________________.
   브라이언이 벌써 집에 (갔다)________________.
   [벌써 already]

Express your spontaneous reaction to the following information.

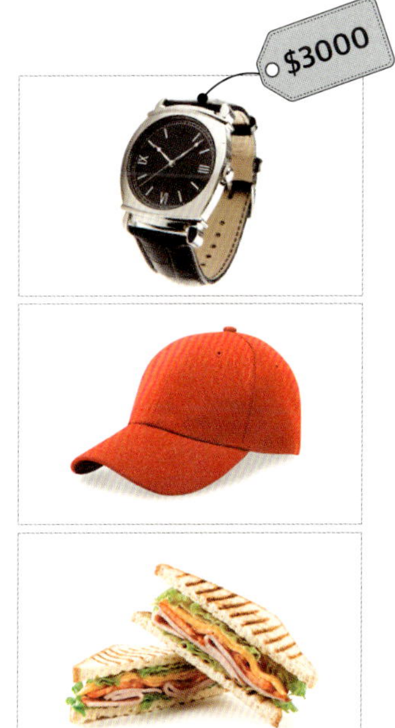

1. A: 이 시계 3,000불이에요.
   B: ________________________.

2. A: 이 모자 어제 샀어요. 어때요?
   B: ________________________.

3. A: 이 샌드위치 제가 만들었어요. 좀 드세요. 맛이 어때요?
   B: ________________________.

4. A: 이 가방 Good Will에서 10불에 샀어요.

   B: ______________________________.

$10

Exercise 12

Listen to the audio and provide your own response using -네요. You may use the words in the box below. 14

싸다 to be cheap	비싸다 to be expensive	멋있다 to be stylish
예쁘다 to be pretty	맛있다 to be delicious	맛없다 to be not tasty
많다 to be a lot	바쁘다 to be busy	

1. A: (Listen.)

   B: 여동생이 너무 예쁘네요.

2. A: (Listen.)

   B: ______________________________.

3. A: (Listen.)

   B: ______________________________.

4. A: (Listen.)

   B: ______________________________.

5. A: (Listen.)

   B: ______________________________.

Useful expressions

아파트 렌트 apartment rent

한복 *Hanbok* (traditional Korean clothing)

III. Culture

Korean food made with 장 (*jang*)

Many Koreans enjoy dishes based on 장 (*jang*). Two of the most popular kinds of 장 are 된장 (*doenjang*) and 고추장 (*gochujang*). Both 된장 and 고추장 are made from fermented soybean paste, which has been identified as "slow food" as opposed to the concept of "fast food." Modern scientists find these 장 ingredients to be one of the healthiest food sources. Koreans frequently make 된장 stew with various vegetable ingredients such as zucchini, onions, green onions, garlic, and tofu often with a choice of seafood or beef. 된장찌개 (*doenjang* stew) is popular among many Koreans and can be consumed any time of the day. 고추장 is the main seasoning for 떡볶이(*tteokboggi*), the sweet and spicy rice cake that has become a very popular snack for the nation.

<된장찌개>

<떡볶이>

장	*Jang* (main sauce)	장 음식	Food made out of *Jang*
된장	soybean paste	된장찌개	soybean paste stew
고추장	spicy sauce	떡볶이	spicy rice cake
간장	soy sauce	잡채	clear noodle with soy sauce, shredded vegetables and meats

Culture

Tteokboggi

Main Ingredients (Servings: 4)
White steamed rice cake 18 ounces (500 g), fish cake 5 ounces (150 g), water 1⅘ cups (360 ml)

Seasoning sauce
Red pepper paste 3T(tablespoons), soy sauce ½T, sugar 2T, starch syrup 1T

Preparation
- 1. If the rice cakes are soft, just rinse and drain it. If it is hard, blanch them in boiling water slightly before cooking.
- 2. Slice the fish cakes into 2 x 1 inches (5 x 2.5 cm) pieces, place on a sieve, and pour hot water on it to drain the oil.

Recipe
- 1. Put water in a pan, add the seasoning sauce, and mix well.
- 2. Bring (1) pan to a boil with rice cakes while stirring them so that they don't stick together.
- 3. Add the fish cakes and boil it until the sauce thickens.

TIP
If you make it with anchovies and kelp broth, you can enjoy a richer flavor. You can add red pepper powder, onions, carrots, green onions, and other ingredients.

<THE TASTE OF KOREA HANSIK. URL: https://www.hansik.or.kr.>

IV. Listen & Discuss

A group of students learning Korean are having a potluck party in a dorm kitchen. Listen to the conversation carefully. Discuss the answers to the following questions with your classmates. Then, write each answer in a full Korean sentence in the space provided.

1. 누가 김밥을 만들었어요?

2. 샤오밍 씨는 무엇을 만들었어요?

3. 떡볶이에는 무엇이 들어가요?

4. 샤오밍 씨는 떡볶이 요리를 어디서 배웠어요? [요리 recipe]

Script

A group of Korean learning students are having a potluck party at a dorm kitchen on a Friday.

01 제시카: 김밥 좀 드세요.

02 샤오밍: 어, 제시카 씨가 만들었어요?[II.1,3]

03 제시카: 아뇨. ㅎㅎ 한국 마트에서 아침에 샀어요.

밥하고 고기, 시금치, 당근이 들어 있어요.

04 샤오밍: 아~. 전 떡볶이를 만들었어요.[II.2] 여기 맛 좀 보세요.

05 제시카: (after trying) 음~ 맛있네요![II.4] 여기는 뭐가 들어갔어요?

06 샤오밍: 떡하고, 설탕하고, 고추장하고... 아 참 그리고 양파요.

07 제시카: 아, 그래요. 떡볶이는 어디서 배웠어요?

08 샤오밍: 인터넷 블로그에서요.

09 제시카: 우와~ 대단해요!

01 Jessica : Please have some gimbap.

02 Xiaoming: Oh, did you (Jessica) make it?

03 Jessica : Nope. (laughing) I bought it at a Korean mart in the morning.

It has rice, meat, spinach, and carrots inside.

04 Xiaoming: Oh~ I made ddeokboggi (spicy rice cake). Here, please taste this.

05 Jessica : (after trying) Mm~ it's delicious!! What did you put in here?

06 Xiaoming: Ddeok (rice cake), sugar, gochujang (red pepper paste).... Oh yeah, and onions.

07 Jessica : I see. Where did you learn it?

08 Xiaoming: From the internet.

09 Jessica : Wow~ Incredible!

V. Guided Conversation

With the organization of the model conversation in Listen & Discuss (Script) in mind, practice the modified conversation below with your partner.

step 1

A group of Korean learning students is having a potluck party at a dorm kitchen on a Friday. Practice the following conversation with your partner, using the information in ( ). Choose one of the options in ( ) to continue the conversation.

01 A: ________________ 좀 드세요.
(떡볶이; 김밥; 잡채; 불고기)

02 B: 어, ________________ 씨가 만들었어요?
(A's name)

03 A: 아뇨. ㅎㅎ 한국 마트에서 아침에 샀어요.

04 B: 전 ________________ 을/를 만들었어요. 여기 맛 좀 보세요.
(떡볶이; 김밥; 잡채; 불고기)

05 A: 음~ 맛있네요!! 여기 뭐 들어갔어요?

06 B: (1) 떡하고 고추장하고 양파요.

(2) 밥하고 김하고 당근하고 불고기요.

(3) 당면하고 소고기하고 시금치하고 당근요.

(4) 소고기하고 양파하고 버섯이요.

Useful expressions

01 불고기 *bulgogi*; 떡 *tteok*
06 밥 cooked rice; 김 seaweed
당근 carrot; 소고기 beef
시금치 spinach;
당면 vermicelli; glass noodles
08 책에서 from a book;
엄마한테서 from my mom
09 멋있어요. (You are) awesome/cool.

07 A: 어디서 배웠어요?

08 B: ________________ 요.
(인터넷에서; 책에서; 친구한테서; 엄마한테서)

09 A: 오 ________________.
(대단해요; 멋있어요)

(Switch roles and continue to practice.)

Guided Conversation

step 2 **Present the conversation from Step 1 in front of the class. Try not to read it!**

VI. Spontaneous Conversation

Now is your chance to have real interactions with your classmates in Korean. You can practice speaking with your classmates, writing, and presenting in front of the class!

Your friend cooked one of the dishes below. Ask your partner the ingredients he/she used. Refer to Ⅴ. Guided Conversation and ask and answer questions about the food and its ingredients.

Please include the following information in your conversation:

- ▶ Show your interest and ask about the dish.
- ▶ Answer with~하고 ~ 하고 ... 들어가다.
- ▶ Ask where he/she bought the ingredients.
- ▶ Ask where he/she learned the recipe.
- ▶ Answer with (~에서; ~한테서) 배우다.

<요리 1>

된장찌개 (된장, 두부, 호박)

<요리 2>

순두부찌개 (순두부, 소고기, 계란, 파)

<요리 3>

비빔밥 (밥, 나물, 고추장, 계란후라이)

<요리 4>

해물파전 (밀가루, 해물, 파)

Fill in the table, using the information you collected from you friend.

Friend's name	
Dish name	
Ingredients	
Where did (s)he learn it?	
How was the taste?	

Write a narrative about your friend's dish, based on the information in the table above.

- ▶ Use "verb/adjective base + ~았어요/~었어요" if possible.
- ▶ Use the "Who ... What ... Verb/Adjective" pattern if possible.
- ▶ Use 그리고 and/or 그런데 when needed.

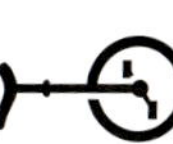

Present what you wrote in Step 2 in front of the class. Try not to read it!

13 저는 이제 스물다섯이 돼요.

I am now becoming 25 years old.

1. Talking about one's age
2. Reading and saying months, dates, and days of the week on a calendar

Preparation & Practice	I. New Words & Expressions II. Patterns, Expressions & Practice 1. Talking about one's age (Korean numerals) 2. Expressing a date 3. Noun + 으로 보여요/로 보여요 to look like ~ 4. Adjective + 아/어 보여요 to look ~ III. Culture Meeting new people and asking about their age
Conversation Activities	IV. Listen & Discuss V. Guided Conversation VI. Spontaneous Conversation

I. New Words & Expressions

 **Study the words and expressions with the audio.**  16

NOUN

고등학생	high school student
나이	age
목요일	Thursday
비밀	secret
수요일	Wednesday
시간	time [시간이 가다 "for time to pass"]

ADJECTIVE

맞다	to be correct; to be right

ADVERB

벌써	already
빨리	fast; quickly
아직	still; (not) yet
정말	really
참	really; very

EXPRESSION

·그러게요.	Yeah, I know.
·에이~	Oh, please!; Come on ~
·(저는 스물다섯)이 돼요.	(I) become (25 years old).

Form

Dictionary form (Word base + 다)	~아요/~어요 form	~으세요/~세요 form
맞다 to be correct; to have an injection	맞아요	맞으세요
되다 to become	돼요	되세요
보이다 to be visible; to look	보여요	보이세요

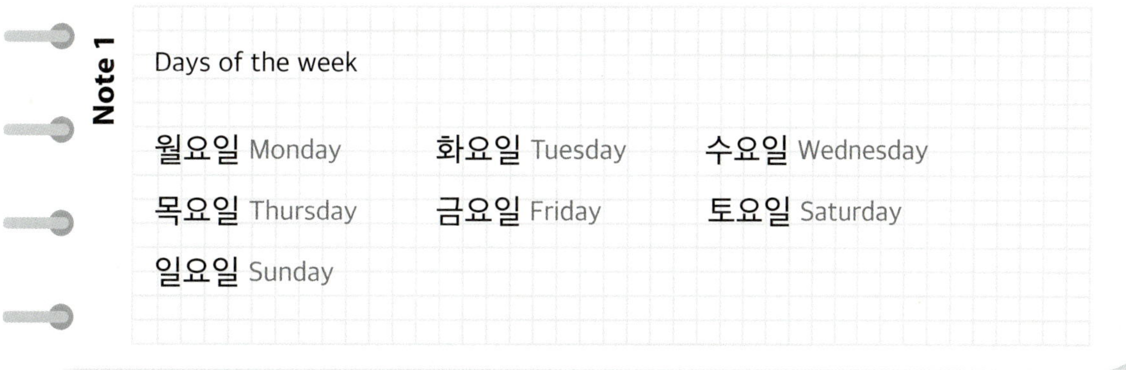

Note 1

Days of the week

월요일 Monday　화요일 Tuesday　수요일 Wednesday

목요일 Thursday　금요일 Friday　토요일 Saturday

일요일 Sunday

Note 2

아직 means "still" or "yet" and can be used in either a positive or a negative sentence. In order to emphasize the meaning of "아직," -"도" may be added, forming 아직도.

저는 아직 학생이에요.	I'm still a student.
마크는 아직 안 자요.	Mark is not sleeping yet.
마크는 아직 안 왔어요.	Mark has not come yet.
아직도 일해요?	Are you still working?
전 아직도 수지를 사랑해요.	I still love Suji.
마크는 아직도 공부하고 있어요.	Mark is still studying.
마크가 아직도 안 자요.	Mark isn't sleeping yet.

Note 3

그러게요 (or 그러게 말이에요) is an expression of agreement. 그러게요 and 그러게 말이에요 are frequently used when you chime in with the other speaker echoing what he/she said. 맞아요 is used when you affirm or acknowledge that what was said is right or true. 맞아요 can also be used to enthusiastically agree with the other speaker.

맞아요.	That is correct; That is right. (=I agree with you.)
그러게요.	Yeah, I know. (=You bet.)
그러게 말이에요.	That's what I'm saying; I know; I hear you.

1. A: 에이미 씨, 뉴욕대학교에 다녀요? Amy, do you go to New York University?
   B: 네, 맞아요. Yeah, that's right.

2. A: 이 식당 음식이 너무 비싸네요. The food at this restaurant is too expensive.
   B: 그러게요. Yeah, I know.

3. (Waiting for Minjoon)
   A: 민준 씨는 항상 늦네요. Minjoon is always late.
   B: 그러게 말이에요. That's what I'm saying.

Listen to the audio and fill in the blanks. 17

1. 시간 참 __________ 가네요.

2. __________ 12월이 다 갔어요.

3. 제 나이는 __________ 이에요.

4. 지영 씨 __________ 고등학생으로 보여요.

Listen to the audio and fill in the blanks.  18

1. A: 오늘이 수요일이에요, ____________________?

   B: 목요일이요.

2. A: 오늘 30일이에요?

   B: 네. ____________________.

3. A: 시간 참 빨리 가네요! 벌써 12월이 다 갔어요!

   B: ____________________.

4. A: 지영 씨 아직 고등학생으로 보여요!

   B: 에이~ 정말 ______________?

II. Patterns, Expressions & Practice

1. Talking about one's age (Korean numerals)

In Lesson 13, we will focus on how to talk about one's age with Korean numerals.

For the introduction to native Korean and Sino-Korean numerals, you may look at Lesson 8 and 10.

1. When telling one's age, you can use **a native Korean numeral** and 살 (the age counter).

1. 아들이 **한** 살이에요. My son is one year old.
2. 저는 **스무** 살이에요. I'm twenty years old.
3. 저는 이제 **스물다섯** 살이에요. I'm twenty-five years old now.

The counter 살 is often dropped when it is obvious that the speaker is talking about someone's age (as in examples 4 and 5 below). In the case that 살 is dropped, "**한**/**두**/**세**/**네**" is not reduced. You must use "**하나**/**둘**/**셋**/**넷**/"(as example 6 below).

4. 여동생은 **열여덟**이에요. My younger sister is eighteen years old.
5. 제 아버지는 **마흔아홉**이세요. My father is forty-nine.
6. 저 아이 나이는 **하나**예요 (**둘**/**셋**/**넷**이에요). The baby's age is one (two/three/four).

1	한 살	11 (10+1)	열한 살	21 (20+1)	스물한 살	31 (30+1)	서른한 살
2	두 살	12 (10+2)	열두 살	22 (20+2)	스물두 살	32 (30+2)	서른두 살
3	세 살	13 (10+3)	열세 살	23 (20+3)	스물세 살	33 (30+3)	서른세 살
4	네 살	14 (10+4)	열네 살	24 (20+4)	스물네 살	34 (30+4)	서른네 살
5	다섯 살	15 (10+5)	열다섯 살	25 (20+5)	스물다섯 살	35 (30+5)	서른다섯 살
6	여섯 살	16 (10+6)	열여섯 살	26 (20+6)	스물여섯 살	36 (30+6)	서른여섯 살
7	일곱 살	17 (10+7)	열일곱 살	27 (20+7)	스물일곱 살	37 (30+7)	서른일곱 살
8	여덟 살	18 (10+8)	열여덟 살	28 (20+8)	스물여덟 살	38 (30+8)	서른여덟 살
9	아홉 살	19 (10+9)	열아홉 살	29 (20+9)	스물아홉 살	39 (30+9)	서른아홉 살
10	열 살	20	스무 살	30	서른 살	40	마흔 살

50 (**쉰** 살), 60 (**예순** 살), 70 (**일흔** 살), 80 (**여든** 살), 90 (**아흔** 살), 100 (**백** 살)

2. There is another age counter 세. A Sino-Korean numeral and 세 (the age counter) can be used to express someone's age.

Use the honorific ~세요 ending when speaking about older-people's ages.

1. 제 할머니는 지금 팔십이 세세요. My grandmother is eighty-two years old.
2. 저희 아버지는 올해 나이가 칠십오 세 되세요. My father turns seventy-five this year.
3. 큰아버지가 지금 육십칠 세세요. My uncle is sixty-seven years old.

3. When asking someone's age, choose an appropriate expression according to his/her age or a social relation/rank between you and the other.

1. 몇 살이에요? (how old is) How old are you? [direct question, e.g., used to peers]

2. 나이가 어떻게 되세요? (age how become) May I ask your age? [indirect question, e.g., used to adults]

3. 연세가 어떻게 되세요? (age how become) May I ask how old you are? [indirect question, e.g., used to elders]

Note 연세 is the honorific word for 나이.

Tell us how old each person is using the dialogue in (1) as an example.

1. 

1 year old

A: 몇 살이에요?

B: 한 살이에요.

2. 

5 years old

A: 몇 살이에요?

B: ______________.

3. 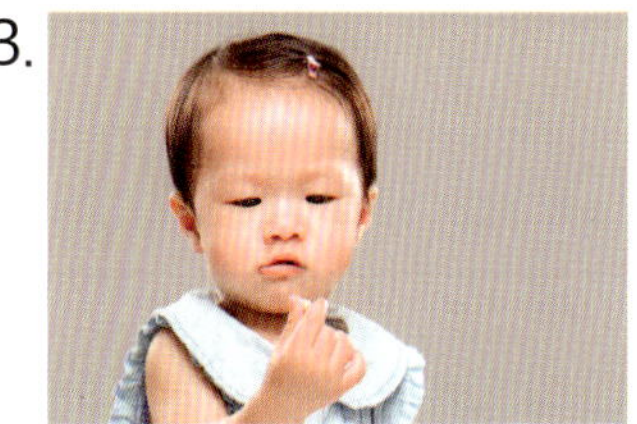

4 years old

A: 몇 살이에요?

B: ______________.

4. 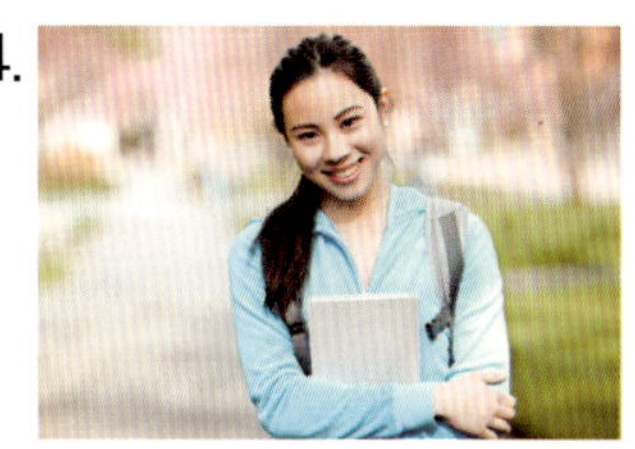
21 years old

A: 몇 살이에요?

B: ____________________.

5. 
53 years old

A: 연세가 어떻게 되세요?

B: ____________________.

6. 
84 years old

A: 연세가 어떻게 되세요?

B: ____________________.

Amy and Minjoon are talking about people's ages. Listen to the conversation and write the age of each person in the blanks. 19

1. 수미 씨는 ______________________________.

2. 제시카 씨는 ______________________________.

3. 민준 씨 형은 ______________________________.

4. 에이미 씨 오빠는 ______________________________.

Useful expressions

동갑	the same age
~하고 동갑이다	to be the same age as ~
저희 형	my older brother [Lit., our older brother] (spoken by a man)
우리 오빠	my older brother (spoken by a woman) [Lit., our older brother]

2. Expressing a date

1. The order of dates

A date is expressed in Korean in the order [year (년)-month (월)-date (일)] in which the biggest concept comes first and the smallest last. For example,

▶ 2025년 5월 10일 (Reading: 이천이십오 년 오 월 십 일)

▶ 1993년 11월 24일 (Reading: 천구백구십삼 년 십일 월 이십사 일)

2. The months (월) of the year

3. The days in a month

Sunday 일요일	Monday 월요일	Tuesday 화요일	Wednesday 수요일	Thursday 목요일	Friday 금요일	Saturday 토요일
			1 일 일	2 이 일	3 삼 일	4 사 일
5 오 일	6 육 일	7 칠 일	8 팔 일	9 구 일	10 십 일	11 십일 일
12 십이 일	13 십삼 일	14 십사 일	15 십오 일	16 십육 일	17 십칠 일	18 십팔 일
19 십구 일	20 이십 일	21 이십일 일	22 이십이 일	23 이십삼 일	24 이십사 일	25 이십오 일
26 이십육 일	27 이십칠 일	28 이십팔 일	29 이십구 일	30 삼십 일	31 삼십일 일	

Note

To ask a date (month and day), you might say **몇 월 며칠이에요?**

1. A: 생일이 **몇 월** **며칠이에요?** — What date is your birthday?
   birthday / what month / what date is

   B: **오월 팔 일**이에요. — It's May 8.

2. A: 오늘 **며칠이에요?** — What is the date today?
   today / what date is

   B: **삼십 일**이에요. — It's 30th.

Talk about the following people's birthdays, as shown in (1).

1. Minjoon: March 5th

   A: 민준 씨, 생일이 몇 월 며칠이에요?

   B: 삼 월 오 일이에요.

2. Steve: August 14th

   A: 스티브 씨, 생일이 언제예요?

   B: ______________________________.

3. Shana: June 8th

   A: ______________________________.

   B: ______________________________.

4. Xiaoming: October 2nd

   A: ______________________________.

   B: ______________________________.

5. Jessica: December 21th

   A: ______________________________.

   B: ______________________________.

Exercise 4

The following dates are Korean holidays. Complete the dialogues about Korean holidays, as shown in (1).

1. [설날 New Year's Day: January 1st]

   A: 설날은 언제예요?

   B: 설날은 일 월 일 일이에요.

2. [한글날 Hangul Day: October 9th]

   A: ______________________________?

   B: ______________________________.

3. [어린이날 Children's Day: May 5th]

A: ______________________________?

B: ______________________________.

4. [부처님 오신 날 Buddha's Birthday: April 8th (on the lunar calendar "음력")]

A: ______________________________?

B: ______________________________.

5. [추석 Harvest Day: August 15th (on the lunar calendar "음력")]

A: ______________________________?

B: ______________________________.

6. [크리스마스 Christmas: December 25th]

A: ______________________________?

B: ______________________________.

Exercise 5

Listen to the conversation between James and Michelle and answer the questions in Korean. 20

1. A: 오늘은 몇 월 며칠이에요?

B: ______________________________.

2. A: 미셸 씨 생일은 언제예요?

B: ______________________________.

3. A: 제임스 씨 생일은 언제예요?

B: ______________________________.

3. Noun + 으로 보이다/로 보이다 "to look like ~"

Form

- After a noun ending in a consonant, attach -**으로 보이다**
- After a noun ending in a vowel, attach -**로 보이다**
- After a word ending in ㄹ, -**로 보이다** is used.

1. **보이다** literally means "to be seen" or "to be visible." -**으로**/-**로 보이다** means "to look like ~" or "to appear as ~."

1. 샤나 씨, 고등학생**으로 보여요**. [ㅇ + 으로] — Shana, you look like a high school student.
2. 샤나 씨는 열여덟**으로 보여요**. — Shana looks like an 18-year-old.
3. 우리 애가 몇 살**로 보여요**? [ㄹ + 로] — How old does my child look?
4. 무슨 색**으로 보여요**? — What color does it look like? [색 color]
5. 김 선생님은 삼십 대**로 보여요**. [ㅐ + 로] — Mr. Kim looks like he is in his 30s. [삼십 대 people in their 30s]

2. [Noun + **으로 보여요**/**로 보여요**] can be replaced with [Noun + **처럼 보여요**], [Noun + **같이 보여요**], or [Noun **같아요**] for the same or similar meaning.

1. 샤오밍 씨는 한국 사람**으로 보여요**. — Xiaoming looks like a Korean.
2. 샤오밍 씨는 한국 사람**처럼 보여요**. — Xiaoming looks like a Korean.
3. 샤오밍 씨는 한국 사람**같이 보여요**. — Xiaoming looks like a Korean.
4. 샤오밍 씨는 한국 사람 **같아요**. — Xiaoming is like a Korean.

Look at the pictures below and respond to the questions by saying what each person or object looks like.

1. 

A: 수지 씨가 고등학생으로 보여요, 대학생으로 보여요?

B: ______________________________.

2. 

A: 무슨 색으로 보여요? 회색으로 보여요, 검은색으로 보여요?

B: ______________________________.

[회색 gray color; 검은색 black color]

3. 

A: 김 사장님이 40대로 보여요, 50대로 보여요?

B: ______________________________.

4. 

A: 남자 아이로 보여요, 여자 아이로 보여요?

B: ______________________________.

Look at the pictures of the following people and tell us what he/she looks like using the words in the box below.

초등학생 elementary school student	중학생 middle school student
고등학생 high school student	대학생 college student
직장인 salaryman	

1. 

____

2. 

____

3. 

____

4. 

____

Listen to the audio and answer the following questions in Korean.

1. A: 소피아 씨는 어느 나라 사람이에요?

   B: ______________________________.

2. A: 김 선생님은 연세가 어때 보여요?

   B: ______________________________.

3. A: 마크 씨는 고등학생처럼 보여요?

   B: ______________________________.

4. A: 사진을 어디서 찍었어요? [사진을 찍다 to take a photo]

   B: ______________________________.

4. Adjective + 아 보이다/어 보이다 "to look ~"

Usage Use [Adjective + **아 보여요**/**어 보여요**] "someone/something looks adjective" to comment on the appearance of someone or something.

1. 어려 **보여요**.	(He/she) looks young.	[어리다 to be young]
2. 얼굴이 좋**아 보여요**.	(Your) face looks good.	[얼굴 face]
3. 옷이 비**싸 보여요**.	The clothes look expensive.	
4. 맛있**어 보여요**.	(It) looks delicious.	
5. 일이 어려**워 보여요**.	The job looks difficult.	

How does he or she look? Make a comment about how each person looks, using ~아 보여요/~어 보여요. You may use the adjectives in the box below.

화나다 to be upset 슬프다 to be sad 좋다 to be good 바쁘다 to be busy

1.

마크 씨가 ____________________.

2.

마키샤 씨가 기분이 ____________________.

3.

영수 씨가 ____________________.

4.

현주 씨가 ____________________.

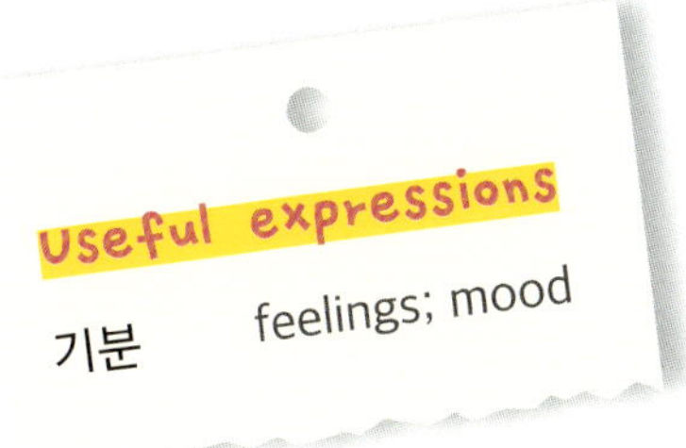

Describe how the thing in each picture looks. Make a comment using ~아 보여요/~어 보여요. You may use the words in the box below.

맛있다 to be delicious	멋있다 to be stylish	어렵다 to be difficult
크다 to be big	작다 to be small	싸다 to be cheap
복잡하다 to be complex, to be complicated		비싸다 to be expensive

1.

옷이 ____________________.

2.

케이크가 ____________________.

3.

문제가 ____________________.
[문제 problem; question]

4.

차가 ____________________.

III. Culture

Meeting new people and asking about their age

When meeting a new person, Koreans don't seem to hesitate to ask their age. Due to the frequent use of honorifics in grammar, most Koreans prefer to decide the appropriate level of speech earlier in the conversation so that they do not offend an older person. There are various indirect ways to ask about a person's age in Korean. For example, the year of one's university entrance is casually mentioned as a way of identifying the age of a person. "몇 학번이세요?" (What is your university entrance year?) is one way of asking about age indirectly. The answer is expressed in two serial numbers, such as 18 학번 (일팔 학번), meaning his or her university entrance year was 2018. But some people don't go to a university. In this situation, people may ask about age using the Zodiac sign, as in "무슨 띠세요?" ("What is your Zodiac sign (띠)?") The 12 animals of the zodiac repeat every 12 years, so you can guess the approximate age of a person if you simply ask their zodiac signs.

[The 12 Zodiac signs that Koreans use]

"What is your Zodiac sign (띠)?"

Find out what your zodiac sign is in the chart below. The date below each year is January 1st of the lunar calendar of that year. If you were born between January 1 in the solar calendar and January 1 in the lunar calendar, you are considered to be born the previous year in the lunar calendar. Therefore, the you will have the zodiac sign of the previous year.

Example: The zodiac sign of a person born on February 5, 1991 is 말띠.

Year	Zodiac Sign	Year	Zodiac Sign	Year	Zodiac Sign
1990년 1월 20일	말띠	2002년 2월 12일	말띠	2014년 1월 31일	말띠
1991년 2월 15일	양띠	2003년 2월 1일	양띠	2015년 2월 19일	양띠
1992년 2월 4일	원숭이띠	2004년 1월 22일	원숭이띠	2016년 2월 9일	원숭이띠
1993년 1월 23일	닭띠	2005년 2월 9일	닭띠	2017년 1월 28일	닭띠
1994년 2월 10일	개띠	2006년 1월 30일	개띠	2018년 2월 16일	개띠
1995년 1월 31일	돼지띠	2007년 2월 18일	돼지띠	2019년 2월 5일	돼지띠
1996년 2월 19일	쥐띠	2008년 2월 7일	쥐띠	2020년 1월 25일	쥐띠
1997년 2월 8일	소띠	2009년 1월 26일	소띠	2021년 2월 12일	소띠
1998년 1월 28일	호랑이띠	2010년 2월 14일	호랑이띠	2022년 2월 1일	호랑이띠
1999년 2월 15일	토끼띠	2011년 2월 3일	토끼띠	2023년 1월 22일	토끼띠
2000년 2월 5일	용띠	2012년 1월 23일	용띠	2024년 2월 10일	용띠
2001년 1월 24일	뱀띠	2013년 2월 10일	뱀띠	2025년 1월 29일	뱀띠

IV. Listen & Discuss

Minjoon and his American colleague Shana are chatting at a coffee shop after a regular meeting of the Korean Conversation Club. Shana is 30 years old. Listen to the conversation carefully. Discuss the answers to the following questions with your classmates. Then, write each answer in a full Korean sentence in the space provided.

1. 민준과 샤나는 몇 월 며칠, 무슨 요일에 이야기를 하고 있어요? (Don't write in Arabic numbers.)

2. 민준은 올해 몇 살이에요?

3. What was 민준's comment on the time passing? Write his line here.

4. How does 민준 comment on 샤나's age? Write his line here.

Script

Minjoon and his American colleague Shana are chatting at a coffee shop after a regular meeting of the Korean Conversation Club. Shana is 30 years old.

01 샤나: 오늘이 수요일이에요, 목요일이에요?

02 민준: 목요일이요.

03 샤나: 그럼, 오늘 21일이에요?[II.2]

04 민준: 네, 맞아요.

05 샤나: 어휴~ 그럼 내일까지 보고서를 끝내야 되네요.

06 민준: 네. 시간 참 빨리 가네요.

07 샤나: 그러게요. 벌써 12월이 다 갔어요!

08 민준: 이제 저는 스물다섯이 돼요.[II.1]

09 샤나: 그래요? 음..., 제 나이는 ㅎㅎ 비밀이에요~

10 민준: 샤나 씨 아직 고등학생으로 보여요![II.3,4]

11 샤나: 에이~ ㅎㅎ 정말 왜 그래요.

01 Shana : Is today Wednesday or Thursday?

02 Minjoon: It is Thursday.

03 Shana : Then is today the twenty-first?

04 Minjoon: Yes, that's right.

05 Shana : Oh no! (sigh) Then we have to finish the report by tomorrow.

06 Minjoon: Yeah, time goes by really quickly.

07 Shana : Yeah, I agree. December has gone by already.

08 Minjoon: I am now becoming 25 years old.

09 Shana : Are you? Um, my age (laughing) is a secret~

10 Minjoon: Miss Shana, you still look like a high school student!

11 Shana : Oh come on~ Why are you being like that?

V. Guided Conversation

With the organization of the model conversation in Listen & Discuss (Script) in mind, practice the modified conversation below with your partner.

step 1 **Two close friends are chatting with each other. Practice the following conversation with your partner, using the information in ( ). Choose one of the options to make the conversation move naturally.**

01 A: 오늘이 ________ (~요일) 이에요, ________ (~요일) 이에요?

02 B: ________ (~요일) 이요.

03 A: 그럼, 오늘 ________ (...; 20; 21; 22 ...) 일이에요?

04 B: 네, 맞아요.

05 A: 와~ 시간 참 빨리 가네요! 벌써 12월이 다 갔어요!

06 B: 그러게요. 저는 ________ (이제; 다음 달이면; 내년이면) ________ (your age) 이 돼요.

07 A: 그래요? ________ (B's name) 씨는 생일이 언제예요?

08 B: ____ ( ) 월 ____ ( ) 일이에요. ________ (A's name) 씨는요?

09 A: 저는 ____ ( ) 월 ____ ( ) 일이에요.

10 B: 아, 그래요? 근데 ________ (A's name) 씨는 아직 ________ (중학생; 고등학생; 대학생) 으로 보여요!

11 A: 고마워요. ________ (B's name) 씨도 ________ (중학생; 고등학생; 대학생) 으로 보여요!

12 B: ㅎㅎ 농담하지 마세요. 근데 고마워요!

(Switch roles and continue to practice.)

Useful expressions
12 농담하지 마세요! Don't make fun of me!

step 2 **Present the conversation from Step 1 in front of the class. Try not to read it!**

Guided Conversation

VI. Spontaneous Conversation

Now is your chance to have real interactions with your classmates in Korean. You can practice speaking with your classmates, writing, and presenting in front of the class!

Using the family trees of you (A) and your classmate (B) below, talk about each other's family members in terms of their age, birthday (month & day), and how they look. Make sure to include the expressions from the box below in your conversation.

- ▶ ~ 은/~는 몇 살이에요?
  생일이/은 언제예요?
- ▶ ~은/~는 나이가 어떻게 돼요?
  생일이/은 언제예요?
- ▶ ~께서는 연세가 어떻게 되세요?
  생신이/생신은 언제세요?
- ▶ ~은/~는 (고등학생처럼; ...) 보여요!
- ▶ ~은/~는/~께서는 (젊어; 삼십 대로; 사십 대로; 오십 대로) 보이세요!
  [젊다 to be young; 삼십 대 one's thirties; 사십 대 one's forties; 오십 대 one's fifties]

While asking each family member's age and date of birth, fill in the blanks with the information you collected from your classmate.

(A's family)

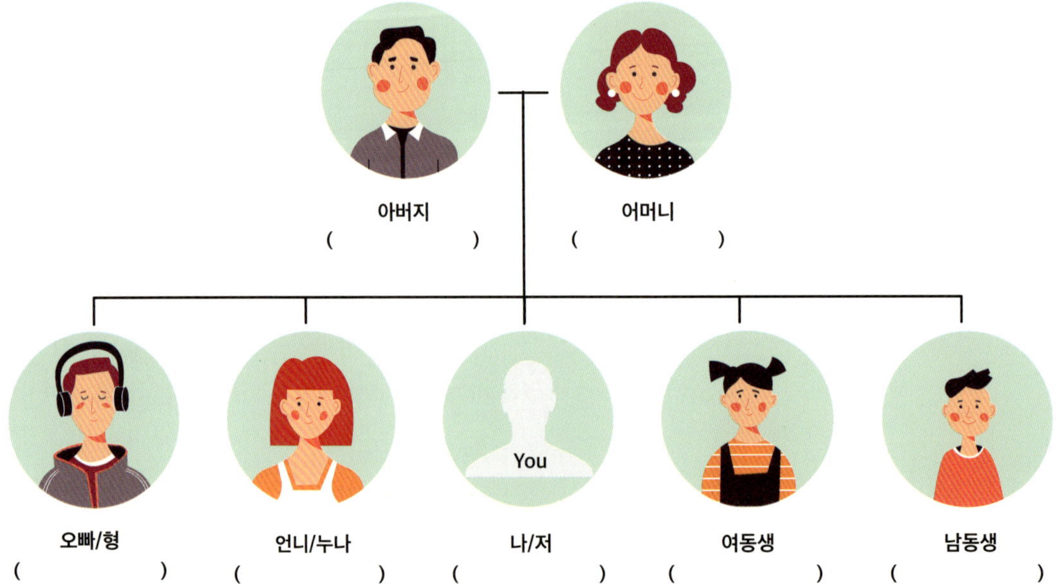

(B's family)

아버지
(   )

어머니
(   )

오빠/형
(   )

언니/누나
(   )

You

나/저
(   )

여동생
(   )

남동생
(   )

step 2

Write a narrative that introduces your classmate's family members and their age, date of birth and more.

Example: (Name of your classmate) 씨 아버지는 연세가 쉰둘(52)이세요. 그런데, 사십 대 (his forties)로 보이세요. 생신은 오 월 (May) 십삼 일 (13)이세요.

step 3

Based on what you wrote in Step 2, introduce your classmate's family members to the class. Try not to read what you wrote in Step 2.

14 오늘 정말 춥네요.

It is really cold today.

1. Talking about weather conditions
2. Talking about temperature

Preparation & Practice	I. New Words & Expressions II. Patterns, Expressions & Practice 1. ~이면/~면, ~으면/~면 if ... or when ... 2. Weather expressions 3. ~아지다/~어지다 to become ~ 4. ~아 죽다/~어 죽다 ~ to death III. Culture Weather conditions in Korea
Conversation Activities	IV. Listen & Discuss V. Guided Conversation VI. Spontaneous Conversation

I. New Words & Expressions

 **Study the words and expressions with the audio.**  23

NOUN		**ADVERB**	
여름	summer	그냥	just
올해	this year	더	more
표현	expression	많이	a lot
		원래	originally
VERB		유난히	unusually; particularly
모르다	to not know	진짜/정말	really (spoken)/ really (spoken or written)
죽다	to die		
		EXPRESSION	
ADJECTIVE		· 14도	fourteen degrees
따뜻하다	to be warm	· 네?	What?
따뜻해지다	to become warm	· 뭐라구요?	What did you say?
춥다	to be cold (used for weather)	· 언제쯤 ...?	Around when ...?
		· 이렇게	like this

Form

Dictionary form (Word base + 다)		~아요/~어요 form	~으세요/~세요 form
모르다	to not know	몰라요 (See Rule 6. in Appendix V.)	모르세요
죽다	to die	죽어요	돌아가세요
따뜻하다	to be warm (weather)	따뜻해요	--
춥다	to be cold (weather)	추워요	--

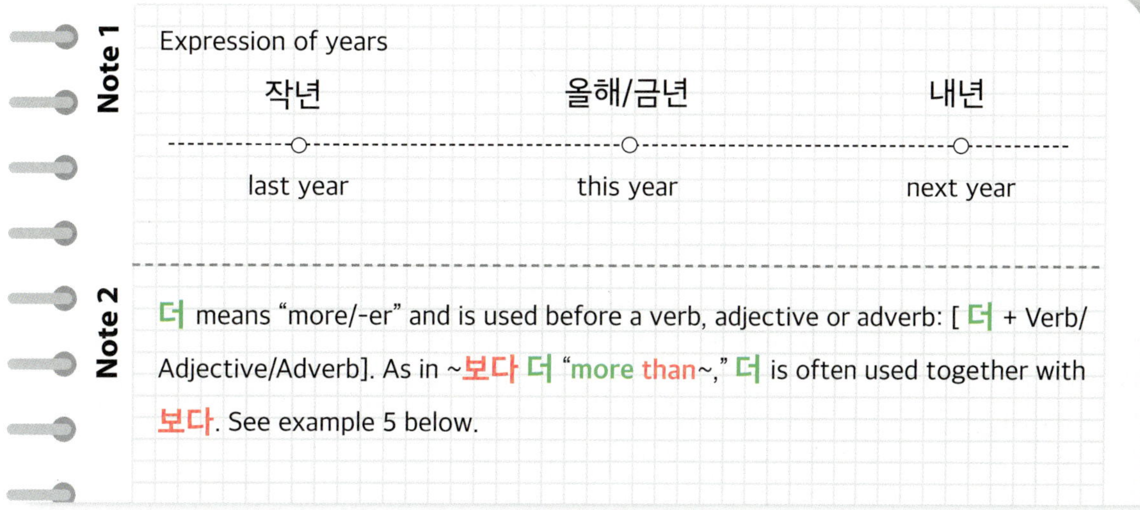

Note 1

Expression of years

작년	올해/금년	내년
last year	this year	next year

Note 2

더 means "more/-er" and is used before a verb, adjective or adverb: [더 + Verb/Adjective/Adverb]. As in ~보다 더 "more than~," 더 is often used together with 보다. See example 5 below.

1. A: 크림 좀 더 드릴까요? (드릴까요: verb) — Should I give you a little more cream?
   B: 네, 더 주세요. (주세요: verb) — Yes, please give me more.
2. A: 뭘 더 주문할까요? (주문할까요: verb) — Should we order more?
   B: 이제 됐어요. — It's fine.
3. A: 손님, 뭐가 더 필요하세요? (필요하세요: adjective) — Sir, do you need anything else? [Lit., what is more necessary?]
   B: 포크 하나만 더 주세요. (주세요: verb) — Please give us one more fork.
4. A: 뉴욕은 겨울에 많이 추워요? — Is New York very cold in the winter?
   B: 네. 근데 올해가 더 춥네요. (춥네요: adjective) — Yes, but it is colder this year.
5. 저는 민준 씨보다 더 열심히 공부해요. (열심히: adverb) — I study harder than Minjoon.

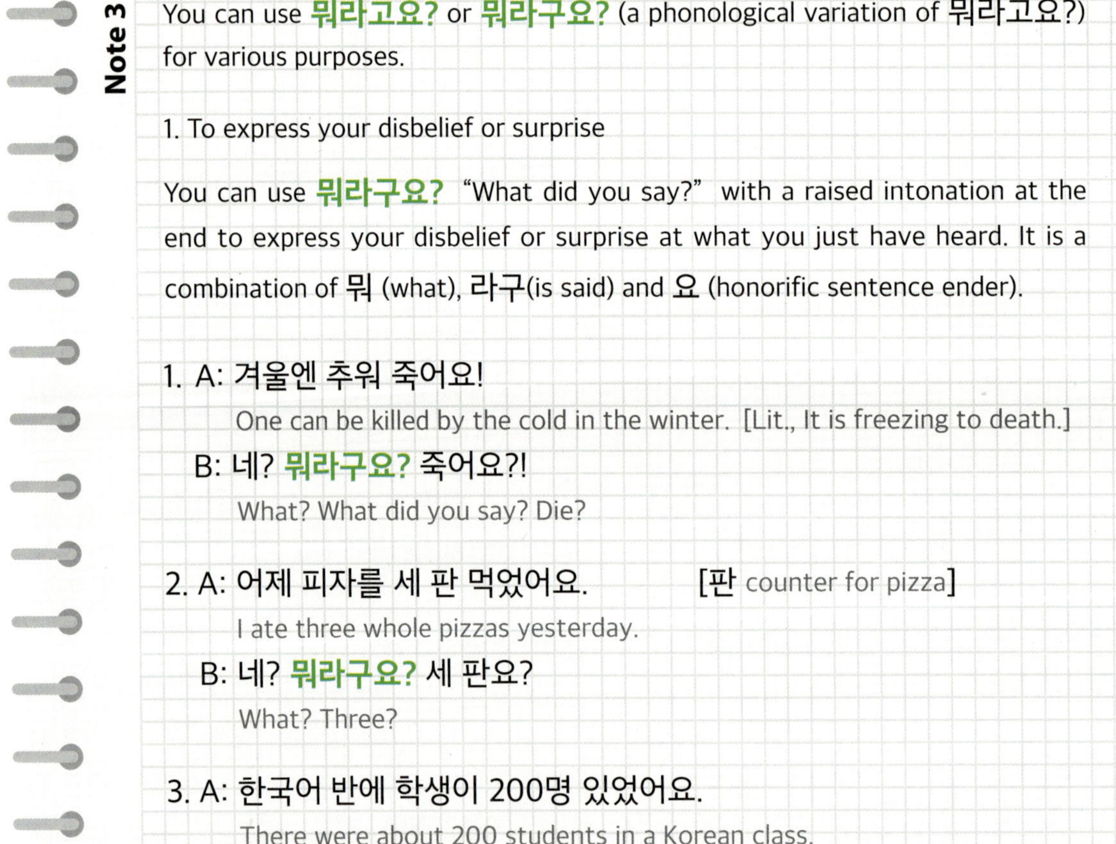

Note 3

You can use 뭐라고요? or 뭐라구요? (a phonological variation of 뭐라고요?) for various purposes.

1. To express your disbelief or surprise

You can use 뭐라구요? "What did you say?" with a raised intonation at the end to express your disbelief or surprise at what you just have heard. It is a combination of 뭐 (what), 라구(is said) and 요 (honorific sentence ender).

1. A: 겨울엔 추워 죽어요!
   One can be killed by the cold in the winter. [Lit., It is freezing to death.]
   B: 네? 뭐라구요? 죽어요?!
   What? What did you say? Die?
2. A: 어제 피자를 세 판 먹었어요. [판 counter for pizza]
   I ate three whole pizzas yesterday.
   B: 네? 뭐라구요? 세 판요?
   What? Three?
3. A: 한국어 반에 학생이 200명 있었어요.
   There were about 200 students in a Korean class.
   B: 뭐라구요? 200명이요?
   What? That many? 200 people?

2. To show you are upset

You can also use **뭐라구요?** with a raised intonation at the end to show that you are upset because what you have heard is absurd.

(Conversation between an employee and a boss.)

A: 요즘 너무 바빠서 리포트를 아직 못 끝냈어요.

I couldn't finish the report yet because I've been busy these days.

B: **뭐라구요?** 오늘까지인데요.

What? It's due by today!

3. To indirectly request the other speaker to repeat what they said

You can also use **뭐라구요?** when you misheard or didn't hear something in order to request the speaker to repeat it.

(Conversation between a bank teller and a customer)

A: 성함이 어떻게 되세요? What is your name?

B: (didn't hear) **뭐라구요?** What did you say?

Exercise 1

Listen to the audio and fill in the blanks.  24

1. 오늘 진짜 ____________. 오늘 아침이 14도예요.
2. 한국은 여름에 많이 ____________?
3. 5월이면 ____________.

Exercise 2

Listen to the audio and fill in the blanks. 25

1. A: 뉴욕은 ____________ 추워요?
   B: 네. 올해가 유난히 더 춥네요.
2. A: ____________ 따뜻해져요?
   B: 5월이면 따뜻해져요.
3. A: 한국은 여름에 더워 죽어요.
   B: 네? ____________?
4. A: 죽어요?
   B: 하하. __________________ 그래요.

II. Patterns, Expressions & Practice

1. Verb or adjective base + ~이면/면, ~으면/면 "if ..." or "when ..."

Usage Use ~으면/~면 to indicate conditional/hypothetical situations or those that are certain to take place. ~으면/~면 is equivalent to the English "if" or "when."

Form1 NOUN + 이면/면 (Lit., If it is NOUN)

- NOUN + 이면 (When NOUN ends in a consonant)
- NOUN + 면 (When NOUN ends in a vowel) [이 *is dropped*]

1. 5월이면 날씨가 따뜻해요. [ㄹ+ 이면] In May, it is warm. [Lit., If (it) is May, the weather is warm.]
2. 두 시간이면 가요. In two hours, you can get there. [Lit., If (it) is two hours, (you) go.]
3. 한 시면 좋을까요? [ㅣ+ 면] Will 1 o'clock be good? [Lit., If (it) is 1 o'clock, will (it) be good?]
4. 학생이면 무료예요. For a student, it is free. [Lit., If (one) is a student, (it) is free.]
5. 다음 주면 방학이에요. It's a school break next week. [Lit., when (it) is next week, it is a school break]

Useful expressions

무료 no charge; free
방학 school break

Form2 Verb/Adjective + 으면/면

- Verb/Adjective + 으면 (When Verb/Adjective ends in a consonant)
- Verb/Adjective + 면 (When Verb/Adjective ends in a vowel)

* Verb/Adjective base (ending in ㄹ) + 면

1. 내일 날씨가 좋으면 등산 가요. [ㅎ + 으면]
   If the weather is good tomorrow, let's go mountain climbing.
2. 이번 주말에 바쁘면 다음 주말에 만나요. [ㅡ + 면]
   If (you) are busy this weekend, let's meet next weekend.
3. 일이 끝나면 저한테 문자하세요.
   When your work is over, please text me.
4. 뉴욕에 오면 저한테 전화하세요.
   When you come to New York, please call me.
5. 한국에 살면 한국어를 빨리 배워요. [ㄹ + 면]
   If you live in Seoul, you learn Korean quickly.

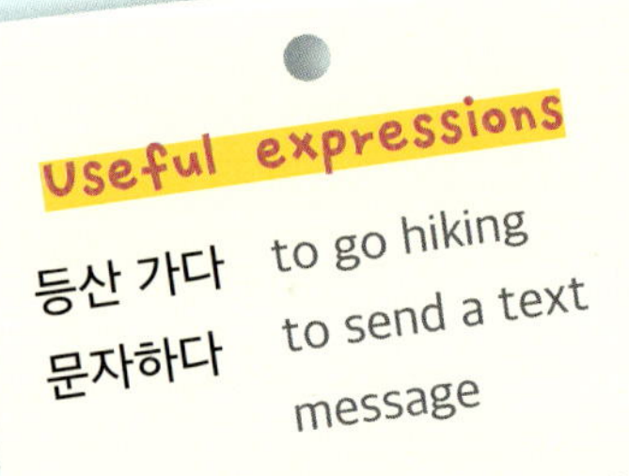

Complete each dialogue with the "NOUN + 이면/면" form using the information provided in ( ).

1. A: 한국은 7월에 날씨가 어때요?
   B: (7월이다)____________ 아주 더워요.

2. A: 오늘 몇 시에 일이 끝나요?
   B: 아마 (여섯 시이다)____________ 끝나요.

3. A: 시카고까지 얼마나 걸려요?
   B: 차로 (세 시간이다)____________ 가요.

4. A: 테니스 자주 치세요?
   B: (토요일이다)____________ 항상 테니스 쳐요.

Complete the following dialogues using ~으면/~면.

1. A: 시간 (있다)____________ 보통 뭐하세요?
   B: 저는 보통 운동해요. 수업이 (없다)____________ 학교 수영장에서 수영해요.

2. A: 커피를 안 (마시다)____________ 차를 드세요.
   B: 무슨 차 있어요?

3. A: 서울에서 부산까지 얼마나 걸려요?
   B: KTX를 (타다)____________ 세 시간 반 걸려요.

4. A: 내일 날씨가 (좋다)____________ 등산 갈까요?
   B: 내일 비 와요.
   A: 그래요? 내일 비 (오다)____________ 영화 볼까요?
   B: 네. 좋아요.

Useful expressions

수영장	swimming pool
KTX를 타다	to take the KTX (Korea Train Express)
타다	to ride
비(가) 오다	to rain
(시간이) 걸리다	to take (time)

Patterns, Expressions & Practice

Listen to the conversation between Amy and Minjoon and answer the questions in Korean. 26

1. When does Minjoon usually do on weekends?

____.

2. What kind of exercise does Minjoon do?

____.

3. What does Amy do when she has time?

____.

Useful expressions

농구	basketball
보통	usually
온라인 게임	online game

2. Weather expressions

There are four seasons (사계절) in Korea.

계절 (Seasons)	
봄	spring
여름	summer
가을	fall
겨울	winter

Here are some of the words that can be used to express weather.

Words expressing weather		~어요/~아요 form
덥다	to be hot	더워요
춥다	to be cold	추워요
따뜻하다	to be warm	따뜻해요
시원하다	to be cool	시원해요
서늘하다	to be cool; be refreshing	서늘해요
쌀쌀하다	to be chilly	쌀쌀해요

맑다	to be clear; to be sunny	맑아요
흐리다	to be cloudy	흐려요
구름이 끼다	to be cloudy	구름이 껴요
비가 오다	for rain to come	비가 와요
눈이 오다	for snow to come	눈이 와요
바람이 불다	for the wind to blow	바람이 불어요
기온이 낮다	for the temperature to be low	기온이 낮아요
기온이 높다	for the temperature to be high	기온이 높아요

Temperatures (기온) in Korea are measured in Celsius (섭씨, °C) and not Fahrenheit (화씨, °F). For example, "thirty-five degree Celsius" is 섭씨 35도.

1. 지금 서울 기온은 28도예요. The temperature in Seoul is 28 °C now.
2. 오늘 서울 낮 기온은 31도예요. The mid-day temperature in Seoul today is 31 °C.
3. 오늘 서울 밤 기온은 23도예요. The temperature tonight in Seoul is 23 °C.

Describe the following weather in Korean.

1. ____________________

2. 

3. 

4. ____________________

5. ____________________

Look at the weather map and report the weather conditions of each city today, as in (1).

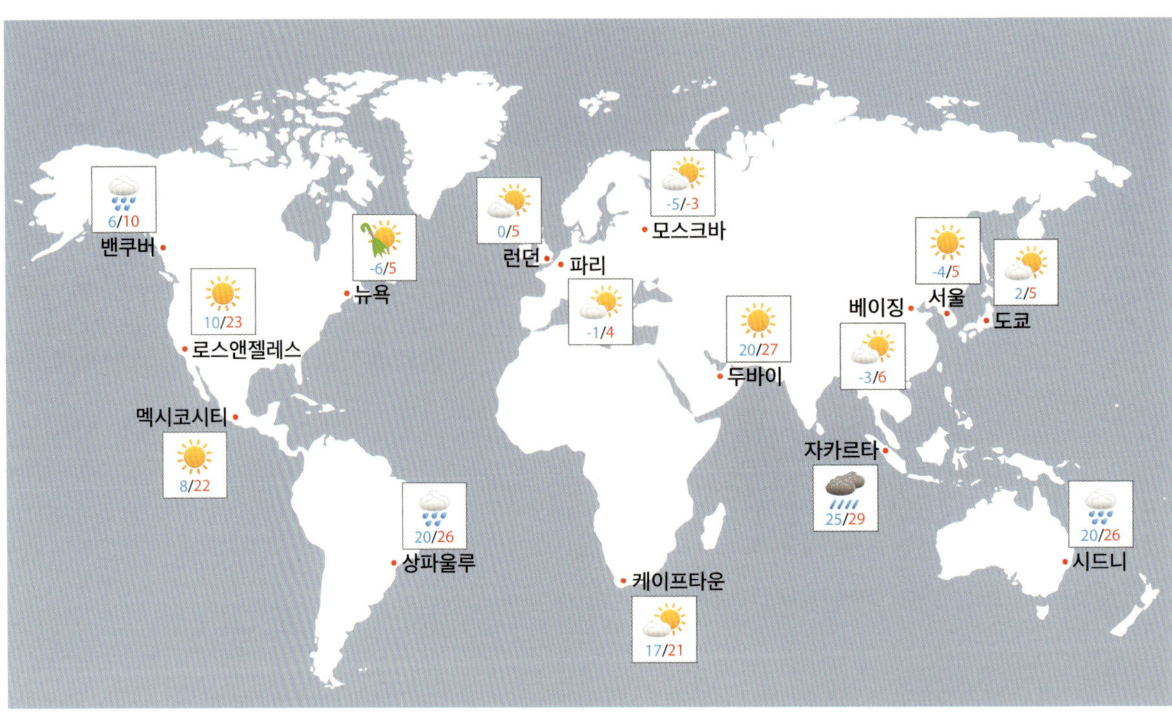

1. 뉴욕은 오늘 영하 육 도에서 영상 오 도예요. 아침에 비가 오고 오후에 맑아져요.

2. 런던은 오늘 ______________________. ______________________.

3. 모스크바는 오늘 ______________________. ______________________.

4. 밴쿠버는 오늘 ______________________. ______________________.

5. 서울은 오늘 ______________________. ______________________.

Listen to the conversation about winter weather in Chicago, Hawaii, and Busan and answer the following questions in Korean. 27

1. 제시카 씨 고향이 어디예요?

______________________________.

2. 시카고 겨울 날씨가 어때요?

______________________________.

3. 제시카 씨는 얼마 동안 하와이에 살았어요?

______________________________.

4. 하와이 겨울 날씨가 어때요?

______________________________.

5. 민수 씨 고향은 어디예요?

______________________________.

6. 부산 겨울 날씨가 어때요?

______________________________.

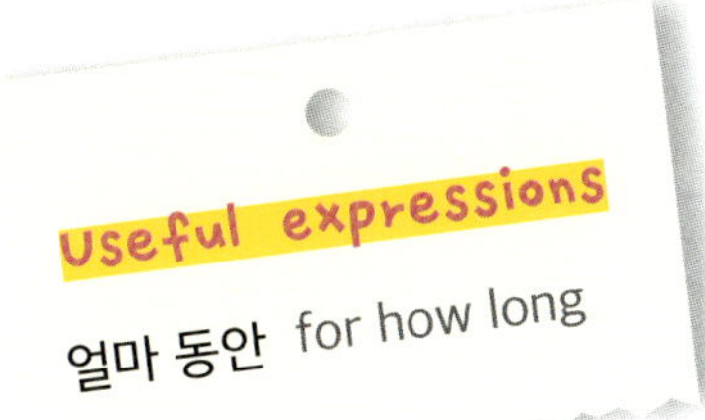

3. Adjective base + ~아지다/~어지다 "to become ~"

Usage Use "Adjective + 아지다/어지다" to express a change of someone or something from one state/condition to another.

Form The choice between ~아지다/~어지다 depends on the last vowel of the dictionary form of an adjective.

▶아 or 오 ending adjective + 아지다

▶Other vowel-ending adjective base + 어지다

▶~하다 ending adjectives → ~해지다

The rule for the choice between ~아지다 and ~어지다 is the same as that of the choice between ~아요/~어요, which you studied in "2. Sentence ending:~어요/~아요" in Lesson 4. See the example sentences below.

1. 낮(day)이 많이 짧아졌어요. The day became very short.
[ㅏ + 아지다]

2. 저와 애니는 사이가 멀어졌어요. The relationship between Annie and me became distant. [사이 relationship; 멀다 to be far or distant]
[ㅓ + 어지다]

3. 내일은 날씨가 추워져요. The weather for tomorrow will become cold.

4 오늘 날씨가 갑자기 추워졌어요. The weather has become cold today.
[추우 + 어지다]

5. 요즘 집 값이 싸졌어요. These days the housing price has become cheap.

6. 옷이 작아졌어요. The clothes became small.

7. 다니엘하고 친해졌어요. I became close with Daniel. [친하다 to be close]

8. 요즘 경기가 많이 나빠졌어요. The economic conditions became worse recently. [경기 economic conditions]

Note If a current state or condition is the result of a change in the past, you must use the past form "~아졌어요/~어졌어요."

How has the weather changed? Tell us the changes of the weather using "Adjectives + 아졌다/어졌다," as in (1).

따뜻하다 to be warm	덥다 to be hot	서늘하다 to be cool
춥다 to be cold	맑다 to become clear	

1.

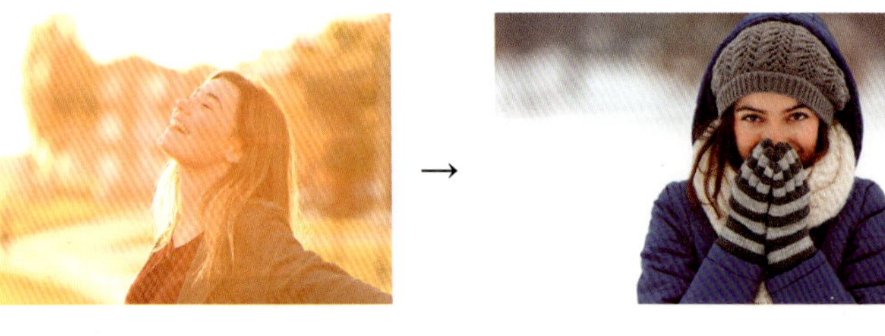

날씨가 추워졌어요.

2.

→

______________________________.

3.

→ ______________________________.

4.

→ ______________________________.

5.

→ ______________________________.

A restaurant near your house is now under the new ownership and you noticed some changes. Tell the changes of state using "Adjective + 아졌다/어졌다" as shown in (1). You may use the following adjectives in your answer.

많다 to be a lot	좋다 to be good	맛있다 to be delicious
깨끗하다 to be clean	비싸다 to be expensive	

1. 식당이 깨끗해졌어요.
2. 음식이 ______________________________.
3. 음식값이 ______________________________.
4. 서비스가 ______________________________.
5. 직원이 ______________________________.

Listen to the conversation between Amy and Minjoon and answer the questions in Korean. 28

1. How is the weather?

______________________________.

2. How is Amy these days? Why?

______________________________.

3. How is Minjoon's workload these days?

______________________________.

4. Adjective + ~아 죽다/~어 죽다 "~ to death"

Usage 죽다 means "to die." ~아 죽다/~어 죽다 literally means "to die from ~." It is used to emphasize the intensity of a certain state or condition.

A: 서울 여름 날씨 어때요?	How is the summer weather in Korea?
B: 더워 죽어요.	It is really hot. [Lit., It is hot to death.]

When emphasizing one's emotion or state, ~아 죽겠어요/~어 죽겠어요 is frequently used, which literally means "I will die from ~."

덥다 to be hot	더워 죽겠어요.	I feel so hot.
춥다 to be cold	추워 죽겠어요.	I feel so cold.
바쁘다 to be busy	바빠 죽겠어요.	I'm busy to death.
배고프다 to be hungry	배고파 죽겠어요.	I'm hungry to death.
배부르다 to be full	배불러 죽겠어요.	I'm so full.
시끄럽다 to be noisy	시끄러워 죽겠어요.	It's so noisy.
졸리다 to be sleepy	졸려 죽겠어요.	I'm so sleepy.
피곤하다 to be tired	피곤해 죽겠어요.	I'm so tired.
힘들다 to be strenuous	힘들어 죽겠어요.	It's so backbreaking/hard.

Imagine that you are the person in the pictures below. Express your emotions by exaggerating them using ~아 죽겠어요/~어 죽겠어요. You may use the words in the box below.

졸리다 to feel sleepy	배부르다 to be full	배고프다 to be hungry
바쁘다 to be busy	무겁다 to be heavy	시끄럽다 to be noisy
힘들다 to be strenuous	피곤하다 to be tired	

1.

2.

3.

4.
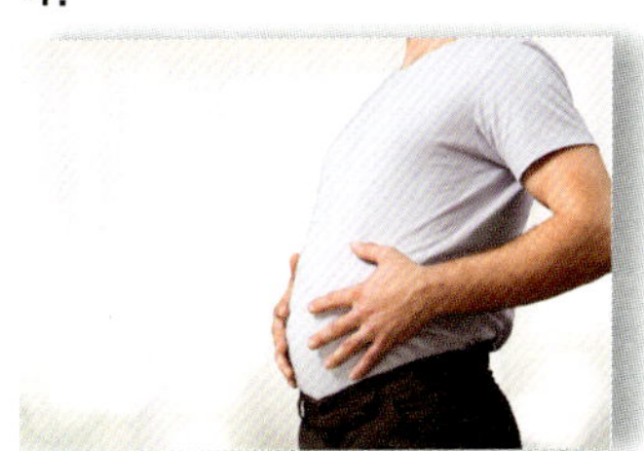

5.

6.

III. Culture

Weather conditions in Korea

Korea has four seasons (봄 spring, 여름 summer, 가을 fall, and 겨울 winter). Koreans often refer to the change of the weather as a good conversation starter as the weather changes frequently. 한반도 (The Korean peninsula) is located in the temperate climate region. In hot summer months, the weather condition changes close to the tropical climate. The temperature changes from the winter averaging -6~3°C (21°F~37°F) in January to the summer averaging 23~ 26°C (73°F~78°F) in August. The typical time of Korean summer is from July to August and is characterized as humid and hot with a long rainy season in July. This rainy season is called 장마 (*jangma*). Winter in Korea is generally cold, relatively dry, and clear.

In winter, many Koreans celebrate 첫눈 오는 날 (the day of the first snow) with their loved ones. Koreans think the first snow is good news and a true beginning of winter. On this day they call friends and loved ones for a friendly get-together after work. They usually go out and have dinner and share drinks to celebrate the nature's gift.

IV. Listen & Discuss

Minjoon and Amy are at the office talking about the recent weather in New York. Listen to the conversation carefully. Discuss the answers to the following questions with your classmates. Then, write each answer in a full Korean sentence in the space provided.

1. 오늘 아침은 몇 도예요?

____

2. 뉴욕은 올해 날씨가 어때요?

____

3. 뉴욕 날씨가 언제면 따뜻해져요?

____

4. 한국의 여름 날씨는 어때요?

____

Script

☞ **Minjoon and Amy are at the office talking about the recent weather in New York.**

01 민준 : 으~, 오늘 정말 춥네요.[II.2]

02 에이미: 네, 진짜 추워요! 오늘 아침이 14도예요.

03 민준 : 뉴욕은 원래 이렇게 추워요?

04 에이미: 네, 올해가 유난히 더 춥네요.

05 민준 : 그래요? 그럼 언제쯤 따뜻해져요?[II.3]

06 에이미: 음... 5월이면 따뜻해져요.[II.1]

07 민준 : 와~ 한국은 5월이면 벌써 더워요.

08 에이미: 아 그래요? 몰랐어요. 한국은 여름에 많이 더워요?

09 민준 : 네, 정말 더워요. 더워 죽어요![II.4]

10 에이미: 네? 뭐라구요? 죽어요?!

11 민준 : 하하. 그냥 표현이 그래요.

01 Minjoon: Brr, today is really cold.

02 Amy : Yes, it's really cold! It's 14 degrees this morning.

03 Minjoon: Is New York always this cold?

04 Amy : Yeah. This year is particularly colder.

05 Minjoon: Really? Around when does it become warmer then?

06 Amy : Um··· It becomes warm by May.

07 Minjoon: Wow~ In Korea, by May, it is already hot.

08 Amy : Is that right? I didn't know. Is summer in Korea very hot?

09 Minjoon: Yes, it is really hot. One can get killed!

10 Amy : What? What did you say? Die?

11 Minjoon: Haha. It is just an expression.

V. Guided Conversation

With the organization of the model conversation in Listen & Discuss (Script) in mind, practice the modified conversation below with your partner.

step 1 **Two close friends are talking about the recent weather in a city. Practice the following conversation with your partner, using the information in (   ).**

01 A: ________ (으~; 헉!; 음~), 오늘 정말 ________ (춥네요; 덥네요; 시원하네요).

02 B: 네, 진짜 ________ (추워요!; 더워요!; 시원해요!) 오늘 아침이 ________ (14도; 99도; 54도) 예요.

03 A: ________ (뉴욕; 서울, 밴쿠버; ...) 은/는 원래 이렇게 ________ (추워요?; 더워요?; 시원해요?)?

04 B: 네. ________ (올 겨울; 올 여름; 올 가을) 이 유난히 ________ (더 춥네요; 더 덥네요; 더 시원하네요).

05 A: 그래요? 그럼 언제쯤 ________ (따뜻해져요?; 시원해져요?; 추워져요?)?

06 B: 음... ________ (5월; 9월; 11월; ...) 이면 ________ (따뜻해져요?; 시원해져요?; 추워져요?)?

07 A: 와~. ________ (your town) 은/는/도 ________ (5월; 9월; 11월; ...) 이면 ________ (벌써) ________ (더워요; 시원해요; 추워요).

For lines 08-11, choose (1) or (2) to make your conversation move naturally.

Guided Conversation

08 B: 아 그래요? 몰랐어요.

(1) ______ (A's town) 은/는 ______ (여름;겨울) 에 많이 ______ (더워요?; 추워요?) ?

(2) ______ (A's town) 은/는 가을에 어때요?

09 A: (1) ______ (더워; 추워) 죽어요!

(2) 여기보다 더 ______ (추워요; 더워요).

10 B: (1) 네? 뭐라구요? 죽어요?!

(2) 부러워요!

11 A: (1) 하하. 그냥 표현이 그래요.

(2) 하하 그래요? 언제 ______ (따뜻해지다; 시원해지다) 으면/면 ______ (your town) 에 한번 놀러 오세요~

Useful expressions

10 부럽다	to be envious
11 언제	someday
한번	once
놀러 오세요!	Come and enjoy the visit

(Switch roles and continue to practice.)

step 2 Present the conversation from Step 1 in front of the class. Try not to read it!

VI. Spontaneous Conversation

Now is your chance to have real interactions with your classmates in Korean. You can practice speaking with your classmates, writing, and presenting in front of the class!

step 1

Using the expressions in the box below and some additional expressions from the Guided Conversation, talk to one another in groups of three. Exchange information about the weather conditions of each person's hometown.

- ▶ (뉴욕; 텍사스; LA; 서울 ...)의 (봄; 여름; 가을; 겨울) 날씨는 어때요?
- ▶ (봄; 여름; 가을; 겨울)에는 보통 몇 도까지 (올라 가요; 내려가요)?
- ▶ (봄; 여름; 가을; 겨울)에는 보통 몇 도예요?
- ▶ (여름; 가을)에는 많이 (더워요; 추워요; 습해요; 건조해요)?
- ▶ (봄; 가을)에는 많이 (따뜻해요; 시원해요)?
- ▶ (봄; 여름; 가을; 겨울)은 (길어요; 짧아요; 어때요)?
- ▶ Additional expressions from the Guided Conversation.

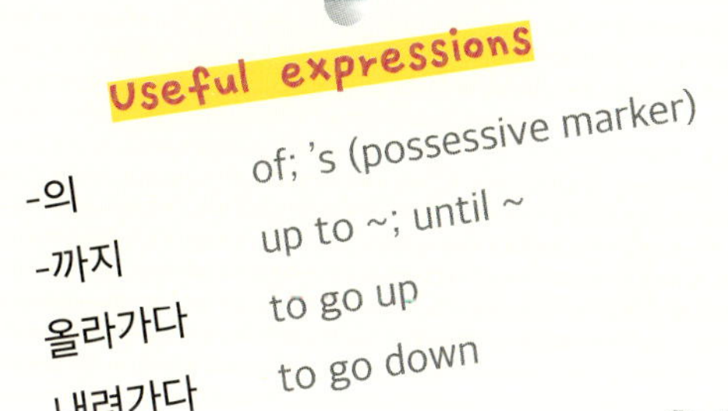

Complete the table with the information you collected from each classmate about the weather/climate conditions in their hometown.

	Weather/Climate conditions	
	Classmate 1	Classmate 2
봄		
여름		

가을		
겨울		

Now let's write a narrative about the weather/climate conditions of each classmate's town, based on the information in the table.

For example,

Classmate 1의 고향은 LA예요. LA의 봄은 따뜻해요. 보통 화씨 54도예요. 낮에는 70도까지 올라가고, 밤에는 47도까지 내려가요. 봄은 길어요. 여름은 ...

Based on what you wrote in Step 2, present the weather/climate conditions of each classmate's town. Try not to read what you wrote in Step 2.

15 우리 점심 먹으러 가요.

Let's go to eat lunch.

Talking about what to eat for lunch

Preparation & Practice	I. New Words & Expressions II. Patterns, Expressions & Practice 1. Responding to a negative question 2. ~으러 가다/~러 가다 — to go for the purpose of ~ 3. ~아 봤다/~어 봤다 — to have done ~ 4. ~는데, ~은/~ㄴ데, ~인데 — Giving background information III. Culture Everyday Korean meals
Conversation Activities	IV. Listen & Discuss V. Guided Conversation VI. Spontaneous Conversation

I. New Words & Expressions

 **Study the words and expressions with the audio.** 

30

NOUN

근처 neighborhood; vicinity
[이 근처: *nearby*]

배 stomach; belly

불닭 spicy chicken *[Lit., fire chicken]*

순두부 soft tofu

점심 (1) lunch; (2) lunch time

정도 about ~; around ~ [*Lit., degree*]

PRONOUN

거기 there; that place [거기서: *at there*]

우리 we; our; us

ADJECTIVE

배고프다 to be hungry

비싸다 to be expensive

ADVERB

아직 yet; still

EXPRESSION

· 거긴

as for that place [*shortened form of* 거기는]

· (코리아 하우스) 말이에요?

Do you mean (Korea House)?

Form

Dictionary form (Word base + 다)		~아요/~어요 form	~으세요/~세요 form
배고프다	to be hungry	배고파요	배고프세요
비싸다	to be expensive	비싸요	--
-에 가 봤다	to have been to ~	가 봤어요	가 보셨어요
... 말이다	to mean ~	... 말이에요	... 말씀이세요

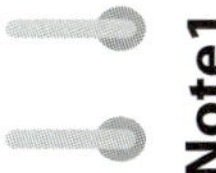

Note1

Use ~**말이에요?** "Do you mean ~?" in a question to check or confirm your understanding of the information in the given context.

1. A: 도서관에서 만나요. — Let's meet at the library.
   B: 중앙 도서관 **말이에요?** — Do you mean the Central Library?

2. A: 학생이세요? — Are you a student?
   B: 저 **말이에요?** — Are you talking to me?

In a statement, use ~말이에요 (I mean ~; I am saying ~; What I am saying is ~) to confirm or emphasize what you meant or just said.

3. A: 아직 안 왔어요?	Hasn't she come yet?
B: 수미 씨 말이에요?	Are you talking about Sumi? (Question)
A: 아뇨. 제시카 씨 말이에요.	No, I mean Jessica. (Statement)
4. A: 민준 씨 벌써 왔죠?	Minjoon already came, right?
B: 누구요?	Who?
A: 민준 씨 말이에요.	I mean Minjoon.

Note 2

하다 literally means "to do," but In the context of "8불에서 12불 정도 해요," 하다 means "to cost."

A: 요즘 순두부찌개 얼마죠?	How much is 순두부찌개 these days?
B: 8불에서 12불 정도 해요.	It costs around 8 to 12 dollars. [Lit., It does 8 dollars to 12 dollars.]

Note 3

정도 "around/about ~" is interchangeable with -쯤.

A : 요즘 된장찌개 얼마죠?	How much is 된장찌개 these days?
B1: 12불 정도 해요.	It cost about 12 dollars.
B2: 12불쯤 해요.	It cost about 12 dollars.

Note 4

그럼 means "if so; well, then" or "of course" depending on the context.

1. 그럼 means "if so" or "well, then." 그럼 is a shortened form of 그러면. In colloquial speech, 그러면은 is also used for the same meaning.

1) A: 오늘은 제가 살게요.	It's on me today.
B: 그럼, 다음에 제가 살게요.	Then I will buy next time.
2) A: 오늘은 바빠요.	As for today, I am busy.
B: 그럼, 다음에 만나요.	Then let's meet next time.

3) A: 햄버거 먹을래요? 피자 먹을래요? Would you like to have hamburger? (Or) would you like to have pizza?

B: 피자요. Pizza.

A: 그러면, 피자 주문할게요. Then I will order pizza.

4) A: 배 고파요? Are you hungry?

B: 네. Yes.

A: 그럼, 같이 점심 먹어요. Then let's have lunch together.

2. 그럼 means "of course." 그럼요 is a combination of 그럼 and the honorific sentence ender 요. Use 그럼 between close friends.

1) A: 내일 파티에 와요? Are you coming to the party tomorrow?

B: 그럼요. Of course.

2) A: 한국 음식 괜찮아요? Are you alright with Korean food?

B: 그럼요. Of course.

3) A: 마이클 씨 알아요? Do you know Michael?

B: 그럼요, 알아요. Of course, I know him.

4) (Between close friends)

A: 마이클 알아? Do you know Michael?

B: 그럼, 알아. Of course, I know him.

Listen to the audio and fill in the blanks. 31

1. 배 안 고파요? 우리 ______________ 가요.

2. 거기 음식 괜찮은데 거기서 ______________?

3. 이 근처 한국 식당에 ______________?

Listen to the audio and fill in the blanks. 

1. A: 이 근처 한국 식당에 가 봤어요?

   B: "코리아 하우스" ______________________________?

   A: 네.

2. A: 코리아 하우스 가 봤어요?

   B: ________________________ 안 가 봤어요.

3. A: 거긴 _____________________________?

   B: 비빔밥하고 불닭이 맛있어요.

4. A: 거기 _____________________________?

   B: 네. 8불에서 12불 정도 해요.

II. Patterns, Expressions & Practice

1. Responding to a negative question

Usage Negative questions in Korean are phrased differently from English. When a negative question contains correct information, respond with "네" or "예." When it contains incorrect information, respond with "아뇨" or "아니요" and then you may provide the correct information.

English: A: Don't you study?
B1: No, (I don't study).
B2: Yes, (I study).

The same response in English above is phrased in a different way in Korean.

한국어: A: 공부 안 해요?
B1: 네, (안 해요). [Lit., Yes, (I don't study).]
B2: 아니요/아뇨, 해요. [Lit., No, I study.]

Look at more examples below.

1. A: 영화 보러 안 가요? Aren't you going to see the movie?
B: 네. 전 벌써 그 영화 봤어요. No. I've already seen the movie. [Lit., Yes. I've already seen the movie.]
Saying "네 (Yes)" because "not going" is true.

2. A: 점심 안 먹었어요? Didn't you have lunch?
B: 네, 안 먹었어요. No, I didn't. [Lit., Yes, I didn't eat.]
Saying "네 (Yes)" because "didn't eat" is true.

3. A: 점심 안 먹었어요? Didn't you have lunch?
B: 아뇨, 먹었어요. Yes, I did. [Lit., No. I ate.]
Saying "아뇨 (No)" because "didn't eat" is not true.

Respond to the following questions in Korean using 네 or 아니요/아뇨.

1. A: 한국에 안 가 봤어요?

   B: ____________. 안 가 봤어요.

2. A: 한국 음식 안 먹어 봤어요?

   B: ____________. 먹어 봤어요.

3. A: 내일 미팅에 안 가요?

   B: ____________. 못 가요.

4. A: 아이스크림 안 좋아하세요?

   B: ____________. 좋아해요. 근데 지금은 배가 좀 불러서요.

Exercise 2

Respond to the following questions in Korean, as in (1).

Useful expressions

취소되다 to be cancelled
한국 문화 Korean culture

1. A: 운전 못 해요?

   B: 네, 운전 못 해요.

2. A: 남자 친구는 한국말 못 해요?

   B: ______________________________.

3. A: 내일 미팅 없어요?

   B: ________________________. 취소됐어요.

4. A: 초콜릿 케이크 안 좋아해요?

   B: ________________________.

5. A: 다음 학기에 한국 문화 수업 안 들어요?

   B: ________________________.

2. Verb base + ~으러 가다/~러 가다 "to go for the purpose of ~"

Usage Use "Verb base + ~으러 가다/~러 가다" to express the purpose of going. It means "to go in order to do ~" or "to go for the purpose of doing ~." You may put some other information between 으러/러 and 가다, which is indicated with (...) below.

Verb base + 으러/러 (...) 가다/오다 to go for the purpose of ~

Form Use the rule below to choose between ~으러 (...) 가다 and ~러 (...) 가다.

- ▶ Consonant-ending verb base + 으러 (...) 가다/오다
- ▶ Vowel-ending verb base + 러 (...) 가다/오다
- * Verb base (ending in ㄹ) + 러 (...) 가다/오다

1. 이번 여름에 한국어 배우러 서울에 가요.
   [우+러]
2. 오늘 오전에 친구하고 같이 커피 마시러 카페에 가요.
3. 그룹 프로젝트가 있어서 친구들 만나러 도서관에 가요.
4. A: 어디 가세요?
   B: 식당에요. 점심 먹으러요.
   [ㄱ+으러]
5. A: 어디 가세요?
   B: 체육관에요. [체육관 gym]
   A: 운동하러 가세요? [운동하다 to exercise]
   B: 네. 농구 하러 가요. [농구하다 to play basketball]
6. A: 학교 앞 이탈리아 식당에 가 봤어요?
   B: La Mancha 말이에요? 아직 안 가 봤는데⋯.
   A: 그럼, 오늘 같이 저녁 먹으러 갈까요?
7. 김밥 만들러 와요.

Respond to the following questions in Korean, as in (1).

1. A: 점심 먹으러 보통 어디 가세요?
   B: 저는 보통 학교 식당에 가요.

2. A: 운동하러 어디 가세요?
   B: ______________________.

3. A: 옷 사러 보통 어디 가세요?

   B: ______________________________.

4. A: 영화 보러 보통 어디 가세요?

   B: ______________________________.

   "AMC 영화관"

5. A: 데이트하러 보통 어디 가세요?

   B: ______________________________.

6. A: 한국 음식 먹으러 보통 어디 가세요?

   B: ______________________________.

   "코리아 하우스"

You are going to places to do different activities. Respond with "~으러/~러 [place]에 가요." as in(1).

1. (도서관에서 공부해요.)

   공부하러 도서관에 가요.

2. 
   (백화점에서 쇼핑해요.)

   ______________________________.

3. 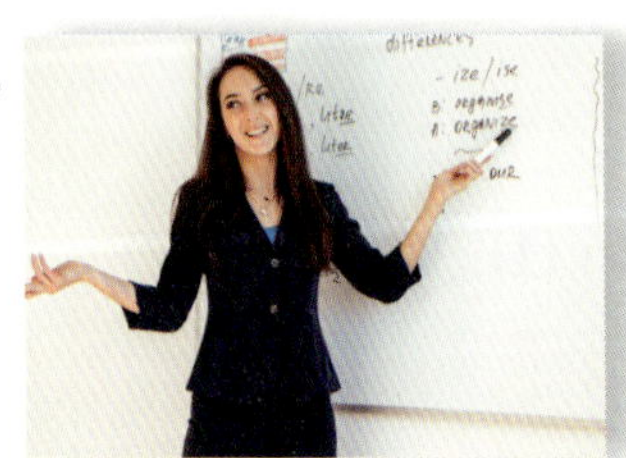
   (한국에서 영어를 가르쳐요.)

   ______________________________.

4. 
(카페에서 친구를 만나요.)

______________________________________.

5. 
(친구 집에서 저녁을 먹어요.)

______________________________________.

A group of your classmates is going to Korea this summer. Share each person's purpose for going to Korea using the information given in the box.

제니 : 한국어하고 한국 문화를 배우다
스티브: 서울에서 영어를 가르치다
제임스: 여행도 하고 쇼핑도 하다
리사 : 친구가 대전에 살아서 친구를 만나다
준호 : 부산대학교에서 한국 역사 수업을 듣다

Useful expressions

-도 하고 -도 하다	to do ~ and also do ~
대전	*Daejeon* (a city in South Korea)
한국 역사	Korean history

Question: 왜 한국에 가요?

1. 제니 : 한국어하고 한국 문화를 배우러 가요.
2. 스티브: ______________________________.
3. 제임스: ______________________________.
4. 리사 : ______________________________.
5. 준호 : ______________________________.

Patterns, Expressions & Practice

3. Verb base + ~아 봤다/~어 봤다 "to have done ~" [expressing past experiences]

Usage To express one's past experience, use the past tense form: "Verb base + ~아 봤다/~어 봤다."

1. 순두부찌개 먹어 봤어요.	I have tried soft tofu stew.
2. 한국에 가 봤어요?	Have you been to Korea?
3. 아르바이트 해 봤어요.	I've worked a part-time job.
4. 한국 노래 들어 봤어요.	I have listened to K-pop.
5. A: Peet's Coffee에 가 봤어요?	Have you been to Peet's Coffee?
B: 아뇨, 안 가 봤어요.	No, I haven't.
6. A: 한국어 수업 들어 봤어요?	Have you taken Korean class?
B: 네, 지난 학기에 들었어요.	Yes, I took last semester.

Ask your co-worker whether she/he has tried the following Korean dishes, as in (1).

1.	2.	3.	4.	5.
불고기	잡채	된장찌개	육개장	불닭

1. 불고기 먹어 봤어요?

2. ______________________________?

3. ______________________________?

4. ______________________________?

5. ______________________________?

Listen to the conversation between Minjoon and Jessica and answer the following questions. 33

<Conversation 1>

1. Circle all the dishes that Jessica has tried.
   a. 만두 b. 갈비 c. 불고기 d. 잡채

2. Circle the dish that Minjoon recommended to Jessica.
   a. 만두 b. 갈비 c. 불고기 d. 잡채

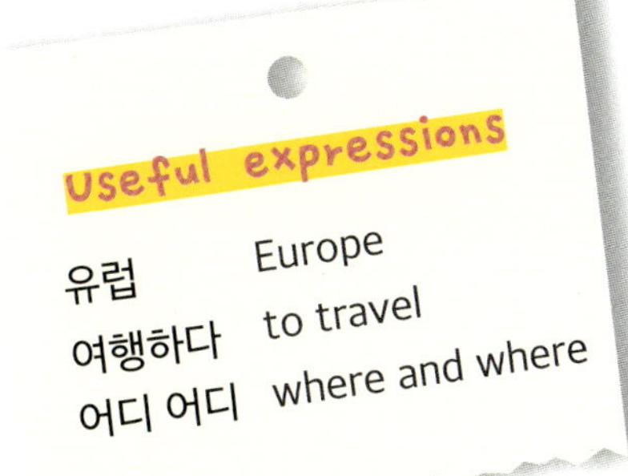

<Conversation 2>

3. Which countries has Minjoon NOT traveled to?
   a. 스페인 Spain b. 영국 United Kingdom c. 이탈리아 Italy d. 프랑스 France

4. Circle the places that Minjoon has visited.
   a. 바르셀로나 Barcelona b. 로마 Rome c. 밀라노 Milano d. 파리 Paris e. 런던 London

4. ~는데, ~은/~ㄴ데, ~인데 "... and/so/but"

Usage Use "Verb + 는데" or "Adjective + 은데/ ㄴ데" in the following situations.

1. To provide background information before saying the information to follow it:

   1. 어제 불닭을 먹어 봤는데 정말 매웠어.
      I have tried to eat 불닭. It was really spicy.

   2. 지금 비 오는데 우산 있어요?
      It's raining now; do you have an umbrella?

   3. 요즘 한국 드라마 보는데 재미있어요.
      I'm watching a Korean drama lately and it is fun.

2. To provide background information that contrasts with the information to follow it:

   1. 옷이 예쁜데 너무 비싸요.
      The clothes are pretty, but they are too expensive.

   2. 비 오는데 우산이 없어요.
      It's raining but I don't have an umbrella.

3. 공부했는데 시험을 못 봤어요.

   I studied but I didn't do well on the exam.

4. 크리스는 미국 사람인데 한국말을 잘 해요.

   Chris is an American but he speaks Korean well.

5. 한국어가 어려운데 재미있어요.

   Korean is difficult but it is fun.

3. To provide background information to justify your request or proposal: :

1. 시간이 없는데 택시를 타세요.

   You are running out of time; take a taxi.

2. 거기 음식 괜찮은데 거기서 먹을까요?

   The food there is good; shall we eat there?

3. 오늘은 바쁜데 내일 만나요.

   I'm busy today; let's meet tomorrow.

Form When you use a verb to provide background information, use "verb + 는데."

▶ Verb base + 는데, ...

가다 to go	: 가-		는데	→	가는데
공부하다 to study	: 공부하-		는데	→	공부하는데
보다 to see	: 보-		는데	→	보는데
먹다 to eat	: 먹-	+	는데	→	먹는데
오다 to come	: 오-		는데	→	오는데
있다 to have; exist	: 있-		는데	→	있는데
없다 to not have/exist	: 없-		는데	→	없는데

Form When you use an adjective to provide background information, use "adjective + 은데/ㄴ데."

▶ Adjective base (ending in a consonant) + 은데

▶ Adjective base (ending in a vowel) + ㄴ데

* Adjective base (ending in ㄹ, ㅎ) + ㄴ데

좋다 be good	: 좋-		은데	→	좋은데 [ㅎ+ 은데]
바쁘다 be busy	: 바쁘-		ㄴ데	→	바쁜데 [ㅡ+ ㄴ데]
예쁘다 to be pretty	: 예쁘-	+	ㄴ데	→	예쁜데
멀다 to be far	: 멀-(ㄹ drops)		ㄴ데	→	먼데
노랗다 to be yellow	: 노랗-(ㅎ drops)		ㄴ데	→	노란데

Form When you use 이다 to provide background information, use "NOUN + 인데/ ㄴ데."

▶NOUN (ending in a consonant) + 인데

▶NOUN (ending in a vowel) + 인데 or ㄴ데

대학생이다 to be a college student → 대학생인데

가수이다 to be a singer → 가수인데 or 가순데 (spoken)

Form When you use the past tense to provide background information, use " Adjective/Adjective base + 었는데/ 았는데."

알다 know : 알 + 았- + 는데 → 알았는데

읽다 read : 읽 + 었- + 는데 → 읽었는데

Note

Some verbs or adjectives that have bases ending in "ㅂ" do not follow the usual rules. (For ㅂ- irregular, see Rule 3. in Appendix Ⅴ.)

어렵다 to be difficult : 어렵 + 은데 → 어려우 + ㄴ데 → 어려운데

가깝다 to be close : 가깝 + 은데 → 가까우 + ㄴ데 → 가까운데

Give some background for what you want to say next. Connect each expression in the the left column with the related expression in the right column.

1. 이번 주는 좀 바쁜데 ·	· a. 시작할까요?
2. 좀 추운데 ·	· b. 다음 주에 만나요.
3. 요즘 요가 배우는데 ·	· c. 재미있어요.
4. 이제 10시인데 ·	· d. 연습을 많이 못 했어요.
5. 오늘 프레젠테이션이 있는데 ·	· e. 아주 맛있었어요.
6. 어제 한국 친구 집에서 김밥을 먹었는데 ·	· f. 창문 닫을까요?

Useful expressions

요가를 배우다 to learn yoga

창문을 닫다 to close the window

시작하다 to start

프레젠테이션 presentation

연습을 하다 to practice

Choose phrases from the box below and write them in the appropriate blanks in order to make a contrast between the two clauses.

이 선글라스가 예쁜데	한국 사람인데	차는 마시는데
생선은 좋아하는데	이번 주말에는 바쁜데	

1. ______________________ 커피는 안 마셔요.
2. ______________________ 다음 주말에는 시간이 있어요.
3. ______________________ 좀 비싸요.
4. ______________________ 영어를 아주 잘 해요.
5. ______________________ 고기는 안 좋아해요.

Useful expressions

선글라스 sunglasses
생선 fish

Exercise 10

Complete the following sentences using ~는데/~은데/~ㄴ데/인데 with the verb or adjective given in (   ).

1. A: 오늘 한국 마트에 (가다)______________ 같이 갈까요?
   B: 어, 오늘은 좀 바빠서요.
2. A: 기숙사는 어때요?
   B: (좋다)______________ 좀 작아요.
3. A: 이거 뭐예요?
   B: 이거 한국 음식(이다)______________ 조금 매워요.
4. A: 코리아 하우스 어때요?
   B: 거기 음식은 (맛있다)______________ 조금 비싸요.
5. A: 여기 에이미 씨하고 민준 씨 왔어요?
   B: 에이미 씨는 (왔다)______________ 민준 씨는 안 왔어요.

Useful expressions

작다 to be small
맵다 to be spicy

III. Culture

Everyday Korean meal

A typical everyday meal in Korea includes a bowl of steamed rice as a staple for the table, accompanied by a Korean-style soup. There are usually 2-3 side dishes (반찬) made from different seasonal cooked vegetables or seasoned dried seafood products, such as 오징어채 (dry squid) or 김 (roasted seaweed sheets). At the center, one main dish, such as 찌개 (a stew) or 구이 (a grilled meat), is presented for sharing around the table. Some of the popular main dishes are 된장찌개 (a soybean stew with different kinds of meats), 불고기 (sweetly marinated sliced beef), 생선구이 (pan fried fish), and 갈비찜 or 갈비구이 (steamed or grilled ribs with sweet soy sauce).

Kimchi (김치), the national dish of Korea

One can say that the single most important national dish that most Koreans eat everyday would be 김치 (*Kimchi*). Styles of 김치 vary widely from region to region, and the main ingredients for 김치 also including vegetables such as 무 (radish), 배추 (napa cabbage), 총각무 (small radish) or even 파 (scallion). The kinds of 김치 that Koreans eat differ seasonally. In the summer, they make 열무김치 (young radish water *kimchi*). In the winter they typically make 동치미 (radish water brine *kimchi*). However, for all seasons, 배추김치 (napa cabbage *kimchi*) is the most popular. 배추김치 (napa cabbage *kimchi*) is prepared in several steps.

First, cut napa cabbages into 4 pieces and brine them for a while.

Rinse them in cold water and season the salted napa cabbages with 마늘 (garlic), 고춧가루 (hot pepper flakes), 젓갈 (fish sauce), 무 (radish), and 생강 (ginger) seasoning.

Now just put the cabbage in a cool place and wait for a few days for the appropriate fermentation process to occur, and there is your 김치!

IV. Listen & Discuss

34

Jessica and her friend Xiaoming are talking about what to eat for lunch. Listen to the conversation carefully. Discuss the answers to the following questions with your classmates. Then, write each answer in a full Korean sentence in the space provided.

1. 샤오밍 씨와 제시카 씨는 어느 식당에서 점심 먹어요?

2. 샤오밍 씨에 따르면, 그 식당은 무슨 음식이 맛있어요? [-에 따르면 according to ~]

3. 제시카 씨는 어느 음식을 좋아해요?

4. 제시카 씨가 좋아하는 음식은 얼마 정도 해요? [좋아하는 음식 favorite food]

Script

Jessica and her friend Xiaoming are talking about what to eat for lunch.

01 제시카: 배 안 고파요? 우리 점심 먹으러 가요.[II.2]

02 샤오밍: 그래요. 이 근처 한국 식당에 가 봤어요?[II.3]

03 제시카: "코리아 하우스" 말이에요?

04 샤오밍: 네.

05 제시카: 아뇨. 아직 안 가 봤어요.

06 샤오밍: 거기 음식 괜찮은데 거기서 먹을까요?[II.4]

07 제시카: 거긴 뭐가 맛있어요?

08 샤오밍: 비빔밥하고 불닭이 맛있어요.

09 제시카: 음... 전 순두부 좋아하는데...

10 샤오밍: 어, 순두부도 있어요!

11 제시카: 안 비싸요?[II.1]

12 샤오밍: 네. 8불에서 12불 정도 해요.

13 제시카: 좋아요! 그럼, 거기 가요.

01 Jessica : Aren't you hungry? Let's go to eat lunch!

02 Xiaoming: Okay. Have you been to the Korean restaurant nearby?

03 Jessica : Do you mean "Korean House?"

04 Xiaoming: Yes.

05 Jessica : No, I haven't been there yet.

06 Xiaoming: The food there is all right, should we eat there?

07 Jessica : What is delicious there?

08 Xiaoming: *Bibimbap* (mixed rice bowl) and *buldak* (spicy chicken stir fry) are delicious.

09 Jessica : Um··· I like *soondubu* (soft tofu dish)...

10 Xiaoming: Oh, they have *soondubu* too!

11 Jessica : Is it not expensive?

12 Xiaoming: Yeah. The food costs 8 to 12 dollars.

13 Jessica : Okay! Then let's go there.

V. Guided Conversation

☞ **With the model conversation in Listen & Discuss (Script) in mind, practice the modified conversation using the food items below with your partner.**

초밥 | 짜장면 | 짬뽕

스테이크 | 햄버거 | 핫도그

스파게티 | 프라이드 치킨 | 순두부찌개

해물칼국수 | 떡볶이 | 육개장

It's getting close to meal time and two friends are trying to decide what to eat. Practice the following conversation with your partner, choosing one of the options in (   ) to make the conversation flow naturally.

01 A: ________ 씨, 배 안 고파요? 우리 ________ 먹으러 가요~
(B's name) (아침; 점심; 저녁)

02 B: 그래요. 이 근처 ________ 식당에 가 봤어요?
(중국; 한국; 미국; 일본; ..)

03 A: ________ 말이에요?
(name of the restaurant)

04 B: 네.

05 A: 아뇨. 아직 안 가 봤어요.

06 B: 거기 음식 괜찮은데 거기서 먹을까요?

07 A: 거긴 뭐가 맛있어요?

08 B: ________ 하고 ________ 이/가 맛있어요.
(Dish 1) (Dish 2)

09 A: 음... 전 ________ 좋아하는데···
(Dish 3)

10 B: 어, ________ 도 있어요!
(Dish 3)

11 A: 가격은 어때요?

12 B: ________ 불 정도 해요.
(range of the food price; use from~ to~)

13 A: 좋아요! 그럼, 거기 가요.

(Switch roles and continue to practice.)

Present the conversation from Step 1 in front of the class. Try not to read it!

VI. Spontaneous Conversation

Now is your chance to have real interactions with your classmates in Korean. You can practice speaking with your classmates, writing, and presenting in front of the class!

You and your friend are going to have dinner tonight. Share a conversation about your dinner plans with your partner following the instructions below.

1. Please include the following information in your dinner planning conversation.

- What food you/your friend like
- Which restaurant you/your friend have been to
- What dish you/your friend recommend
- What dish you/your friend plan to order at the restaurant
- The price of the dishes you/your friend plan to order at the restaurant

2. Pretend that you and your friend have had the dinner. Now talk to each other about it, including the information below.

- How was the dish you/your friend ordered?
- Why (or Why not) did you/your friend like the restaurant?

Complete the table below, based on the conversation you had in "Step 1."

	Favorite dish	Dish ordered	How it was	Its price
You				
Your friend				

Based on the table you completed in Step 2, write a simple review of the restaurant you and your friend visited.

For example: 오늘 저녁 먹으러 (restaurant name)에 가 봤어요. 친구는 (dish name)을 주문했어요. 저는 (dish name 1)를 좋아하는데, 친구가 (dish name 2)을/를 추천했어요. 그래서, (dish name 2)를 주문했는데, 맛이 없었어요. 가격은 ($$)정도 했어요. (restaurant name)에 가면, (dish name 2)은/는 주문하지 마세요. (dish name 1)을/를 주문하세요.

Useful expressions

추천하다	to recommend
가격	price
~지 말다	Please don't ~

Based on what you wrote in Step 3, present about the restaurant and the dishes in front of the class. Try not to read what you wrote in Step 3!

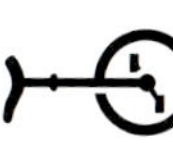

16 생일 축하해요!

Happy birthday!

Celebrating a birthday and giving a gift

Preparation & Practice	I. New Words & Expressions II. Patterns, Expressions & Practice 1. ~한테, ~한테서 — to [person]; from [person] 2. ~지만 — ... but; although ... 3. ~아 보세요/~어 보세요 — Please try (doing) 4. ~아 봐도 돼요?/~어 봐도 돼요? — Is it okay to~ ?; May I try to ~ ? 5. Non-honorific speech level — The "~아" style III. Culture Counting age, birthday food, and important birthdays
Conversation Activities	IV. Listen & Discuss V. Guided Conversation VI. Spontaneous Conversation

I. New Words & Expressions

 **Study the words and expressions with the audio.**  35

NOUN

생일 birthday
핸드폰 케이스 cell phone case

VERB

고르다 to choose
듣다 to hear; to listen to
쓰다 (1) to write; (2) to use
알다 to know
열다 to open
축하하다 to congratulate; to celebrate

ADVERB

마침 just in time

MARKER

~지만 ~ but; although ~
-한테 to [person]
-한테(서) from [person]

EXPRESSION

· 그럼요. For sure; Absolutely.
· ~기(가) 힘들다 to be hard/difficult to do ~
· 별거 아니지만 ... It is nothing special but …
· 생일 축하해요! Happy birthday!

Form

Dictionary form (Word base + 다)		~아요/~어요 form	~으세요/~세요 form
듣다	to hear; to listen to	들어요	들으세요
쓰다	to use	써요	쓰세요
있다	to exist	있어요	계세요 [Lesson 9, II.3]

Exercise 1

Listen to the audio and fill in the blanks.  36

1.  

____

2. 

____

3.  

____

Listen to the audio and fill in the blanks.  37

1. A: 생일 ________________!

   B: 제 생일 어떻게 알았어요?

2. A: 제 생일 어떻게 알았어요?

   B: 샤오밍한테 ________________.

3. A: 이거 선물이에요.

   B: 와~ ________________.

4. A: 지금 열어 봐도 돼요?

   B: ________________.

II. Patterns, Expressions & Practice

1. NOUN + 한테 "to NOUN" vs. NOUN + 한테서 "from NOUN"

Usage The difference between "NOUN + 한테" and "NOUN + 한테서" is shown below.

pattern .... NOUN (goal) + 한테 ...

Use "NOUN + 한테" when NOUN is the goal/recipient and the verb is usually a "giving/sending/going" verb.

Subject + 이/가	Goal + 한테		Verb(give/send/go/...)
제시카가 Jessica	샤오밍한테 to Xiaoming	선물을 gift	줘요. give
Jessica gives a gift to Xiaoming.			

As in the example above, Xiaoming is the goal, recipient, or intended person to whom the gift is given.

1. 이거 제시카 씨한테 좀 주세요. Please give this to Jessica.
2. A: 배가 많이 아픈데요. I have a stomachache.
   B: 의사한테 가 보세요. Please go to a doctor.

3. 제 친구 생일이라서 친구한테 선물을 줬어요. It's my friend's birthday so I gave a gift to my friend.

Note 1 Here are some other "verbs of giving/sending/going" that are often used in daily conversation: 보내다 "to send (something) (to someone)," 전화(를) 하다 "to give a call (to someone)," 얘기(를) 하다 "to tell a story (to someone)," 선물(을) 하다/주다 "to give a gift (to someone)," 편지(를) 하다/쓰다 "to write a letter (to someone)."

Note 2 Use "NOUN (goal) + 께" when NOUN is 어머니, 아버지, 선생님, 할머니, etc. who gets honorific expressions.

1. 어제 할머니께 전화를 드렸어요.
   I called my grandmother yesterday.
   [Lit., I gave a phone call to my grandmother yesterday.]

Useful expressions

드리다 to give (something) (to an older person), which is a humble expression of 주다

2. A: 저, 질문이 있는데요. — I have a question.
   B: 한국어 선생님께 물어 보세요. — Please ask the Korean teacher.

pattern ... **NOUN (source) + 한테서** ...

Use "NOUN + 한테서" when NOUN is the source and the verb is usually a "receiving/coming" verb.

Subject + 이/가	Source + 한테서		Verb(receive/take/hear/...)
샤오밍이 Xiaoming	제시카한테서 from Jessica	선물을 gift	받아요. receive
Xiaoming receives a gift from Jessica			

Note 3

Here are some other "verbs of receiving/coming" that are often used in daily conversation: 얘기(를) 듣다 "to hear a story (from someone)," (전화)가 오다 "Lit., (for a telephone call to come (from someone)," (편지)가 오다/도착하다 "Lit., (for a letter) to come/arrive (from someone)."

As in the example above, 제시카 is the source or originating person from whom the gift comes.

1. 샤오밍한테서 좋은 소식을 들었어요.
   I heard good news from Xiaoming.
2. 남자 친구한테서 크리스마스 카드가 왔어요.
   The Christmas card came from my boyfriend.

Note 4

In colloquial speech, 서 in "NOUN (source) + 한테서" can be dropped, resulting in the form "NOUN (source) + 한테." In this situation, you can still understand that NOUN is the source, not the goal, given the context (particularly if you consider the meaning of the verb).

1. 룸메이트한테 소포가 도착했어요. 저는 너무 기뻤어요!
   A package arrived from my roommate. I was so happy!
2. 마크가 제시카한테 선물을 받았어요.
   Mark received a gift from Jessica.

Fill in the blanks with an appropriate marker from the box.

-한테	-한테서	-께

1. 김 선생님________ 한국어 질문을 드렸어요.
2. 민지________ 선물을 받았어요. 너무 좋았어요!
3. 마이클________ 좋은 소식을 들었어요.
4. 어제 밤에 할머니________ 생일 카드를 썼어요.
5. 동생________ 전화가 왔어요.
6. 친구________ 이야기를 했어요.

Useful expressions

소식 news
쓰다 to write
이야기를 하다 to tell; to tell a story

The following sentences are missing some markers. Fill in each blank with the most appropriate marker from the box.

-한테	-한테서	-께	-을/-를	-하고	-에	-에서

1. 어머니________ 어제 문자를 보냈어요. 동생도 저________ 문자를 했어요.
2. 오래간만에 책방에서 잡지 ________ 두 권 샀어요.
3. 형________ 동생이 내일 모두 집에 와요.
4. 서점________ 친구 생일 카드를 샀어요.
5. 오늘은 학교________ 안 가요. 일요일이잖아요.
6. 친구________ 생일 축하 전화를 받았어요.
7. 수학 문제가 어려워요? 제 친구 마이클________ 물어보세요. 마이클이 수학을 잘 해요.

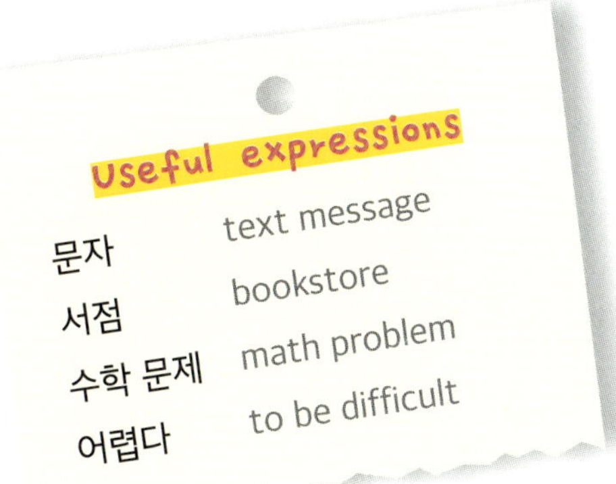

Listen to the audio and fill in the blanks.

1. 오늘 수업 시간에 선생님______ 질문을 드렸어요.

2. 어제 친구가 저______ 전화를 했어요.

3. 샤오밍______ 생일 선물을 받았어요!

4. 언니______ 할머니 소식을 들었어요.

5. 민준 씨______ 무슨 선물을 줄까요?

6. 이거 할아버지______ 드리는 선물이에요.

2. ~지만 "... but; although ..."

Usage Use ~**지만** to express the meaning "but" or "although."

Form Attach ~**지만** to the verb or adjective of the first clause in a sentence.

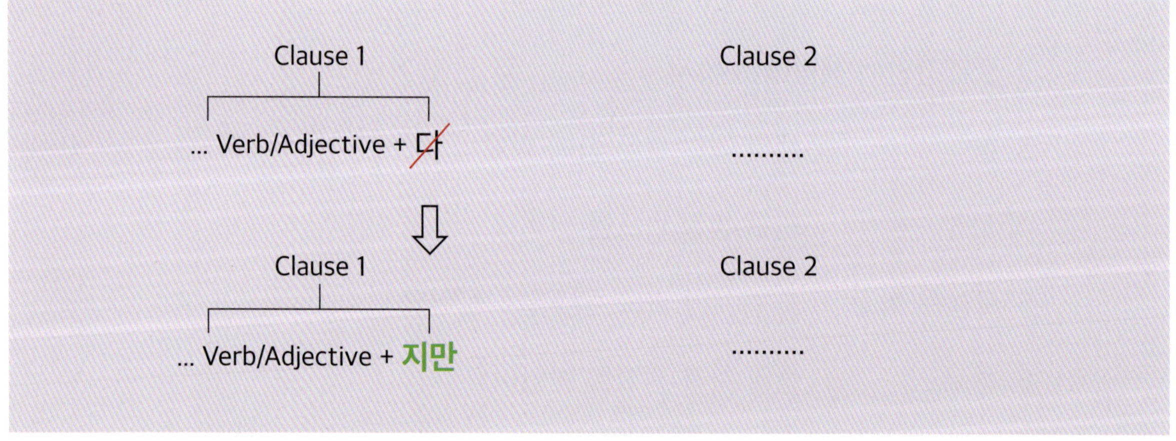

그 식당 음식은 비싸다. 음식이 맛있다

그 식당 음식은 비싸**지만** 음식이 맛있어요.

The food at the restaurant is expensive, **but** it is delicious.

Let us look at the examples below.

1. 일이 어렵지만 재미있어요.
   The job is difficult, but it is fun.

2. 수업이 재미있지만 숙제가 많아요.
   The class is fun, but there is a lot of homework.

3. 그 아파트가 좋지만 비싸요.
   The apartment is good, but it is expensive.

4. 마크는 기숙사에 살지만 제임스는 아파트에 살아요.
   Mark lives in a dorm, but James lives in an apartment.

5. 에이미는 클럽 미팅에 가지만 민준은 못 가요.
   Amy is going to the club meeting, but Minjoon cannot go.

6. 제시카는 미국 사람이지만 한국말을 잘 해요.
   Jessica is American, but she speaks Korean well.

7. 어제는 비가 왔지만 오늘은 맑아요.
   It rained yesterday, but it is clear today.

8. 저는 한국에는 가 봤지만 일본에는 안 가봤어요.
   I've been to Korea, but I haven't been to Japan.

9. 희준은 한국 가수(이)지만 영어를 잘 해요.
   Huijoon is a Korean singer, but he speaks English well.

* NOUN (ending in a consonant) + 이다 → NOUN이지만
* NOUN (ending in a vowel) → NOUN이지만 or NOUN지만

10. 이것은 떡볶이지만 맵지 않아요.
    This is tteokbokki, but it's not spicy.

Match the best suitable clause in Column A with the clause in Column B.

A		B
1. 방이 작지만 ·		· a. 맛있어요.
2. 차는 마시지만 ·		· b. 커피는 안 마셔요
3. 떡볶이가 맵지만 ·		· c. 재미있어요.
4. 한국말이 조금 어렵지만 ·		· d. 깨끗해요.
5. 그 사람은 가수지만 ·		· e. 노래를 못 해요.

Write a sentence describing the information given in the picture.

1.

가방이 예쁘지만 비싸요.

2.

(yesterday)

(today)

____.

3.

(to see often)

(not to see these days)

____.

4.  

(to leave windows open)

____.

You are writing a review of the hotel you stayed at in Seoul. Complete the following review. You may use the words given in the box below.

불편했다	크고 좋았다	오래됐다	없었다	맛있었다

1. 호텔이 ____________ 넓고 깨끗했어요.

2. 방이 ____________ 화장실이 좀 작았어요.

3. 수영장은 ____________ 피트니스 센터하고 사우나가 있어서 편했어요.

4. 호텔 안에 레스토랑이 있었는데 음식이 ____________ 가격이 좀 비쌌어요.

5. 호텔 가까이에 지하철 역이 없어서 조금 ____________ 버스 정류장이 있어서 괜찮았어요.

Useful expressions

불편하다	to be inconvenient; to be uncomfortable
크다	to be big
오래되다	(for something) to be old
넓다	to be wide; to be spacious
깨끗하다	to be clean
화장실	bathroom
피트니스 센터	fitness center
사우나	sauna
레스토랑	restaurant
~가까이에	close to ~
지하철 역	subway station
교통	transportation
버스 정류장	bus stop

Patterns, Expressions & Practice

3. ~아 보세요 /~어 보세요 "Please try (doing)"

As introduced in Lesson 15, ~아 봤다/~어 봤다 is used to express one's past experiences.

1. A: 아르바이트 해 봤어요?
   B: 네, 식당에서 웨이터 일을 해 봤어요.
   A: Have you ever worked a part-time job?
   B: Yes, I've worked as a waiter at a restaurant.
2. A: 학교 앞 일본 식당에 가 봤어요?
   B: 네, 가 봤어요. 우동을 먹어 봤는데 맛있었어요.
   A: Have you been to the Japanese restaurant in front of the school?
   B: Yes, I have. I've tried the *udon* and it was delicious.

When you want to suggest doing an activity, use "Verb base + 아 보다/어 보다," meaning "try it out and see how you like it." In that case, it is often used with 한번 (one time; once). 한번 ~아 보세요/한번 ~어 보세요 means "Please give it a try and see how you like it."

When you want to suggest doing an activity together, you may use 한번 ~아 볼까요?/한번 ~어 볼까요?, meaning "Shall we try doing ~ and see what it is like?"

1. 학교 앞 한국 식당에 한번 가 보세요.
   Please try the Korean restaurant in front of the school.
2. 비빔밥을 먹어 보세요. Please try *bibimbap*.
3. 수미 씨를 한번 만나 보세요. Please try meeting Sumi.
4. 민호 씨한테 물어 보세요. Why don't you ask Minho?
5. 이 바지 한번 입어 보세요. Please try these pants on.
6. 같이 한번 가 볼까요? Shall we go together?

Your friend is not familiar with Korea and Korean culture but he/she is interested in learning more about Korea. Suggest the following activities to your friend using ~아 보세요/~어 보세요 "You should try ~."

1. 한인 타운을 (구경하다) ______________________
2. 김치를 (먹다) ______________________
3. 한국 노래를 (듣다) ______________________
4. 서울에 (가다) ______________________
5. 한국어를 (배우다) ______________________
6. 한국 친구를 (사귀다) ______________________

Useful expressions

친구를 사귀다 to make a friend

Exercise 8

Look at the pictures and suggest an activity to your friend using ~아 보세요/~어 보세요 "You should try ~."

1. 한국 식당에 가 보세요.
2. 한국어 수업을 ______________________.
3. ______________________.
4. ______________________.
5. 창문 좀 ______________________.

Create B's response by giving your suggestion, saying "You should try ~" or "Why don't you ~?." You may use the following verbs. Use the word only once.

가다 to go	묻다 to ask	전화하다 to call
부탁하다 to ask a favor	신청하다 to apply	참가하다 to participate

1. A: 제임스 씨가 아직 안 왔어요.

   B: 제임스 씨한테 ______________________.

2. A: 이번 여름에 말레이시아를 여행할 거예요.

   B: 쿠알라룸푸르에 꼭 ______________________. 정말 멋있어요!

3. A: 컴퓨터가 고장났어요. 컴퓨터를 고쳐야 해요.

   B: 제인 씨가 컴퓨터를 잘 알아요. 제인 씨한테 ______________________.

4. A: 박 선생님 전화번호 아세요?

   B: 저는 모르는데 명진 씨는 알 거예요. 명진 씨한테 ______________________.

5. A: 한국에서 공부하고 싶어요. 그런데 돈이 없어요.

   B: Study abroad 장학금을 ______________________.

6. A: 한국어를 2년 동안 배웠어요.

   B: 한국어 스피킹 콘테스트에 한 번 ______________________.

Useful expressions

고장나다	to break down; to become out of order;
고치다	to repair; to fix
~고 싶다	to want to~
장학금을 신청하다	to apply for a scholarship
스피킹 콘테스트	speaking contest
-에 참가하다	to participate in ~

4. ~아 봐도 돼요?/~어 봐도 돼요? "Is it okay to try to ~?; May I try to ~?"

Usage Use ~아 봐도 돼요?/~어 봐도 돼요? when you ask for permission to try to do something.

Form ~아/~어 봐도 돼요 is the combination of ~아/어 보- (to try ~) + ~아도 돼요? (Is it okay to ~?; May I ~?). To choose between ~아 봐도 돼요? and ~어 봐도 돼요?, follow the same rules for choosing between ~아요 and ~어요, as shown in Lesson 4 (II.3).

Here are the rules from Lesson 4.

When the last vowel of the verb base is 아 or 오, attach ~아 봐도 돼요?
(알다: 알 + 아 봐도 돼요? → 알아 봐도 돼요?)

Dictionary form (Word base + 다)	Base ending in 아/오 + 아 봐도 돼요?	Vowel contraction	~아 봐도 돼요?/ ~어 봐도 돼요 form
가다 to go	가 + 아 봐도 돼요?	가아 →가 봐도 돼요	가 봐도 돼요?
오다 to come	오 + 아 봐도 돼요?	오아 →와 봐도 돼요	와 봐도 돼요?
알다 to know	알 + 아 봐도 돼요?	--	알아 봐도 돼요?
만나다 to meet	만나 + 아 봐도 돼요?	만나아 → 만나 봐도 돼요	만나 봐도 돼요?

When the last vowel of the verb base is not 아 or 오 (but is 어, 이, or 으), attach ~어 봐도 돼요? (먹다: 먹 + 어 봐도 돼요? → 먹어 봐도 돼요?)

Dictionary form (Word base + 다)	Base ending in not 아/오 + 어 봐도 돼요?	Vowel contraction	~아 봐도 돼요? / ~어 봐도 돼요 form
먹다 to eat	먹 + 어 봐도 돼요?	--	먹어 봐도 돼요?
입다 to wear	입 + 어 봐도 돼요?	--	입어 봐도 돼요?
쓰다 to use	쓰 + 어 봐도 돼요?	쓰어 → 써 봐도 돼요? (See Rule 3. in Appendix V.)	써 봐도 돼요?
열다 to open	열 + 어 봐도 돼요?	--	열어 봐도 돼요?

When the verb ends in ~하다, use **해 봐도 돼요**?
(노래하다 →노래**해 봐도 돼요**?)

순두부찌개를 주문하다 to order 순두부찌개 → 순두부찌개를 주문**해 봐도 돼요**?
여기서 운동하다 to exercise here → 여기서 운동**해 봐도 돼요**?

Not all verbs follow the above rules. Here are some verbs that are exceptions to those rules. (See Rule 1. in Appendix V.)

Dictionary form (Word base + 다)	ㄷ changes to ㄹ	~어 봐도 돼요 form
듣다 to listen to	듣 → 들	들어 봐도 돼요?
걷다 to walk	걷 → 걸	걸어 봐도 돼요?

Let us examine the forms with the following examples.

1. A: 이 차 운전해 **봐도 돼요**? May I try to drive this car?
   B: 네, 그러세요. Sure. Go ahead.

2. A: 이 청바지 입**어 봐도 돼요**? May I try to put on these blue jeans?
   B: 네, 저기서 입어 보세요. Sure. Please try it over there.

3. A: 이 모자 써 **봐도 돼요**? May I try to put on this hat?
   B: 그럼요. Sure.

4. A: 저녁에 나가 **봐도 돼요**? May I go out this evening?
   B: 오늘은 안 돼요. You may not today.
   같이 숙제해야 돼요. We need to do homework together.

You want to ask whether you can try to do the following actions. Complete each conversation by asking for permission.

1. (At a restaurant)
A: 이 부대찌개가 정말 맛있네요!
B: ______________________________?

2. (In the kitchen)
A: 여기 김밥 재료가 다 있어요.
B: ______________________________?

3. (At a birthday party)
A: 생일 축하합니다! 여기 선물이에요.
B: ______________________________?

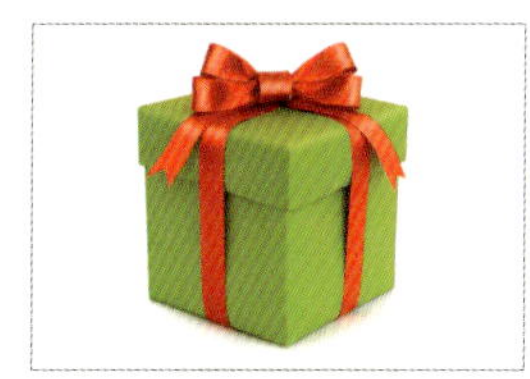

4. (At a music store)
직원 : 여기 새 음악이 나왔어요.
제시카: ______________________________?

5. (At a clothing store)
직원: 뭘 도와드릴까요?
유미: 이 자켓 ______________________________?

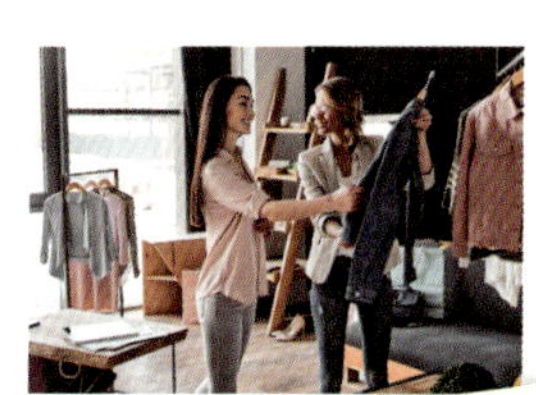

Useful expressions

새 음악	new music
나오다	to come out
자켓	jacket

Note

Use ~**아 봐도 돼요?**/~**어 봐도 돼요?** when you ask for permission to try to do something, meaning "Is it okay to try to ~?; May I try to ~?". Use ~**아도 돼요?**/~**어도 돼요?** when you ask for permission to do something, meaning "Is it okay to ~?; May I ~?".

1. A: 저 ... 펜이 없는데, 에이미 씨 펜 좀 써**도 돼요**?
   Umm... I don't have a pen. Is it okay to use your pen?
   B: 네, 쓰세요.
   Sure, you can.

2. A: 이 펜 진짜 잘 써지네요.
   This pen writes pretty well.
   B: 그래요? 저도 써**봐도 돼요**?
   Really? Is it okay to try to write with it?

Listen to the audio and write what 리사 and 에이미 will do together next week.

____

____

____

____

____

____

Ask your teacher permission using either "~아도/~어도 돼요?" or "~아/~어 봐도 돼요?"

1. You　: 영어를 써도 돼요? (영어, 쓰다)
   선생님: 아니요. 한국어만 쓰세요!

2. You　: ______________________? (화장실, 가다)
   선생님: 네, 갔다 오세요.

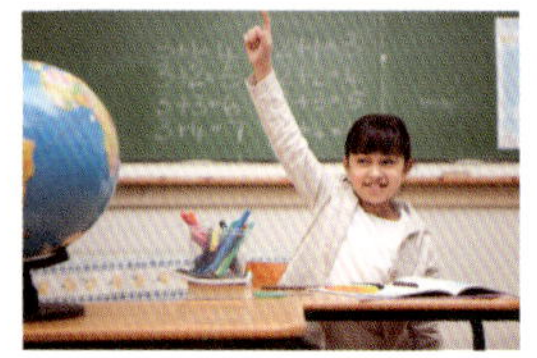

3. You　: ______________________? (여기, 앉다)
   선생님: 네, 거기 앉아 보세요.

4. 선생님: 숙제 주세요.
   You　: 혹시 ______________________? (내일, 드리다)
   선생님: 왜요?
   You　: 숙제를 했는데 집에 있어요. 죄송해요.

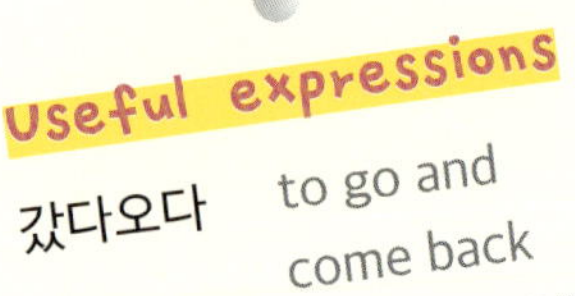

5. Non-honorific speech level: The "~아" style

Usage The "~아" speech style, as in the table below, is a speech style used toward a listener with whom the speaker feels close or intimate. This speech style is often observed from an adult talking to his/her close friend of a similar or younger age, an adult talking to a child, or a child talking to another child.

(Types) There are four types of the "~아" speech style according to the sentence types(e.g., statement), as shown in the table below.

Sentence types	Speech levels			
	Honorific		Non-honorific	
	More Formal ⟪ ⟫ More Informal		More Formal ⟪ ⟫ more Informal	
	"~습니다" style [Lesson 19]	"~아요" style [Lesson 4]	"~는다" style [Intermediate, L1]	"~아" style [Lesson 16]
Statement (with falling intonation)	~습니다/~ㅂ니다.	~아요/~어요.	~는다/~ㄴ다/~다.	~아/~어.
	1. 책을 읽습니다. 2. 친구를 만납니다. I read a book. I meet a friend.	1. 친구를 만나요. 2. 책을 읽어요. I meet a friend I read a book.	1. 친구를 만난다. 2. 책을 읽는다. I meet a friend I read a book.	1. 친구를 만나. 2. 책을 읽어. I meet a friend I read a book.
Question (with rising intonation)	~습니까?/~ㅂ니까?	~아요/~어요?	~니? or ~(으)냐/~느냐?	~아/~어?
	1. 책을 읽습니까? 2. 친구를 만납니까? Do you read a book? Do you meet a friend?	1. 친구를 만나요? 2. 책을 읽어요? Do you meet a friend? Do you read a book?	1. 친구를 만나니? 2. 책을 읽니? Do you meet a friend? Do you read a book?	1. 친구를 만나? 2. 책을 읽어? Do you meet a friend? Do you read a book?
Proposal	~읍시다/-ㅂ시다.	~아요/~어요.	~자.	~아/~어.
	1. 책을 읽읍시다. 2. 친구를 만납시다. Let us read a book. Let us meet a friend.	1. 친구를 만나요. 2. 책을 읽어요. Let us meet a friend. Let us read a book.	1. 친구를 만나자. 2. 책을 읽자. Let us meet a friend. Let us read a book.	1. 친구를 만나. 2. 책을 읽어. Let us meet a friend. Let us read a book.
Command	~으십시오/~십시오. or ~으시오/~시오.	~아요/~어요.	~아라/~어라.	~아/~어.
	1. 책을 읽으십시오. 2. 친구를 만나십시오. Please read a book. Please meet a friend.	1. 친구를 만나요. 2. 책을 읽어요. Please meet a friend. Please read a book.	1. 친구를 만나라. 2. 책을 읽어라. Meet a friend. Read a book.	1. 친구를 만나. 2. 책을 읽어. Meet a friend. Read a book.

Form By dropping the 요 that appears in ~아요/~어요, you can switch your speech style from the honorific style (존댓말) to the non-honorific style (반말), as in examples 1~3 below.

1. Verb/Adjective + 아요/어요 → Verb/Adjective + 아/어

Honorific form (~ + 아요/ 어요)	Non-honorific form (~ + 아/ 어)	Meaning
가요.	가.	I go.
공부해요.	공부해.	I study.
장 볼까요?	장 볼까?	Shall we go grocery shopping?
줄게요.	줄게.	I will give (to you).
많아요.	많아.	There are a lot.
어려워요.	어려워.	It is difficult.
어때요?	어때?	How is it?

2. a. Noun + 이에요/예요 → Noun + 이야/야
   b. Noun 이/가 아니에요 → Noun 이/가 아니야

Honorific form (~ + 이에요/예요)	Non-honorific form (~ + 아/ 어)	Meaning
팀은 미국 사람이에요.	팀은 미국 사람이야.	Tim is American.
뭐예요?	뭐야?	What is it?
한국 음식이에요.	한국 음식이야.	It's Korean food.
한국 음식이 아니에요.	한국 음식이 아니야.	It's not Korean food.

3. Verb/Adjective + 을/ㄹ 거예요 → Verb/Adjective + 을 거야

Honorific form (~ + 을/ㄹ 거예요)	Non-honorific form (~ +을/ㄹ 거야)	Meaning
먹을 거예요.	먹을 거야.	I will eat.
할 거예요.	할 거야.	I will do.

The following tables show honorific and non-honorific forms of adverbs and nouns.

1. Adverbs

Honorific form	Non-honorific form	Meaning
네/예	응/어	Yes.
아니요/아뇨.(shortened form)	아니/아니야	No.

2. Nouns

Honorific form	Non-honorific form	Meaning
댁	집	home
말씀	말	word
성함	이름	name
연세	나이	age
사람	분	person
밥	진지	meal
…	…	…

Note 1 Don't confuse the honorific form with the humble form. Honorific forms are used by speakers to raise the status of listeners, while humble forms are used by speakers to lower themselves in front of their listeners.

Humble form	Non-humble/Plain form	Meaning
· 저	· 나	· I, my, me
제가 (← 저 + 가)	내가	I (as a subject)
저의/제 (← 저 + 의)	나의/내	my (as a possessive)
저를 (← 저 + 를)	나를	me (as an object)
· 저희	· 우리	· we, our, us
저희가 (← 저희 + 가)	우리가	we (as a subject)
저희의 (← 저희 + 의)	우리의	our (as a possessive)
저희를 (← 저희 + 를)	우리를	us (as an object)

Note 2 Remember that the pronoun 당신 "you" is not frequently used in the ~어요/~아요 speech style. In place of 당신 "you," a person's name, title (e.g., 선생님 teacher, 매니저님 manager, 과장님 section chief, etc), or family term (e.g., 형 brother, 누나 sister, 이모 aunt, 이모부 uncle, etc.) is frequently used. In 반말 speech, however, you can use the pronoun 너 "you."

Honorific speech	Non-honorific speech
제시카: 마이클 씨는 요즘 바빠요? 마이클: 네. 좀 바빠요.	제시카: 너는 요즘 바빠? 마이클: 응. 좀 바빠.

Let us compare the honorific and non-honorific speech styles in the following conversation.

Honorific speech	Non-honorific speech
01 에이미: 생일 축하해요!	01 에이미: 생일 **축하해**!
02 민준 : 어! 제 생일 어떻게 알았어요?	02 민준 : 어! **내** 생일 어떻게 **알았어**?
03 에이미: 샤오밍 씨한테 들었어요.	03 에이미: 샤오밍 씨한테 **들었어**.
04 이거 별 거 아니지만...	04 이거 별 거 아니지만...
05 선물이에요.	05 **선물이야**.
06 민준 : 와~ 고마워요! 지금 열어 봐도 돼요?	06 민준 : 와~ **고마워**! 지금 열어 봐도 **돼**?
07 에이미: 그럼요~. 열어 보세요.	07 에이미: **그럼**~. 열어 **봐**.
08 민준 : 우와! 핸드폰 케이스네요!	08 민준 : 우와! 핸드폰 **케이스네**!
09 마침 필요했는데요... 잘 쓸게요!	09 마침 **필요했는데**... 잘 **쓸게**!
10 에이미: 잘 됐네요. 고르기 힘들었는데요.	10 에이미: 잘 **됐네**. 고르기 **힘들었는데**.

Switch the following conversation from honorific speech style to non-honorific style as shown in the first two lines.

01 제시카: 지금 몇 시예요?
(몇 시야?)

02 샤오밍: 1시 45분이에요.
(45분이야)

03 제시카: 어, 그럼 저는 인제 갈게요. 2시에 수업이 있어서요.
( ) ( ) ( )

04 샤오밍: 아, 그래요? (Talking to himself) 어..., 그럼 어떡하지?
( )

05 제시카: 음. 그럼 저녁에 다시 봐요.
( )

06 저는 수업이 4시에 끝나요. 샤오밍 씨는요?
( ) ( ) ( )

07 샤오밍: 전 오늘 수업 없어요. 그럼, 4시반 쯤에 여기서 다시 만날까요?
( ) ( ) ( )

08 제시카: 네, 그래요. 그럼, 제가 나중에 문자할게요.
( ) ( ) ( ) ( )

09 샤오밍: 네~ 그럼 이따가 봐요.
( ) ( )

Switch the following conversation from honorific speech style to non-honorific style by filling in (   ). Lines 01 and 02 are filled in as examples.

01 제시카: 김밥 좀 드세요.
(먹어.)

02 샤오밍: 어, 제시카 씨가 만들었어요?
(네가/니가) (   )

03 제시카: 아뇨. ㅎㅎ 한국 마트에서 아침에 샀어요.
(   ) (   )

04 밥하고 고기, 시금치, 당근이 들어 있어요.
(   )

05 샤오밍: 아~. 전 떡볶이를 만들었어요. 여기 맛 좀 보세요.
(   ) (   ) (   )

06 제시카: (먹은 후) 음~ 맛있네요! 여기는 뭐가 들어갔어요?
(   ) (   )

07 샤오밍: 떡하고, 설탕하고, 고추장하고... 아 참 그리고 양파요.
(   )

08 제시카: 아, 그래요. 떡볶이는 어디서 배웠어요?
(   ) (   )

09 샤오밍: 인터넷 블로그에서요.
(   )

10 제시카: 우와~ 대단해요!
(   )

Rewrite the conversation between the two friends in 반말.

01 제시카: 배 안 고파요? 우리 점심 먹으러 가요~

____.

02 샤오밍: 그래요. 이 근처 한국 식당에 가 봤어요?

____.

03 제시카: "코리아 하우스" 말이에요?

____.

04 샤오밍: 네.

____.

05 제시카: 아뇨. 아직 안 가 봤어요.

____.

06 샤오밍: 거기 음식 괜찮은데 거기서 먹을까요?

____.

07 제시카: 거긴 뭐가 맛있어요?

____.

08 샤오밍: 비빔밥하고 불닭이 맛있어요.

____.

09 제시카: 음... 전 순두부 좋아하는데...

____.

10 샤오밍: 어, 순두부도 있어요!

____.

11 제시카: 안 비싸요?

____.

12 샤오밍: 네. 8불에서 12불 정도 해요.

____.

13 제시카: 좋아요! 그럼, 거기 가요.

____.

III. Culture

Counting age, birthday food, and important birthdays

1. Counting age

Koreans traditionally count age by including the time that the baby was inside of the mother. Therefore, once the baby is born, his or her age is considered to be one year old. This is called 한국 나이 (Korean age). To distinguish 한국 나이 from the age counted from the moment of the birth, people use the biological age after birth called 만 나이 (age from birth). If you ask a Korean person's age, the answer may be 한국 나이 or 만 나이. People may add 한국 나이로 (in Korean age...) or 만으로 (in biological age...) in their answers to clarify the confusion. If a person says "I am *man* 20 years old" (저는 만 스무살입니다), it is his or her biological age which is 20 years old. Most people are older in their Korean ages because they have already gained one more year upon birth. Laws and regulations follow a person's biological age, but people casually use 한국 나이, depending on how they want to present their age.

한국 나이	만 나이
1살	0살
2살	1살
3살	2살
...	...

2. Birthday food

Koreans set a bowl of seaweed soup with a side of rice as a staple birthday food along with other celebratory foods, such as 잡채 (noodle dish), 불고기(sliced beef), 전 (pancakes), 갈비 (ribs), 떡 (rice cakes), 생일 케이크 (a birthday cake).

Typical birthday table

미역국 (Seaweed soup)

3. Important birthdays

Significant birthdays in Korea include 돌 (the first birthday), 환갑 (the sixtieth birthday), 칠순 잔치 (the seventieth birthday), and 팔순 잔치 (the eightieth birthday). On these significant birthdays, Korean families and friends gather to celebrate and share a big meal together.

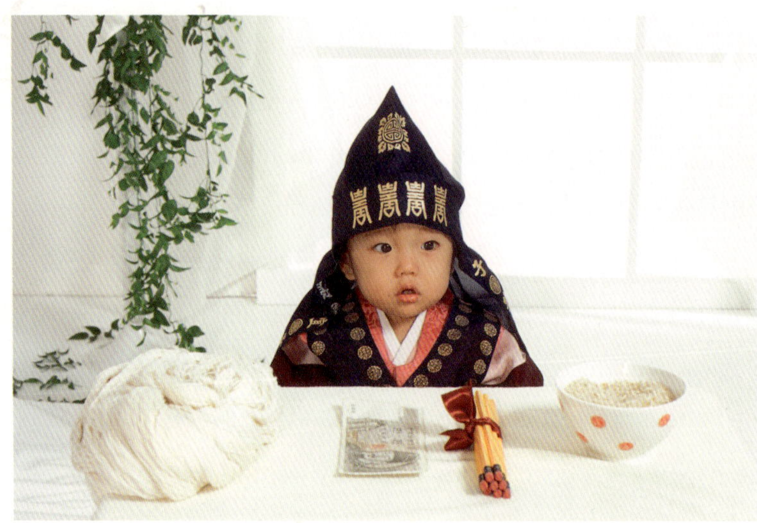

돌 (***Dol*, the first birthday party)**

돌잡이 ***(Doljabi)***

IV. Listen & Discuss

Amy is speaking to Minjoon in the company's break room. They both work as interns. Listen to the conversation carefully. Discuss the answers to the following questions with your classmates. Then, write each answer in a full Korean sentence in the space provided.

1. 오늘은 무슨 날이에요?

2. 에이미는 어떻게 알았어요?

3. 에이미는 민준한테 무엇을 줬어요?

4. 민준은 에이미의 선물을 좋아했어요? 왜요?

Script

Amy is talking to Minjoon in the company's break room. They both work as interns. Watch the video and guess what is happening in this conversation.

01 에이미: 생일 축하해요!

02 민준 : 어! 제 생일 어떻게 알았어요?

03 에이미: 샤오밍한테 들었어요.[II.1]

04 이거 별거 아니지만… 선물이에요.[II.2]

05 민준 : 와~ 고마워요! 지금 열어 봐도 돼요?[II.4]

06 에이미: 그럼요~. 열어 보세요.[II.3]

07 민준 : 우와! 핸드폰 케이스네요!

08 마침 필요했는데 잘 쓸게요!

09 에이미: 잘 됐네요. 고르기 힘들었는데.

01 Amy : Happy birthday!

02 Minjoon: Oh! How did you know it's my birthday?

03 Amy : I heard it from Xiaoming.

04 It's not anything special, but… it is a gift (for you).

05 Minjoon: Wow, thank you! May I open it now?

06 Amy : Of course~. Please open it.

07 Minjoon: Wow! It is a cell phone case!

08 I just needed it recently. I'll really use this well!

09 Amy : That worked out well. It was hard to choose.

V. Guided Conversation

With the model conversation in Listen & Discuss (Script) in mind, practice the modified conversation below with your partner.

step 1

Today you're celebrating a special day with your partner. Practice the following conversation with your partner, choosing the best option in (   ) to make the conversation flow naturally.

01 A: ____________ 축하해요!
(생일; 졸업; 합격; 승진)

02 B: 어! 어떻게 알았어요?

03 A: ____________ 한테 들었어요.
(someone's name)

04 이거 별 거 아니지만… 선물이에요.

05 B: 와~ 고마워요!

06 A: ____________.
(뭘요; 아니에요)

07 B: 지금 ____________
(열어 봐도 돼요?; 봐도 돼요?)

08 A: 그럼요~. ____________.
(열어 보세요; 보세요)

09 B: 우와! ____________ ____________!
(머그 컵; 서점 상품권; 커피 상품권; ...) (이네요)

10 ____________.
(정말 고마워요; 잘 쓸게요!; 너무 마음에 들어요!)

(Switch roles and continue to practice.)

Useful expressions

01	졸업	graduation
01	합격	passing (an exam); being accepted
01	승진	promotion
07	서점 상품권	book store gift card
07	커피 상품권	coffee gift card
08	마음에 들다	to be one's liking

Guided Conversation

Present the conversation from Step 1 in front of the class. Try not to read it!

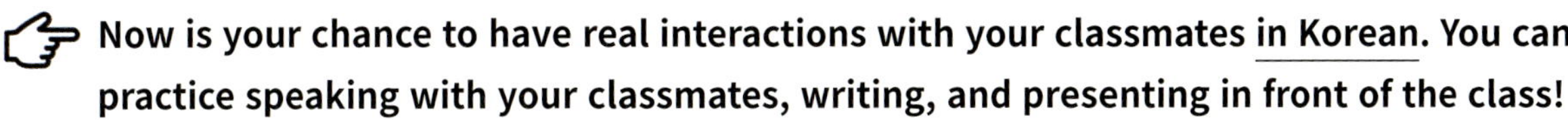

VI. Spontaneous Conversation

Now is your chance to have real interactions with your classmates in Korean. You can practice speaking with your classmates, writing, and presenting in front of the class!

step 1

You (Speaker A) want to congratulate your friend (Speaker B) for the following occasions. Choose an occasion from the box below that you want to congratulate them on:

생일　　졸업　　대학 입학 (university matriculation)　　승진(promotion)

Role-play as Speaker A and B, including the expressions below in your conversation.

(Speaker A)
- ▶ Say congratulations.
- ▶ Give a gift. (Choose one from the gift list below.)
- ▶ Exchange pleasantries for the occasion.

(Speaker B)
- ▶ Express your appreciation.
- ▶ Offer Speaker A to join you for dinner at your favorite restaurant as a token of your appreciation.
- ▶ Ask whether Speaker A has been there before.
- ▶ Ask what dish Speaker A likes.

<Gift List>

시계	wristwatch
카드	card
상품권	gift card
꽃	flowers
명함 지갑	business card wallet
넥타이	necktie
스카프	scarf
향초	aromatic candle
만년필	fountain pen

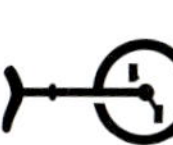

As Speaker A or B, please write a journal entry on the celebration of the occasion from Step 1. The following is a sample writing of Speaker A's journal that you may refer to for your own writing:

오늘은 친구 샤오밍 생일이었어요. 저는 친구한테 상품권을 줬는데, 너무 좋아했어요.
우리는 같이 저녁을 먹으러 코리아 하우스에 갔어요.
친구는 (dish name 1)을/를 주문했어요. 친구가 (dish name 1)을/를 추천했지만, 제가 (dish name 1)을/를 싫어해서 (dish name 2)을/를 주문했어요. (dish name 2)은/는 정말 맛있어요.
가격은 ($$)정도 했어요. 우리는 즐거운 시간을 보냈어요.

Present your journal writing in front of the class. Try not to read what you wrote in Step 2!

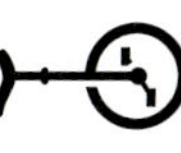

17 한국말 정말 잘하시네요!

You speak Korean very well!

Complimenting one's ability and talking about one's future plans

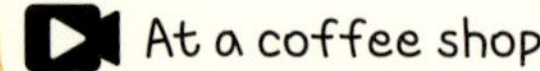

Preparation & Practice	I. New Words & Expressions II. Patterns, Expressions & Practice 1. ~을 거예요/~ㄹ 거예요 — will ~ [prediction; volition] 2. Sentence ending ~지요?/~죠? — Seeking the listener's agreement 3. -으로/-로 — by ~; in ~; with ~ [Instrument/means] 4. 잘해요; 못해요; 잘 못해요 — Expressing one's ability 5. ~으려고 하다/~려고 하다 — intend to ~ ~으려고/~려고 — intending to ~; in order to ~ 6. ~는데도, ~은/ㄴ데도, ~인데도 — even though... /even if ... III. Culture Courteous responses to compliments
Conversation Activities	IV. Listen & Discuss V. Guided Conversation VI. Spontaneous Conversation

I. New Words & Expressions

 **Study the words and expressions with the audio.**  41

NOUN

기자	journalist; reporter
내년	next year
동안	during ~; for ~
영어	English
한국말	the Korean language

VERB

다니다	to attend
알다	to know
전공하다	to major in (at a university)
졸업하다	to graduate

ADVERB

더	more

MARKER

-도	(1) also, too; (2) even

EXPRESSION

- ~을/~를 잘 못해요. (I) am not that good at ~.
- 한국말(을) 참 잘하시네요! Oh, (you) speak Korean really well!
- 한국말로 기자죠? (It) Is *gija* in Korean, right?

Form

Dictionary form (Word base + 다)	~아요/~어요 form	~으세요/~세요 form
졸업하다	졸업해요	졸업하세요
알다	알아요	아세요
전공하다	전공해요	전공하세요
다니다	다녀요	다니세요
필요하다	필요해요	필요하세요

Note1

You learned -도 "also" in Lesson 3. Depending on the contexts, -도 means either "also" or "even." In this lesson, it is used to mean "even."

1. 한국어 문법은 한국 사람한테도 어려워요.
   Korean grammar is difficult even to Koreans.

2. 앨버트는 한국말을 몰라요. "안녕하세요?"도 몰라요.
   Albert doesn't know Korean. He doesn't know even "Hello?" in Korean.

Match the Korean words from column A with their English definition in column B.

A	B
1. 대학원	a. studies of business management
2. 기자	b. graduation
3. 경영학	c. company
4. 졸업	d. graduate school
5. 회사	e. journalist

Listen to the audio and fill in the blanks. 

1. A: 전 내년에 졸업하는데... 제시카 씨는 ____________________?

   B: 저도 내년에요.

2. A: 한국말 참 잘하시네요!

   B: ____________________. 아직 잘 못해요.

3. A: Journalist ____________________ 뭐예요?

   B: 기자예요.

4. A: 민준 씨는 뭐 하실 거예요?

   B: 저는 1년 더 일하고 ____________________ 갈 거예요.

II. Patterns, Expressions & Practice

1. ~을 거예요/~ㄹ 거예요 "will ~" [prediction; volition]

Form Use the rule below to choose between ~을 거예요 and ~ㄹ 거예요.

- ▶ Verb/Adjective + 을 거예요 (When Verb/Adjective base ends in ㄹ)
- ▶ Verb/Adjective + ㄹ 거예요 (When Verb/Adjective base ends in a vowel)
- * Adjective base + 거예요 (When Verb/Adjective base ends in ㄹ, as in 열다 below)

Dictionary form (Word base + 다)	Consonant-ending base + 을 거예요	Dictionary form (Word base + 다)	Vowel-ending base + ㄹ 거예요
찾다 to look for	찾을 거예요	가다 to go	갈 거예요
먹다 to eat	먹을 거예요	졸업하다 to graduate	졸업할 거예요
있다 to exist	있을 거예요	이다 to be	일 거예요
많다 to be many	많을 거예요	열다 to open	열 거예요
좋다 to be good	좋을 거예요	필요하다 to be necessary	필요할 거예요

Not all verbs and adjectives follow the above rules. Here are some examples of irregular verbs and adjectives:

Dictionary form (Word base + 다)	Rules	~을 거예요/~ㄹ 거예요
맵다 to be spicy	ㅂ changes to 우	매울 거예요
춥다 to be cold		추울 거예요
듣다 to listen to	ㄷ changes to ㄹ	들을 거예요
걷다 to walk		걸을 거예요

Usage 1 Use **~을 거예요**/**~ㄹ 거예요** to predict things that will probably happen.
~을 거예요/**~ㄹ 거예요** is often used with 아마 "maybe" or 어쩌면 "perhaps."

1. 영미: 한국 마트는 몇 시에 열어요?
   지현: 아마 여덟 시에 열 **거예요**.

2. 엄마: 저 사람 이름이 기억이 안 나네.
   딸: 민준 씨 아니에요? 아마 민준 씨**일 거예요**.

3. 지미: 영화관에 가고 싶은데 예매가 필요해요?
   진호: 어떤 영화 보려고요? 오늘 주말이잖아요.
   사람이 많**을 거예요**.
   지미: "신과 함께"요. 웹툰이 원작인데, 재미있을까요?
   진호: 네. 그 영화 요즘 인기가 많아요. 재미있**을 거예요**.

4. 민영: 재선 씨, 지금 밖에 날씨는 어때요?
   재선: 글쎄요. 저도 잘 모르지만, 아마 추**울 거예요**.

5. A: 제임스 씨는 아직 싱글이죠?
   B: 아마 그럴 **거예요**.

Useful expressions

기억이 나다	to remember
예매	reservation
신과 함께	Along With the Gods
웹툰	webtoon
원작	original work
인기	popularity

Usage 2 Use ~을 거예요/~ㄹ 거예요 to express your volition (i.e., plan, intention, willingness, insistence) or ask the listener's.

1. 선생님: 다음 학기에는 무슨 언어를 배울 거예요?
   학생 : 한국어 중급반하고 독일어를 배울 거예요. 다음에 이 두 나라를 여행하고 싶어요.

2. 종국: 선미 씨, 대학은 언제 졸업할 거예요?
   선미: 내년에 졸업할 거예요. 그래서 올해부터 직장을 찾고 있어요.
   종국: 선미 씨는 좋은 직장을 빨리 찾을 거예요. 화이팅!

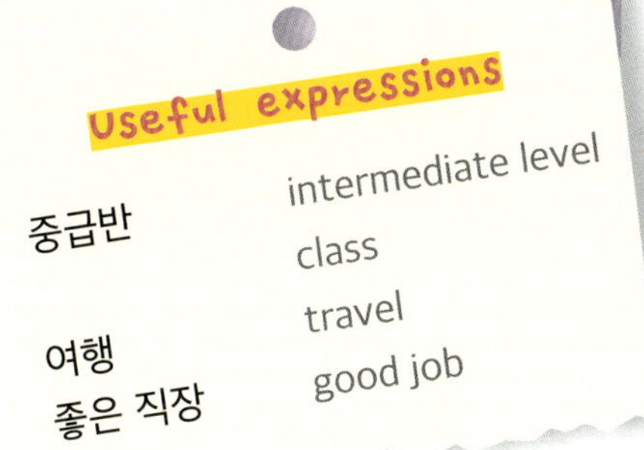

Express your future plans with ~을 거예요/~ㄹ 거예요. Use the given English cues to complete each dialogue.

1. 01 에이미: 내일부터 방학이네요! 좋은 계획 있어요?
   02 제시카: 친구하고 같이 ____________ (will go to NYC).
   03 에이미: 와. 뉴욕은 처음이세요?
   04 제시카: 네. 너무 ____________ (will be fun).
   거기서 친구 제임스도 ____________ (will meet).

2. 01 제시카: 다음 주가 졸업이네요. 졸업하고 ____________ (what will you do)?
   02 샤오밍: 네. 인턴쉽 할 거예요. 그리고 직장을 ____________ (will look for).
   03 제시카: 중국에서 ____________ (will work)?
   04 샤오밍: 직장은 아직 모르겠어요.

3. 01 에이미: 민준 씨, 다음 달부터 무슨 외국어 ______ ?
(will learn)

02 민준: 중국어요. 회사에서 ______ .
(will need)

4. 01 지혜: 주말에 가족들을 보러 시카고에 ______ .
(will go)

02 민준: 아, 좋겠네요! 저도 한국에 있는 가족들과 오늘 밤에 ______ .
(will call)

5. (Use the ~아 speech style)

01 제임스: 생일 축하해! 오늘 ______ ?
(where will you go)

02 민준: 회사 사람들하고 같이 저녁 ______ .
(will eat)

03 제임스: ______ ?
(who will come)

04 민준: 에이미, 줄리, 영민 씨하고 존. 너도 와!

05 제임스: 응, 갈게!

Useful expressions

계획	plan
처음이다	to be the first time
모르겠어요	I don't know.
[time] 부터	from [time]

Exercise 2

Express the speakers' future plans and expectations using the cues in ( ).

1. 01 리사: 금요일 저녁에 ______ ?
(will watch a movie)

02 제리: 네, 영미 씨하고 같이 볼 거예요. 올래요?

03 리사: 미안해요. 전 금요일 저녁에 친구 생일 파티에 ______ .
(will go)

그래서 오늘 선물을 ______ .
(will buy)

2. 01 민준 : 졸업하고 뭐 할 거예요?

02 샤오밍: 전 프로그래머 할 거예요. I will work as a programmer.

03 민준 : 와. 전 ______ .
(will work as a journalist)

04 에이미: 저는 잘 모르겠어요. 대학교 졸업할 때까지 천천히 ______ .
(will find)

3. 01 지영 : 민준 씨는 러시아어를 잘 해요?

02 제시카: ______ .
(Maybe he cannot do well yet)

4. (Use the ~아 speech style)

01 You : 이번 주에 숙제가 ______________.
(will be a lot)

02 Classmate: 아마 ______________.
(will be so)

5. (Use the ~아 speech style)

01 존 : 우리 그룹 프로젝트는 언제 ______________?
(will do)

02 수영: 오늘은 시간이 없는데… 내일은 어때?

03 존 : 내일은 오후 4시가 좋아. 그런데 저녁은 같이 ______________?
(will eat)

04 수영: 그래. 이번에는 내가 살게!

Useful expressions

프로그래머를 하다	to work as a programmer
천천히	slowly
러시아어	Russian language
러시아어를 하다	to speak Russian

Listen to the conversation between two friends and fill in the blanks. 

01 민준 : 내일 (1) ______________?

02 제시카: (2) ______________ 거예요. 이번 주에 숙제가 너무 많아요.

03 민준 : 저녁에 시간 있어요? 내일 저녁에 에이미 씨 생일 파티가 있어요.

04 제시카: 어머 그래요? 저는 시간이 없어서 아마 (3) ______________.

05 민준 : 숙제 빨리하고 생일 파티에 가요. 다른 친구들도

(4) ______________.

06 제시카: 알겠어요. 빨리 해 볼게요.

2. Sentence ending ~지요?/~죠? Seeking the listener's agreement

Form ~**지요**? is a combination of 지 and the sentence ending 요. In spoken discourse, the contracted form ~**죠**? (←지+요) is commonly used.

> ▶ Full form : Verb/Adjective + ~**지요**?
>
> ▶ Contracted form: Verb/Adjective + ~**죠**?

Usage Use ~**지요**?/~**죠**? when you assume or expect that someone should (or might) agree with what you are saying.

> 1. In questions/proposals: When you use ~**지요**?/~**죠**?, you assume that the listener should (or might) agree with what you are asking. Thus, it conveys the meaning of "... **don't you**?; ... **isn't it**?; **can't he**?; etc" depending on the context.

1. A: 반갑습니다! 또 뵙네요! 성함이 황샤오밍 씨**죠**?
   B: 네, 맞습니다. 저도 반갑습니다!

2. A: 벌써 여덟 시예요. 지금 나가서 저녁 먹**죠**?
   B: 벌써 그렇게 됐어요? 좋아요!

- In (2) above, Speaker A assumes that Listener B should agree with his request (having dinner) because it is 8 pm and Speaker B should be hungry at that moment.

> 2. In statements: When you use ~**지요**/~**죠**, you are expecting or assuming that the listener should agree with or might be aware of what you are saying. Thus, it can be translated into "**as you know**; **as you might expect**; etc" depending on the context.

1. A: 한국 여름 날씨는 어때요?
   B: 정말 덥**죠**. 여기와 똑같아요.

2. A: 오늘 정말 많이 춥네요! 사무실 히터 틀었**죠**?
   B: 물론이**죠**! 제가 추위를 잘 타잖아요?

3. A: 오늘 생일 맞죠? 축하해요!
   B: 어! 제 생일 어떻게 알았어요?
   A: 민준 씨한테서 들었**죠**.

Seek the listener's agreement using the -죠 ending.

1. A: 오늘 날씨 (춥다) 춥죠?

   B: 네. 너무 추워요.

2. 마이클: 안녕하세요? 요즘 어떻게 지내요?

   수미 : 좀 바빠요. 마이클 씨도 요즘 (바쁘다)________________?

3. A: 이번 여름에 한국에 (가다)________________?

   B: 네. 6월 20일에 가요.

4. A: 어제 한국 문화 쇼 어땠어요? (재미있었다) ________________?

   B: 네. 재미있었어요. 사람들도 많이 왔어요.

5. A: 오늘 15일(이다) ________________?

   B: 아뇨. 16일이에요.

6. A: 기말고사 다 (끝났다) ________________?

   B: 아니요. 아직 2개 남았어요.

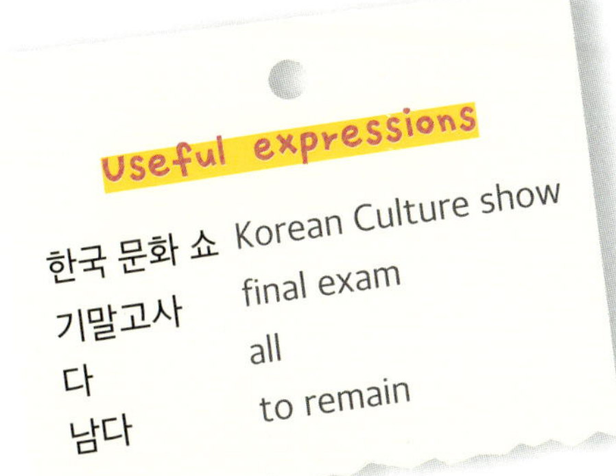

Your Korean friend is asking the following questions. Respond to the questions using the ~죠 ending, which roughly corresponds to "of course" or "for sure."

1. A: 한국에서 2년 사셨죠? 그럼 한국말 하세요?
   B: 그럼요. 한국말 (하다)____________.

2. A: 애틀랜타에서 오셨죠? 애틀랜타에는 한국 사람들 많아요?
   B: 네. (많다)____________. 한국 가게들도 많아요.

3-4. A: 한국 음식 좋아하세요?
   B: 네. (물론이다)____________.
   A: 매운 음식도 드세요?
   B: 네. 잘 (먹다)____________.

Useful expressions

애틀랜타	Atlanta
한국 가게	Korean store
매운 음식	spicy food

3. -으로/-로 "by ~; in ~; with ~; as ~" [instrument/means]

Usage Attach -으로/-로 to nouns to mark them as instruments or means by which a task is performed. Such nouns or instruments can be tools, modes of transportation, materials, ingredients, etc.

Form

- ▶ Consonant-ending NOUN + 으로
- ▶ ㄹ or Vowel-ending NOUN + 로

Look at the following examples.

1. 볼펜으로 쓰세요.	Please write it with a ball-point pen.
2. 한국말로 하세요.	Please speak in Korean.
3. 영어로 말할까요?	Shall we speak in English?
4. A: 불고기는 뭐로 만들어요?	What is *bulgogi* made from?
B: 불고기는 소고기로 만들어요.	*Bulgogi* is made from beef.
5. A: 뉴욕에 어떻게 갔어요?	How did you get to New York?
차로 갔어요?	Did you go by car?
B: 아니요. 비행기로 갔어요.	No. I went by airplane.

The following items are Korean dishes and their ingredients. Create sentences about how each dish is made, using -으로/-로 as shown in (1).

1. 

[떡, 고추장]

떡볶이는 떡하고 고추장으로 만들어요.

2. 

[야채, 계란]

비빔밥은 ______________________.

3. 

[배추]

김치는 ______________________.

4. 

[소고기]

불고기는 ______________________.

5. 

[김, 야채, 밥]

김밥은 ______________________.

Listen to the audio and provide the corresponding Korean words for the English words from the conversation. 44

1. Graduate school ______________________

2. Master's degree ______________________

3. Journalism ______________________

4. International studies ______________________

Fill in the blanks with the means of transportation choosing from the pictures in the box.

1. 집에서 학교까지 가까워요. 그래서 저는 보통 __________으로/로 학교에 가요.

2. 뉴욕에서 시카고까지 __________으로/로 2시간쯤 걸려요.

3. 서울에서 부산까지 __________으로/로 3시간쯤 걸려요.

4. A: 버스로 갈까요?
   B: 지하철이 더 빨라요. __________으로/로 가요.

4. 잘해요; 못해요; 잘 못해요 Expressing one's ability

Usage Use **잘하다**, **못하다**, or **잘 못하다** to express your or another person's ability. They literally mean "to do well," "cannot do," and "cannot do well," respectively. Depending on the contexts, they can be translated as "to be good at," "to be bad at," and "to be not that good at."

Look at the following examples:

1. 저는 스페인어 **잘해요**. I am good at Spanish.
2. 저는 스페인어 **못해요**. I can't speak Spanish.
3. 저는 스페인어 **잘 못해요**. I am not that good at Spanish.
4. 마크는 미국 사람인데, 한국말을 아주 **잘해요**.
   Mark is American but he speaks Korean very well.
5. 저는 수학은 **못하지**만, 영어는 **잘해요**. [~지만 ~ but]
   I am not good at math but I am good at English.
6. 저는 탁구는 아주 잘하는데, 배드민턴은 **잘 못해요**.
   I am very good at ping-pong but not that good at badminton.

Listen to the narration by Steve, and mark the following statements as T(True) or F(False). 45

1. ______________ Steve is good at Japanese.

2. ______________ Steve is good at tennis.

3. ______________ Steve is not that good at basketball.

4. ______________ Steve is poor at cooking Korean food.

Talk to each other about what you are good at, what you are bad at, and what you are not that good at. Use the names of sports, skills, or languages provided through the pictures below. You may also use names of sports, skills, or languages that are not listed below.

스포츠 sports

기술 skills

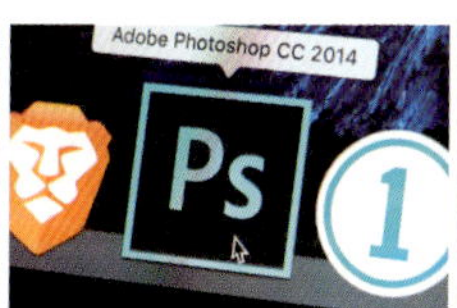

외국어 foreign languages

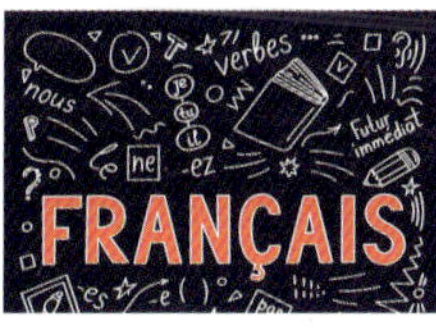

1. A: 저는 테니스 잘해요.

   B: 그래요? 저는 잘 못해요.

2. A: 요리 잘하세요?

   B: 아뇨, 잘 못해요. 그런데, 맛있게 잘 먹어요.

3. A: ____.

   B: ____.

4. A: ____.

   B: ____.

5. A: ____.

   B: ____.

6. A: ____.

   B: ____.

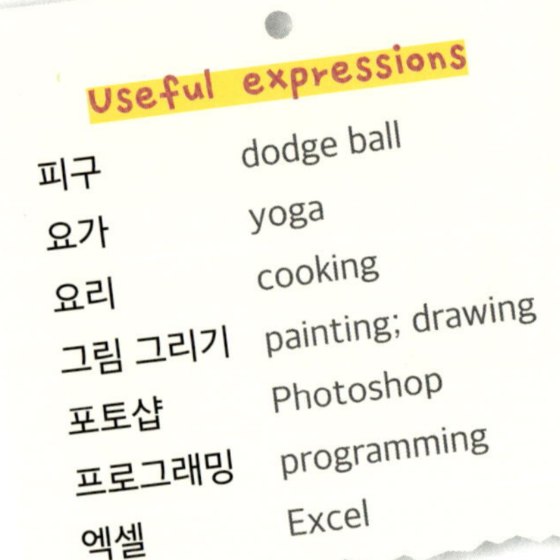

Interview two classmates and find out whether they are good or bad at doing the following activities. Check one box for each category according to their responses.

Interviewee 1: (Classmate's name) ____________________

Category	잘해요	못해요	잘 못해요
수영 swimming			
골프 golf			
탁구 table tennis			
요리 cooking			
인터넷 게임 Internet games			
노래 singing			
바이올린 violin			
수학 math			

Interviewee 2: (Classmate's name) ______________________

Category	잘해요	못해요	잘 못해요
수영 swimming			
골프 golf			
탁구 table tennis			
요리 cooking			
인터넷 게임 Internet games			
노래 singing			
바이올린 violin			
수학 math			

5. ~으려고 하다/~려고 하다 "intend to ~"
~으려고/~려고 "intending to ~; in order to ~"

Usage ~으려고 하다/~려고 하다 means "intend to ~." ~으려고/~려고 without 하다 also similarly means "intending to ~; in order to ~." Use either form to express your or another person's intention.

1. 저는 대학원에 가려고 해요. — I intend to go to graduate school.
2. 저는 대학원에 가려고, GRE를 공부해요. — Intending to go to graduate school, I'm studying for the GRE.

Note1 When you provide just an intention without repeating what has already been shared with the other person during the conversation, you can say ~으려고요/~려고요 (as in B2 below). ~으려고요/~려고요 is the combination of ~으려고/~려고 and the sentence ender 요. [Compare with ~아서요/~어서요 in Lesson 11 (II.2).]

1. A: 왜 GRE를 공부해요?

   B1: 대학원에 가**려고** (GRE를 공부해)**요**.
   (GRE를 공부해: already shared)

   B2: 대학원에 가**려고요**.

Remember A the "honorific" speech style 요 is optional depending on who you are talking to. As in (2) and (3) below where two close friends are talking to each other, 요 is dropped.

2. A : 왜 GRE를 공부해?

   B1 : 대학원에 가**려고** (GRE를 공부해).
   (GRE를 공부해: already shared)

   B2: 대학원에 가**려고요**. (speaking to older people)

3. 주희 : 이 상품권은 뭐야?

   What is this gift card?

   제시카: 응. 박 선생님께 선물하**려고**. 나 이제 졸업하잖아.

   Yes. I **intend to** give it to Mrs. Pak. I am graduating soon, you know.

Form Use the rule below to choose between ~**으려고 (하다)** and ~**려고 (하다)**.

- ▶ Consonant-ending verb base + **으려고 (하다)**
- ▶ Vowel-ending verb base + **려고 (하다)**
- * Verb base (ending in ㄹ) + **려(고)** or **려(고) 하다**

Look at the following examples.

1. 졸업하고 취직하**려고** 열심히 공부해요.

   I am studying hard **in order to** get a full-time job after graduation.

2. 한국말을 잘하**려고** 매일 연습해요.

   I practice it everyday **in order to** speak Korean well.

3. 미나: 희정 씨, 이번 달에 대학원 졸업하시죠? 좋은 계획 있으세요?

   희정: 네. 교수가 되**려고 해요**. 그래서 연구 논문을 열심히 써요.

   Mina : Hee-jeong, you are graduating from graduate school this month, right? Do you have a good plan?

   Hee-jeong: Yes. I **intend to** become a professor. So I am diligently writing a research paper.

4. 준섭: 수진아, 요즘 학원에 다니니?

수진: 응. 컴퓨터 학원에 다녀. 컴퓨터 자격증 좀 따**려고 해**.

Junseop: Sujin, have you been attending a training program lately?

Sujin : Yes. I attend a computer training program. I intend to get a computer certificate.

5. 호준: 여자 친구한테 주**려고** 꽃을 샀어요.

제시카: 잘 했어요. 꽃을 받으면 좋아할 거예요.

Hojun : I bought flowers intending to give them to my girlfriend.

Jessica: Good job. She will like them when she receives them.

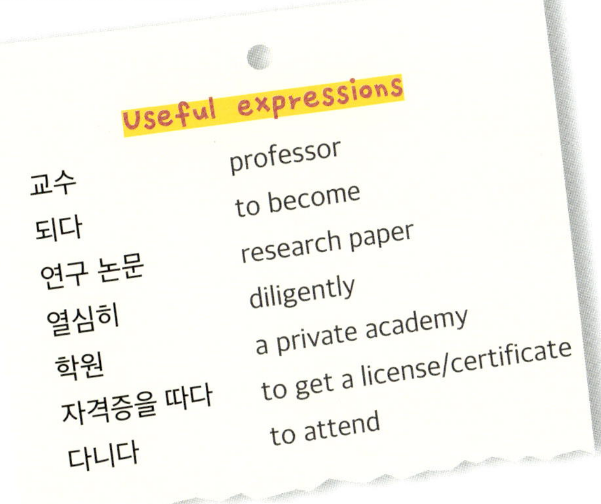

Complete the conversation using ~으려고/~려고 as shown in the following example.

A: 왜 한국어를 배우세요?

B: BTS하고 이야기하려고 배워요 (이야기하다).

1. A: 왜 한국 요리를 배워요?

B: 한국 요리 블로그를 ______________________ (쓰다).

2 A: 지금 어디 가세요?

B: 운전을 ______________________ (배우다) 운전 학원에 가요. [운전 driving]

3. A: 졸업하고 뭐 하실 거예요?

B: 대학원에 ______________________ (가다).

4. A: 어, 이탈리아어는 왜 공부해요?

B: 이번 여름에는 이탈리아를 ______________________ (여행하다).

Listen to the audio and fill in the blanks with the appropriate information. 

01 제임스: 준희 씨, 2월에 졸업이죠?

02 준희 : 네. 벌써 그렇게 됐네요.

03 제임스: 졸업하고 좋은 계획 있어요?

04 준희 : 네. 한 달 동안 여자 친구하고 유럽을 (1)__________________.
프랑스, 독일, 이탈리아, 그리스에 가 볼 거예요.

05 제임스: 와, 좋은데요. 외국어 잘하세요?

06 준희 : 조금요. 고등학교에서 프랑스 말을 배웠는데, 다음 주부터 다시
(2)__________________.

07 제임스: 그래요. 돈은 있어요?

08 준희 : 네. 조금 있지만 많이는 없어요. 그래서 카페에서 (3)__________________.

09 제임스: 여자 친구도 일해요?

10 준희 : 여자 친구도 아르바이트를 (4)__________________.

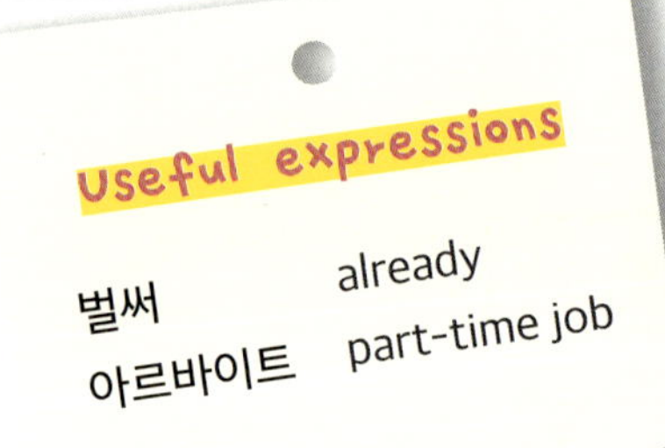

Express each person's intention to carry out the tasks specified in the table, and then write the dialogue in the blanks below, as in (1).

Name	1. 민지	2. 제임스	3. 소라	4. 준	5. 미라	6. 지성
Intention	Get a full time job (취직하다)	Get a part time job	Find a boyfriend	Study Korean	Cook Korean food	Run a marathon (마라톤을 하다)
Action to take to achieve	Study Chinese	Search the Internet (인터넷에서 검색하다)	Go on a blind date	Look for a Korean movie club	Learn to cook from her mother	Practice running (running: 달리기)

1. A: 민지는 왜 중국어를 공부해요?

   B: 민지는 취직하려고 중국어를 공부해요.

2. A: ______________________

   B: ______________________

3. A: ______________________

   B: ______________________

4. A: ______________________

   B: ______________________

5. A: ______________________

   B: ______________________

6. A: ______________________

   B: ______________________

6. ~는데도, ~은/~ㄴ데도, ~인데도 "even though .../even if ..."

Usage ~는데도, ~은/~ㄴ데도, ~인데도 expresses the meaning "even though ~." "도" here carries a meaning similar to "although ..." Remember that you learned the clause connector ~는데, ~은/~ㄴ데, ~인데 in Lesson 15 (Ⅱ.4). By adding 도 to ~는데, ~은/~ㄴ데, ~인데, the meaning of contrast or contradiction is emphasized.

Form Use the rules below to choose among ~는데, ~은/~ㄴ데, ~인데.

▶ Verb + 는데도

▶ consonant-ending NOUN + 인데

▶ Vowel-ending NOUN + 인데 or ㄴ데

▶ Adjective + ㄴ데도 (When Adjective base ends in a vowel)

▶ Adjective + 은데도 (When Adjective base ends in a consonant)

▶~있다/~없다 → 있는데도/없는데도

- The past tense for verb/adjective is ~았는데도/~었는데도.
- The past tense form of NOUN 이다 is ~이었는데도/~였는데도.

1. 미국 사람**인데도** 한국말을 잘 해요.
   Although he is American, he speaks Korean well.

2. 바쁜**데도** 와 줘서 고마워요.
   Thank you for coming even though you are busy.

3. 제임스는 나이가 많**은데도** 어려보여요. [어리다 to be young]
   In spite of being old, James looks young.

4. 공부를 안 했**는데도** 시험을 잘 봤어요.
   Although I didn't study, I did well on the exam.

5. 영어를 10년 동안 배웠**는데도** 아직 잘 못해요.
   Although I learned English for 10 years, I'm still not that good at it.

6. 점심을 많이 먹**었는데도** 아직 배가 고파요.
   I had a big lunch, but I am still hungry.

7. 영화가 재미있**는데도** 인기가 없어요.
   Although the movie is entertaining, it is not popular.

8. 오늘 수업이 없**는데도** 학교에 가세요?
   Are you going to school even though you don't have class today?

Complete the following sentences by matching each clause from column A with the appropriate clause from column B.

A	B
1. 아침, 점심을 안 먹었는데도 ·	· a. 영화관에 사람이 많아요.
2. 에이미는 바쁜데도 ·	· b. 피곤해요.
3. 주말이 아닌데도 ·	· c. 배가 안 고파요.
4. 많이 잤는데도 ·	· d. 아직 날씨가 추워요.
5. 4월인데도 ·	· e. 매일 운동해요.
6. 발표 연습을 많이 했는데도 ·	· f. 떨려요

Exercise 16

Listen to the audio and circle the picture that best describes what you hear.  47

1. a. 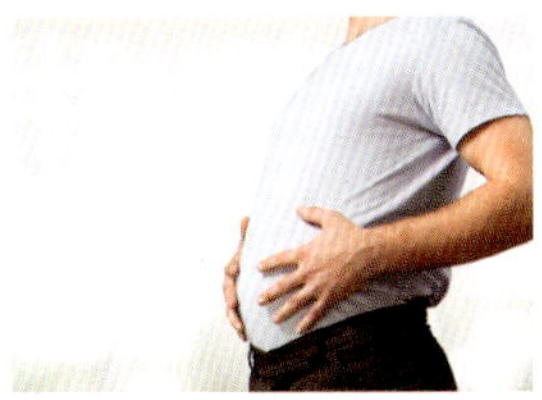 b.  c. 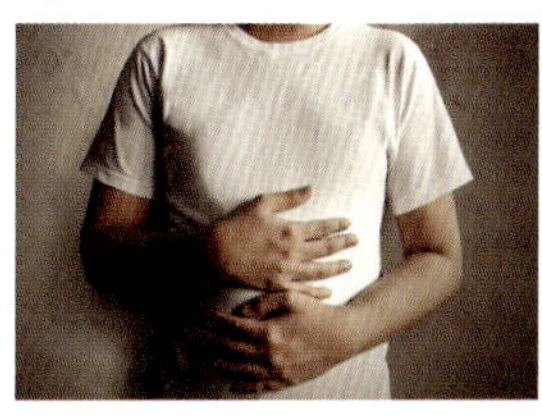 d. 

2. a.  b.  c.  d. 

3. a.  b.  c.  d. 

4. a.  b.  c.  d. 

Useful expressions

영화관	movie theater
피곤하다	to be tired
배가 고프다	to be hungry
운동하다	to exercise
발표	presentation
떨리다	to feel nervous
졸리다	to feel sleepy

Complete the following sentences using your own words.

1. 공부를 했는데도 ______________________.

2. 아픈데도 ______________________.

3. 중국어 전공인데도 ______________________.

4. 머리가 아파서 약을 먹었는데도 ______________________.

Useful expressions

약을 먹다 to take medicine
아프다 to be sick

III. Culture

Courteous responses to compliments

In English, when a compliment is given to you, you usually accept the compliment and respond to it by saying "thank you!' However, in Korean, the most common way of responding to a compliment is to reject the compliment by (1) saying "no," (2) downgrading it or (3) attributing it to someone else. Even if you highly deserve the compliment, you may reject or deprecate the compliment. This shows your humbleness and modesty, virtues highly appreciated in Korean society.

Here are some examples:

1. Saying "no." (Speaker A compliments Speaker B on his face today.)

A: 얼굴 좋아보이시네요.	Your face looks great.
B: 에이, 뭘요. / 에이, 아니에요.	Oh, don't mention it. / Oh, not at all.

2. Downgrading it (Speaker A compliments Speaker B on her scarf.)

A: 스카프가 아주 예쁘네요.	Your scarf is so pretty.
B: 에이, 아니에요. 싼 거예요.	Oh, not at all. It is cheap.

3. Attributing it to someone else (Speaker A compliments Speaker B on his suit.)

A: 양복이 아주 멋있어요.	Your suit is so stylish.
B: 아, 그래요? 어머니께서 사주셨어요.	Oh, really? My mom bought it for me.

Culture

On the other hand, speakers from younger generation may respond with a simple **감사합니다!** (Thank you!) in the similar way to that of English speakers. Nevertheless, a majority of Koreans still tend to reject a compliment rather than immediately accept it.

A: 얼굴 좋아보이시네요. Your face looks great.
B: **감사합니다!** Thank you!

IV. Listen & Discuss

Minjoon and Jessica are chatting at a coffee shop after a Korean Conversation Club meeting. Listen to the conversation carefully. Discuss the answers to the following questions with your classmates. Finally, write each answer in a full Korean sentence in the space provided.

1. 민준 씨가 제시카 씨한테 어떻게 칭찬(compliment)했어요? 표현(expression)을 쓰세요.

2. 제시카 씨는 언제 졸업해요? 그리고 민준 씨는 얼마 동안 회사에서 일할 거예요?

   제시카 씨는 __________. 그리고 민준 씨는 __________

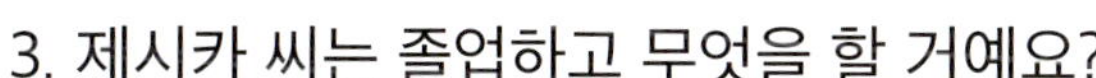

3. 제시카 씨는 졸업하고 무엇을 할 거예요?

4. Journalist는 한국말로 뭐예요?

5. 민준 씨는 대학원에서 무엇을 전공하려고 해요?

Script

Jessica is talking to Minjoon in the company's break room. They both work as interns. Watch the video and guess what is happening in this conversation.

01 민준 : 전 내년에 졸업하는데... 제시카 씨는 언제 졸업하세요?

02 제시카: 저도 내년에요.

03 민준 : 졸업하고 뭐 하실 거예요?[II.1]

04 제시카: Journalist요. 근데 journalist는 한국말로 "기자"죠?[II.2,3]

05 민준 : 네, 기자요. 제시카 씨, "기자"도 아시고... 한국말 참 잘하시네요![II.4]

06 제시카: 아니에요. 아직 잘 못해요. 민준 씨는 뭐 하실 거예요?

07 민준 : 저는 1년 더 일하고 대학원에 갈 거예요.

08 제시카: 아~ 뭐 전공하실 거예요?

09 민준 : 경영학 전공하려고 해요. 회사를 다녔는데도 아직 공부가 더 필요해서요.[II.6]

01 Minjoon: I am graduating next year... When do you graduate, Jessica?
02 Jessica : I am also graduating next year.
03 Minjoon: After graduation, what are you going to do?
04 Jessica : (I'm going to be) a journalist. By the way, "journalist" in Korean is "*gija*," right?
05 Minjoon: Yes, it is "*gija*." Jessica you even know the word "*gija*."... You speak Korean really well!
06 Jessica : No. I don't speak that well yet. What are you going to do Minjoon?
07 Minjoon: I am going to work one more year and (then) go to graduate school.
08 Jessica : Oh~ What are you going to major in?
09 Minjoon: I intend to major in business. I have been working at a company but I feel the need to study further.

V. Guided Conversation

With the organization of the model conversation in Listen & Discuss (Script) in mind, practice the modified conversation below with your partner.

step 1

Two friends are going to graduate soon and are chatting about their future plans. Practice the following conversation with your partner, choosing the best option in ( ) to make the conversation flow naturally.

Useful expressions

6개월 [육 개월]	6 months
1개월 [일 개월]	1 month
2개월 [이 개월]	2 months
10개월 [십 개월]	10 months
개월	counter for a number of months

01 A: 전 ______ 에 졸업하는데...
(올해; 이번 봄; 이번 여름; 이번 가을; 내년)

02 ______ 씨는 언제 졸업하세요?
(B's name)

03 B: 저도/저는 ______ 에요.
(올해; 이번 봄; 이번 여름; 이번 가을; 내년)

04 A: 졸업하고 뭐 하실 거예요?

05 B: ______ (이)요. 근데 ______ 은/는
(job name 1 in English) (job name 1 in English)

06 한국말로 ______ 죠?
(Korean word for job name 1)

07 A: 네. ______ (이)요.
(Korean word for job name 1)

08 ______ 씨, ______ 도 아시고... 한국말 참 잘하시네요!
(B's name) (Korean word for job name 1)

09 B: ______. ______ 씨는 뭐 하실 거예요?
(a courteous response to the compliment) (A's name)

10 A: 저는 ______ 더 일하고 대학원에 갈 거예요.
(6개월; 여름까지; 올해까지; 1년)

11 B: 아~ 뭐 전공하실 거예요?

12 A: ______ 전공하려고 해요. ______.
(your preferred major) (State a reason in one sentence why you need to study)

(Switch roles and continue to practice.)

step 2

Present the conversation from Step 1 in front of the class. Try not to read it!

Guided Conversation

VI. Spontaneous Conversation

Now is your chance to have real interactions with your classmates in Korean. You can practice speaking with your classmates, writing, and presenting in front of the class!

step 1 Interview two classmates one at a time. Choose roles as A or B, and talk to each other about future plans after graduation.

Please create a meaningful conversation, including at least three grammar points in your sentences, such as ~을 거예요/~ㄹ 거예요; -으로/-로; ~지요?/~죠?; 잘 해요; 못 해요; 잘 못해요; ~으려고/~려고; ~으려고 하다/~려고 하다; ~는데도/은데도/인데도.

step 2 Complete the following table with the information you shared in Step 1.

	Classmate's name	When graduating	Plans after graduation	Future job (in Korean words)
Classmate 1				
Classmate 2				

Let's write a narrative about Classmate 1 and 2's plans, based on the above table. Write a 10-sentence paragraph.

Based on what you wrote in Step 2, present the narrative you wrote in front of the class. Try not to read from your script!

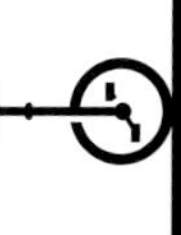

18 소개팅 하실래요?

Would you like to go on a blind date?

Introducing a person and setting up an appointment

At the company's cafeteria during a lunch time

Preparation & Practice	I. New Words & Expressions	
	II. Patterns, Expressions & Practice	
	1. NOUN + 동안; Verb base + 는 동안	during/for~; while ~ing
	2. Noun-modifying forms of verbs	~은/~ㄴ; ~는; ~을/~ㄹ
	3. Noun-modifying forms of adjectives	~던; ~은/~ㄴ;~을/~ㄹ
	4. Describing people's appearances	
	5. 이; 그; 저	this; that; that over there
	6. ~거든요	It is because …; … , you see.
	III. Culture	
	Culture of blind dating in Korea	
Conversation Activities	IV. Listen & Discuss	
	V. Guided Conversation	
	VI. Spontaneous Conversation	

I. New Words & Expressions

Study the words and expressions with the audio. 
49

NOUN

남자 친구	boyfriend
베트남계 미국인	Vietnamese American
사진	photo
소개팅	blind date
엔지니어	engineer
자동차	car; automobile

PRE-NOUN

무슨	what kind of ~; what ~ (e.g., 무슨 일)

ADVERB

되게	really; very (colloquial)
진짜(로)	really

MARKER

-이랑/-랑	(1) with ~; (2) ~ and [colloquial form of -하고/-와/-과]

EXPRESSION

· 소개팅(을) 하실래요? Would (you) like a blind date?

· 잘나가다 to be successful; to be in high demand

· 잘생기다 to be handsome; good-looking

Form

Dictionary form (Word base + 다)	~아요/~어요 form	~으세요/~세요 form
살다 to live	살아요	사세요
잘나가다 to be successful	잘나가요	잘나가세요

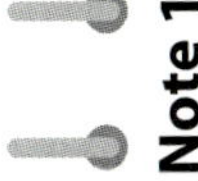

Note 1

Just like -하고 which was introduced in Lesson 8 (Ⅱ.4), -이랑/-랑 means (1) with ~ (2) ~ and. After a word ending in a consonant, use 이랑. After a word ending in a vowel, use 랑.

1. 어제 린다랑 같이 쇼핑했어요.
   I went shopping with Linda yesterday.

2. 린다랑 제시카는 룸메이트예요.
   Linda and Jessica are roommates.

3. 오늘 마이클이랑 같이 점심 먹었어요.
   I ate lunch with Michael today.

4. 민준이랑 마이클은 한국영화클럽 멤버예요.
   Minjoon and Michael are Korean Movie Club members.

Note 2

"-계" means "a family line, descent or lineage." 베트남계 미국인 means "American of Vietnamese descent" or "Vietnamese American."

한국계 미국인 Korean American
이탈리아계 미국인 Italian American

Note 3

그렇구나 "I see" is used as a reaction to what you just heard or learned. You may say 그렇구나 when you realize a new piece of information during a conversation. 그렇구나 is a non-honorific form. Its honorific form is 그렇군요.

Note 4

잘나가다 literally means "to go out well." But it means "(for someone) to be popular" or "(for someone) to be successful or highly-sought-after."

1. 그 영화배우는 요즘 잘나가요. That movie actor is really popular these days.
2. 그 사람은 잘나가는 영화배우예요. He/she is a really popular movie actor.

Match each picture from column A with a word from column B.

1. · · a. 자동차
2. · · b. 사진
3. · · c. 잘생겼어요
4. · · d. 소개팅

Listen to the audio and fill in the blanks. 

1. A: 에이미 씨, ______________ 있어요?

   B: 아니요. 없어요.

2. A: 어떻게 한국말을 잘 해요?

   B: 한국에서 ______________ 살았거든요.

3. A: 그 친구는 무슨 일 해요?

   B: ______________ 자동차 엔지니어예요. 그리고 되게 ______________.

4. A: 혹시 그 친구 사진 있어요?

   B: 에이~ 그냥 한 번 ______________!

II. Patterns, Expressions & Practice

1. Noun + 동안 "during/for ~"
Verb base + 는 동안 "while ~ing"

Usage

NOUN 동안 means "during/for NOUN." When NOUN is a number, **NOUN 동안** is translated as "for NOUN" (e.g., 10년 동안 "for ten years"). Otherwise, **NOUN 동안** is translated as "during NOUN" (e.g., 여름 방학 동안 "during the summer").

If you use 동안 with a verbal phrase (not NOUN), use "**Verb base** + **는 동안**" form which means "while Verb base-ing" (e.g., 가는 동안 "while going," 공부하는 동안 "while studying").

Form

- NOUN + 동안: during + NOUN (of non-numeral expression); for + NOUN (of numeral expression)
- Verb base + 는 동안: while + Verb base-ing

Let us look at the examples below.

1. **10년 동안** 영어를 배웠는데도, 말하기가 쉽지 않아요.
   Although I learned English **for 10 years**, it is not easy to speak.

2. **한 달 동안** 친구하고 같이 요리를 배웠어요.
   I learned cooking **for a month** with a friend.

3. **3주 동안** 학교에서 제시카 씨를 못 봤어요. 제시카 씨한테 무슨 일 있어요?
   I haven't seen Jessica on campus **for three weeks**. Has anything happened to Jessica?

4. 한국영화클럽에서 **여름 방학 동안** 북한 영화 시리즈를 상영할 거예요. 거기 같이 갈래요? [상영하다 to play; show]
   There will be a North Korean movie screening series **during the summer break** at the Korean movie club. Would you like to go there together?

5. 기차 타고 부산에 **가는 동안** 계란하고 김밥을 먹었어요. [기차 train]
   I ate eggs and *gimbap* **while riding** a train to Busan.

6. **그동안** 잘 있었어요?
   Have you been doing well? [그동안 Lit., during that time; in the meantime]

Complete the conversation with the appropriate expressions.

1. 에이미: 선생님, 안녕하세요? ______________ 어떻게 지내셨어요?

   선생님: 잘 지냈어요. 에이미 씨는요?

2. 존　: 한국에서 ______________ (for 1 year) 한국인 룸메이트 친구하고 같이 지냈어요.

   민준: 그랬어요? 한국말 참 많이 늘었겠어요!

3. 샤오밍: ______________ (during the winter break) 스키를 배울 거예요.

   에이미: 어디서요?

   샤오밍: 뉴햄프셔에 스키 학교가 있어요. ______________ (for 2 weeks) 레슨을 받을 거예요.

4. 제시카: 어, 맛있는데요? 어디서 한국 요리 배우셨어요?

   민준　: ______________ (during the summer break) 저희 할머니한테서 배웠어요.

   제시카: 정말 맛있네요!

5. 에이미: 제주도에 ______________ (while going) 비행기에서 책을 읽었어요.

   민준　: 어! 전 워싱턴에서 ______________ (while coming) 한국 영화를 봤어요.

Useful expressions

레슨을 받다	to receive lesson
지내다	to spend (time); to live with
잘 지내다	to be doing well
요즘 어떻게 지내세요?	How are you doing these days?
그동안 어떻게 지내셨어요?	How have you been doing?
제주도	Jeju Island
워싱턴	Washington

Patterns, Expressions & Practice

Fill in the chart with missing expressions.

For a month	한 달 동안; 1개월 동안	During class time	
For three months		During the lunch hour	
During this year		During the meeting time	미팅 시간 동안
During that (time); meanwhile		While dating	데이트하는 동안

Listen to the conversation and fill in the blanks with the time expressions. 51

브라이언: 에이미 씨는 한국에 (1)__________ 있었어요?

에이미 : (2) ______________________ 있었어요.

브라이언: 언제가 제일 더웠어요?

에이미 : (3) __________ 이요.

브라이언: 전 (4) __________ 한국에 있었어요.

근데 그 때 정말 추웠어요!

2. Noun-modifying forms of verbs

Form When you use a verb (e.g., 먹다, 가다) directly before a noun to describe/modify the noun, you must use it in the form of "Verb base + 은/ㄴ," "Verb base + 는," or "Verb base + 을/ㄹ" as shown in the following table.

Dictionary form	Past tense form	Present tense form	Future tense form
Verb base + 다	Verb base + 은/ㄴ + NOUN	Verb base + 는 + NOUN	Verb base +을/ㄹ + NOUN
Verb base (ending in a consonant): 먹다	먹은 음식	먹는 음식	먹을 음식
Verb base (ending in a vowel): 가다	간 식당	가는 식당	갈 식당

The forms (i.e., 은/ㄴ/는/을/ㄹ) above, combined with verbs, enable the verbs to modify the nouns that follow. Thus, they are called "noun-modifying (verb) forms."

Look at the following examples.

1. 제가 먹은 음식은 순두부찌개예요. The food that I ate is 순두부찌개.
   Verb base-은 + NOUN

2. 제가 먹는 음식은 순두부찌개예요. The food that I eat is 순두부찌개.
   Verb base-는 + NOUN

3. 제가 먹을 음식은 순두부찌개예요. The food that I will eat is 순두부찌개.
   Verb base-을 + NOUN

4. 제가 간 식당은 서울 식당이에요. The restaurant that I went to is 서울 식당.
   Verb base-ㄴ + NOUN

5. 제가 가는 식당은 서울 식당이에요. The restaurant that I go to is 서울 식당.
   Verb base-는 + NOUN

6. 제가 갈 식당은 서울 식당이에요. The restaurant that I will go to is 서울 식당.
   Verb base-ㄹ + NOUN

Patterns, Expressions & Practice

The following table shows noun-modifying verb forms with different tenses.

Dictionary form		Past tense form	Present tense form	Future tense form
Verb base + 다		Verb base + 은/ㄴ	Verb base + 는	Verb base + 을/ㄹ
읽다	(to reda)	읽은	읽는	읽을
보다	(to see)	본	보는	볼
가다	(to go)	간	가는	갈
사다	(to buy)	산	사는	살
주문하다	(to order)	주문한	주문하는	주문할
먹다	(to eat)	먹은	먹는	먹을
드시다	(to eat)	드신	드시는	드실
가르치다	(to teach)	가르친	가르치는	가르칠
만나다	(to meet)	만난	만나는	만날
시작하다	(to begin)	시작한	시작하는	시작할
일어나다	(to get up)	일어난	일어나는	일어날
끝나다	(to end)	끝난	끝나는	끝날
공부하다	(to study)	공부한	공부하는	공부할

Note 1 For the noun-modifying form of a ㄹ irregular verb, first drop ㄹ from the verb base and then attach ㄴ, 는, or ㄹ to the base, as shown in the table below.

Dictionary form	Past tense form	Present tense form	Future tense form
Verb base + 다	Verb base + ㄴ	Verb base + 는	Verb base + ㄹ
살다 (to live) 만들다 (to make) 팔다 (to sell)	(살 → 살 + ㄴ) 산 (만들 → 만들 + ㄴ) 만든 (팔 → 팔 + ㄴ) 판	(살 → 살 + 는) 사는 (만들 → 만들 + 는) 만드는 (팔 → 팔 + 는) 파는	(살 → 살 + ㄹ) 살 (만들 → 만들 + ㄹ) 만들 (팔 → 팔 + ㄹ) 팔

Note 2 The noun-modifying forms of ㄷ irregular verbs are:

Dictionary form	Past tense form	Present tense form	Future tense form
Verb base + 다	Verb base + 은	Verb base + 는	Verb base + 을
듣다 (to hear) 걷다 (to walk) 묻다 (to ask)	(듣 → 들 + 은) 들은 (걷 → 걸 + 은) 걸은 (묻 → 물 + 은) 물은 Rule: 1) ㄷ changes to ㄹ 2) 은 is attached	듣는 걷는 묻는	(듣 → 들 + 을) 들을 (걷 → 걸 + 을) 걸을 (묻 → 물 + 을) 물을 Rule: 1) ㄷ changes to ㄹ 2) 을 is attached

Note 3 The following table shows the noun-modifying forms of the 이다 verbs.

Dictionary form	Past tense form	Present tense form	Future tense form
Noun이다 Noun다	Noun이 + 던 /Noun이었+던 Noun + 던 /Noun였+던	Noun이 + ㄴ Noun이 + ㄴ	Noun이 + ㄹ Noun이 + ㄹ
학생이다 (to be) 가수다 (to be)	학생이던/학생이었던 가수던/가수였던	학생인 가수인	학생일 가수일

Usage In Korean, the information about a noun is located in front of the noun. This is done by placing the noun modifying form of a verb in front of the noun, including all the parts that are related with the verb. In the following examples, note the difference in word order between Korean and English expressions.

KOREAN			ENGLISH		
related elements +	Noun-modifying verb form +	NOUN	NOUN +	which +	related elements
		음식	food		
	먹는	음식	food	which	I eat
혼자	먹는	음식	food	which	I eat alone
집에서 혼자	먹는	음식	food	which	I eat alone at home
....					....
Noun-modifying clause				Noun-modifying clause	

Look at the following examples. For simplicity, the boundaries of the noun-modifying clauses are marked with { }.

1. {어제 학교 식당에서 만난} 친구는 마이클이에요.
   NOUN
   The friend {whom I met at the school cafeteria yesterday} is Michael.

2. {미국에 있는 도시 중에서 제가 가장 좋아하는} 도시는 볼더예요.
   NOUN
   The city {that I like best among the cities in the USA} is Boulder.

3. {내일 미팅에 올} 사람은 마이클이에요.
   NOUN
   The person {who is coming to the meeting tomorrow} is Michael.

4. 저는 {한국말을 아주 잘하는} 미국 사람을 알아요.
   NOUN
   I know an American {who speaks Korean very well}.

Mark the boundary of the noun-modifying clauses with { } and underline the related nouns, as shown in (1).

1. { 제가 사는 } 동네에는 한국 사람들이 많아요.
2. 이 식당에는 마이클이 좋아하는 한국 음식이 없어요.
3. 저기 제시카 씨 옆에서 얘기하는 사람은 누구예요?
4. 저는 어제 저녁에 학교 뒤 식당에서 제 룸메이트를 좋아하는 여학생을 만났어요.
5. 오늘 오후에는 제가 잘 아는 친구를 커피숍에서 만나요.

Using the noun-modifying form ~는, tell your friend who the following people are, as shown in (1).

1.
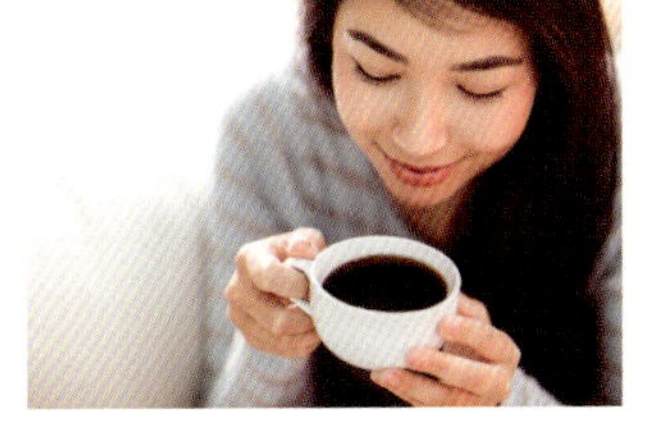
소피아

커피를 마시는 사람은 소피아예요.

2.

제인

음악을 ______________ 제인이에요.

3. 

다이애나

____

4. 

수미

소파에서 ________________________

5. 

마이클

사진을 ____________________

6.

제임스

____

Change the forms of the verbs appropriately so that they can modify the nouns that follow. Pay attention to which tense the noun-modifying verb should use.

1. A: 지난 크리스마스 때 무슨 선물을 받았어요?

   B: 남자 친구한테서 받았는데, ____________(받다) 선물은 카메라였어요.

2. A: 다음 학기부터 이 아파트에서 ____________(살다) 학생은 에이미죠?

   B: 네, 맞아요.

3. A: 지난 여름 방학에 한국에 ____________ (가다) 사람은 마이클이죠?

   B: 네. 이번 여름 방학 때에도 한국에 갈 거예요.

4. A: 민준 씨, 어제 공원에 여자 친구와 같이 갔죠?

   B: 아뇨. 저와 함께 공원에 ____________(가다) 사람은 제 여동생이에요.

5. A: 제가 다음 주에 ____________(가다) 도시는 뉴욕이에요.

   B: 잘 다녀오세요.

6. A: 다음 주가 우리 한국어 수업이 ______________(시작하다) 주예요.

   B: 벌써 그렇게 됐어요? 시간이 참 빨리가요.

7. A: 나중에 봐요.

   B: 네. 그럼 미팅이 ______________(끝나다) 시간에 커피숍 앞에서 기다릴게요.

Complete the following dialogues as in (1).

1. A: 이것은 무슨 음식이에요?

   B: 한국에서 설날에 먹는 음식이에요. (한국, 설날, 먹다, 음식)

2. A: 저기 계시는 분은 누구세요?

   B: ____. (한국어, 가르치시다, 교수님)

3. A: 누가 민지예요?

   B: ____. (생물학, 공부하다, 학생)

4. A: 여기 있는 건물은 무슨 건물이에요?

   B: ____. (학생들, 공부하다, 도서관)

5. A: 한국에 갈 사람들은 어떤 사람들이에요?

   B: ________________________________. (이번 학기, 한국어 수업, 듣다, 사람들)

3. Noun-modifying forms of adjectives

The noun-modifying forms of adjectives are similar to the noun-modifying forms of verbs

Form When you use adjectives (e.g., 좋다, 비싸다) before nouns, you must use them in the form of "Adjective base + 던," "Adjective base + 은/ㄴ," or "Adjective base + 을/ㄹ," as shown in the following table.

Dictionary form	Past tense form	Present tense form	Future tense form
Adjective base + 다	Adjective base + 던	Adjective base + 은/ㄴ	Adjective base + 을/ㄹ
Adjective base (ending in a consonant): 좋다	좋던 음식	좋은 음식	좋을 것
Adjective base (ending in a vowel): 비싸다	비싸던 식당	비싼 식당	비쌀 것

The forms (i.e., 던/은/ㄴ/을/ㄹ) above, combined with the adjectives, enable the adjectives to modify the nouns that follow. Thus, they are called "noun-modifying (adjective) forms."

In particular, note that the form of "adjective base + 던" indicates a situation that continued for a period in the past but no longer exists in the present. Thus, "adjective base + 던" (e.g., 비싸던) can be translated as "**used to** be adjective" (e.g., used to be expensive).

Note 1

The future tense form "을/ㄹ" of adjectives and 이다, except for adjectives ending in ~있다/~없다, is used only before dependent nouns (which cannot be used alone, unlike regular nouns), such as 것(thing, fact, event) / 거(shortened form), 곳 (place), 만큼 (as much/many as), and 듯 (likelihood). In this case, the future tense form carries the meaning of probability, conjecture, or the like rather than the actual future. As an example, refer to "~을 거예요/~ㄹ 거예요" in Lesson 17.(II .1)

1. 내일은 **추울 거예요**. [prediction]
   It may be cold tomorrow.
2. 내일 날씨는 **좋을 거예요**. [prediction]
   Tomorrow's weather might be good.
3. 내년에는 물가가 비**쌀 것이에요**. [prediction]
   The living costs may be expensive in the next year.
4. 내년에는 물가가 **비쌀 듯해요**. [likelihood]
   It is likely that the cost of living will be expensive in the next year.
5. 기분이 **좋을 만큼** 술을 마셨다. [probability]
   He drank as much as it felt good to him.
6. 내일 올 사람은 학생**일 거예요**. [probability]
   The person who comes tomorrow could be a student.

Now look at the examples below.

1. 좋은 음식은 몸에도 좋아요.
   Adj. base-은 + NOUN
   Food that is good is also good for our bodies.

2. 좋던 날씨가 갑자기 나빠졌어요.
   Adj. base-던 + NOUN
   The weather that used to be good suddenly became bad.

3. 비싼 음식은 불고기예요.
   Adj. base-ㄴ + NOUN
   The food that is expensive is 불고기.

4. A: 내일 날씨는 아주 좋을 거예요.
   Adj. base-을 + NOUN
   The weather would be good tomorrow.

   B: 네. 정말 좋을 것 같아요.
   Adj. base-을 + NOUN
   Right. It seems that we would have really good weather.

The following table shows noun-modifying adjective forms.

Dictionary form	Past tense form	Present tense form	Future tense form
Adjective base + 다	Adjective base + 던	Adjective base + 은/ㄴ	Adjective base + 을/ㄹ
좋다 (to be good;nice)	좋던	좋은	좋을
괜찮다 (to be okay)	괜찮던	괜찮은	괜찮을
많다 (to be many)	많던	많은	많을
예쁘다 (to be pretty)	예쁘던	예쁜	예쁠
싸다 (to be cheap)	싸던	싼	쌀
비싸다 (to be expensive)	비싸던	비싼	비쌀
바쁘다 (to be busy)	바쁘던	바쁜	바쁠
크다 (to be big)	크던	큰	클
유명하다 (to be famous)	유명하던	유명한	유명할
편하다 (to be convenient)	편하던	편한	편할
대단하다 (to be incredible)	대단하던	대단한	대단할

Note 2 For the noun-modifying forms of ㅂ irregular adjectives, first change ㅂ in the adjective base to 우 and then attach ㄴ/ㄹ, as shown in the table below. (See Rule 3. in Appendix V.)

Dictionary form	Past tense form	Present tense form	Future tense form
Adjective base + 다	Adjective base + 던	Adjective base + ㄴ	Adjective base + ㄹ
쉽다 (to be easy) 어렵다 (to be difficult) 춥다 (to be cold) 덥다 (to be hot) 반갑다 (to be glad) 맵다 (to be spicy)	쉽던 어렵던 춥던 덥던 반갑던 맵던	(쉽 → 쉬우 + ㄴ) 쉬운 어려운 추운 더운 반가운 매운 Rule: 1) ㅂ changes 우 2) ㄴ is attached	(쉽 → 쉬우 + ㄹ) 쉬울 어려울 추울 더울 반가울 매울 Rule: 1) ㅂ changes 우 2) ㄹ is attached

Note 3 For the noun-modifying forms of ㄹ irregular adjectives , first drop ㄹ from the adjective base and then attach ㄴ/ㄹ, as shown in the table below. (See Rule 2. in Appendix V.)

Dictionary form	Past tense form	Present tense form	Future tense form
Adjective base + 다	Adjective base +던	Adjective base + ㄴ	Adjective base + ㄹ
멀다 (to be far) 길다 (to be long)	멀던 길던	(멀 → 멀 + ㄴ) 먼 (길 → 길 + ㄴ) 긴 Rule: 1) Drop ㄹ 2) ㄴ is attached	(멀 → 멀 + ㄹ) 멀 (길 → 길 + ㄹ) 길 Rule: Drop the second ㄹ

Note 4 The noun-modifying forms of adjectives ending ~있다/~없다 are shown below:

Dictionary form	Past tense form	Present tense form	Future tense form
Adjective base + 다	Adjective base + 던	Adjective base + 는	Adjective base + 을
재미있다 재미없다 맛있다 맛없다	재미있던 재미없던 맛있던 맛없던	재미있는 재미없는 맛있는 맛없는	재미있을 재미없을 맛있을 맛없을

Usage As we learned earlier, the information about a noun is located in front of the noun. This is done by placing the noun modifying form of an adjective in front of the noun, including all the parts that are related with the adjective. In the following examples, note the difference in word order between Korean and English expressions.

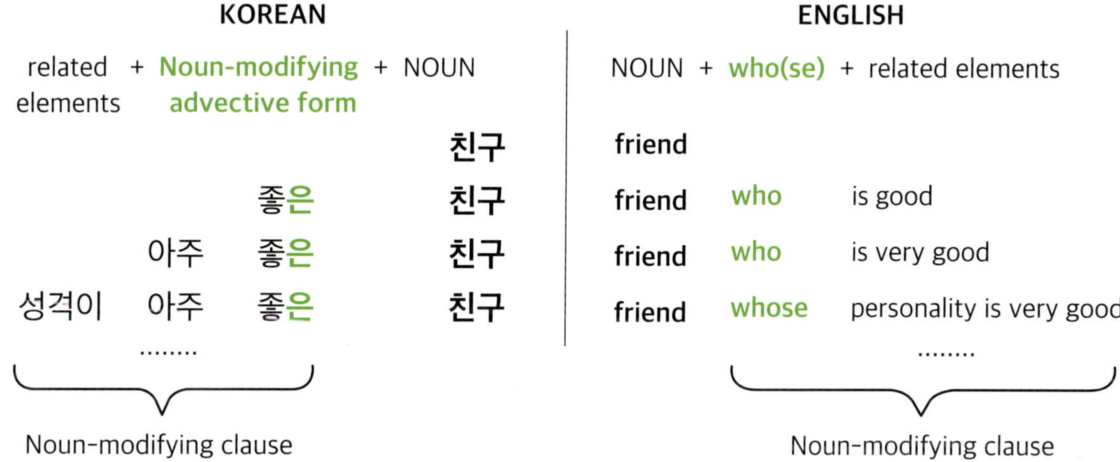

Look at the following examples. For simplicity, the boundaries of the noun-modifying clauses are marked with { }.

1. 마이클은 {성격이 좋은} 친구예요. (NOUN: 친구)
   Michael is a friend {whose personality is good}.

2. {성격이 좋은} 친구는 마이클이에요. (NOUN: 친구)
   A friend {whose personality is good} is Michael.

3. 나는 {성격이 좋은} 친구를 사귀고 싶어요. (NOUN: 친구)
   I'd like to make a friend {whose personality is good}.
   [-을/-를 사귀다 to make a friend; ~고 싶다 to want to ~]

NOUN
4. {1학년 학생인} 브라이언은 뉴욕에서 왔어요.
Brian {who is a freshman} came from New York.

NOUN
5. 저는 {날씨가 좋은} 도시에 살고 싶어요.
I want to live in a city {where the weather is good}.

Change the forms of the adjectives appropriately so that they can modify the nouns that follow.

1. A: 너 어제 본 시험은 어땠어?
B: 정말 (어렵다) ________________ 시험이었어!

2. A: 어제 백화점에서 (싸다) ______________ 가방을 하나 샀어.
B: 괜찮은데!

3. A: 어제는 눈도 오고 정말 (춥다) ______________ 날씨였어.
B: 맞아. 그래서, 난 집에서 안 나갔어.

4. A: 이번 여름 방학 때 한국에 가면, (맛있다) ________________ 한국 음식을 많이 먹을 거야.
B: 넌 정말 좋겠다!

5. A: LA는 겨울에도 (따뜻하다)______________ 도시예요.
B: 저도 당장 LA에 가서 살고 싶어요.

6. A: 배고픈데 (가깝다) ______________ 곳에 점심 먹으러 갈까요?
B: 잘 (드시다)______________ 음식이 뭐예요?

7. A: 수희 씨는 한때 (유명하다)______________ 가수였어요! [한때 at one time; once]
B: 그랬어요? 저는 몰랐어요.

4. Describing people's appearances

The following expressions are commonly used to describe people's current appearances.

Expressions for one's appearance		Noun-modifying form (~은/~ㄴ) of adjectives + NOUN
키가 크다	to be tall [Lit., height is big]	키가 큰 사람
키가 보통이다	to be of average height [Lit., height is average]	키가 보통인 사람
키가 작다	to be short [Lit., height is small]	키가 작은 사람
뚱뚱하다	to be fat	뚱뚱한 사람
통통하다	to be chubby	통통한 사람
날씬하다	to be thin	날씬한 사람
마르다	to be skinny	마른 사람
예쁘다	to be pretty	예쁜 여자
아름답다	to be beautiful	아름다운 여자
잘생기다	to be handsome	잘생긴 남자
못생기다	to be ugly	못생긴 사람
귀엽다	to be cute	귀여운 얼굴
머리가 짧다	(for one's hair) to be short	머리가 짧은 사람
머리가 길다	(for one's hair) to be long	머리가 긴 사람

Note 1 Some adjectives that describe the result of a state are not used in the present tense form. Use the past tense forms instead.

1. 민준 씨는 잘**생겨요**. (Wrong) → 민준 씨는 잘**생겼어요**. (Correct)
2. 민준 씨는 **말라요**. (Wrong) → 민준 씨는 **말랐어요**. (Correct)

Note 2 **예쁘다** "to be pretty" is used for women and **잘생겼다** "to be handsome" is used for men. **미인이다** "to be a beauty" and **미남이다** "to be a handsome man" are also used.

에이미는 **예뻐요**. Amy is pretty.
에이미는 **미인이에요**. Amy is a beauty.
민준이는 **잘생겼어요**. Minjoon is handsome.
민준이는 **미남이에요**. Minjoon is a handsome guy.

Describe the following cat (고양이) using the expressions you learned.

1. 

고양이가 ____________________.

2. 

고양이가 ____________________.

3. 

____________________.

4. 

____________________.

Look at the following pictures and answer the questions.

마크(Mark) Jinsoo(진수)

지영(Jiyoung) 소연(soyeon)

1. A: 키가 작은 사람은 이름이 뭐예요?

   B: ____________________.

2. A: 키가 큰 사람은 누구예요?

   B: ____________________.

3. A: 머리가 짧은 사람은 이름이 뭐예요?

B: ______________________________.

4. A: 머리가 긴 사람은 누구예요?

B: ______________________________.

Listen to the audio and circle the picture that best corresponds to what you hear.

1. a. b.  c.  d. 

2. a.  b.  c.  d. 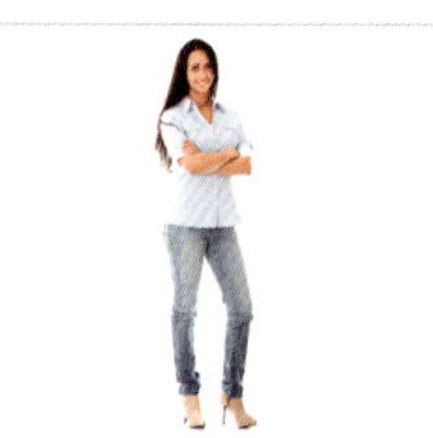

3. a.  b.  c.  d. 

4. a.  b.  c.  d. 

5. 이 + NOUN "this ~"
그 + NOUN "that ~"
저 + NOUN "that ~ over there"

Usage You have learned 여기, 거기, and 저기 as place words which mean "here," "there," and "over there," respectively. (See II.2 in Lesson 9). The words 이, 그, and 저 function similarly.

Use 이 to point out someone or something that is near you (e.g., 이 + NOUN), as in Picture 1 below. Use 그 to point out someone or something that is near the listener (e.g., 그 + NOUN), as in Picture 2 below. 그 is also used to refer to someone or something that is not visually present but is perceptually available. Use 저 to point out someone or something that is away from both the speaker and the listener (e.g., 저 + NOUN), as in Picture 3 below.

Look at the following examples.

1. A: (pointing out the coffee near A) 이 아메리카노 좀 드세요.
   B: 아, 고마워요. 마침 피곤했는데.
2. A: (pointing out the restaurant across the street) 저 순두부집 맛있어요?
   B: 네, 한 번 가 봐요!
3. A: (pointing out the book B is holding in hand) 그 책 재미있어요?
   B: 네, 정말 재미있는 책이에요. 한국 책인데, 읽어 보실래요?
4. A: (pointing out the food B is eating) 그 떡볶이 어때요?
   B: 좀 맵지만 굉장히 맛있는데요?

Complete each conversation using the situation shown in each picture.

1. 상우 : ______________________________?

   Clerk : 이거요? 세일해서 $650이에요.

2. 제니 : ______________________________.

   소피아: 와, 저 배고팠는데! 잘 먹을게요!

3. 왕타오: ______________________________?

   소피아: 혹시 현우 씨 거 아니에요?

4. 제임스: 왕밍 씨, ____________ 어디서 샀어요?

   왕밍 : 이 컴퓨터요? 인터넷에서요.

5. 지혜 : ______________________________?

   민영 : 아, 이거 백화점에서 샀어요. 괜찮죠?

Exercise 13

Create Korean sentences using the English cues.

1. A: (pointing out the smartphone screen) 이 한국어 앱, 얼마예요?

   B: ______________________________.

   That app is not expensive.

2. 유찬: 그 태블릿 PC 언제 샀어요?

   아이린: 아, ______________________________.

   I bought this tablet PC yesterday.

3. 클레어: ______________________________?

   Do you go to that club often?

   선우 : 한국어 클럽이요? 네, 일주일에 한 번 가요.

4. 마이클: ________________________________?

How is that university?

제임스: 괜찮아요. 학생들이 열심히 공부해요.

5. 은서 : 이 쿠키 좀 보세요. 제가 만들었어요.

지아 : 와, ____________________________? 맛있어 보여요.

Did you make that cookie?

Listen to the conversation taking place at a baseball game and fill in the blanks.

01 에이미: 와, 사람이 많네요!

02 민준 : 네, __________ 앉으세요.

03 에이미: __________ 의자에요?

04 민준 : 네. 언제 왔어요?

05 에이미: 지금 왔어요. __________ 사람은 누구예요?

06 민준 : 핫도그 파는 사람이에요. __________ 핫도그 좀 드실래요?

07 에이미: 네, 배고파요. 제가 __________ 핫도그 사 드릴게요.

08 민준 : 좋죠~! __________~!

6. ~거든요 "It's because … , …, you see."

Usage Use ~**거든요** when you provide a reason, justification, or clarification for what has already been said.

Form

▶ Verb/Adjective + **거든요**: 가**거든요**, 싸**거든요**

▶ NOUN 이 (←NOUN이다) + **거든요**: 생일이**거든요**

Look at the following examples. Note that any tense can be used with ~거든요.

1. A : 왜 선물을 사세요? Why do you buy a gift?
   B : 내일이 제 친구 생일이거든요. It's because tomorrow is my friend's birthday.

2. A : 동대문 시장에 갔어요? Have you gone to the Dongdaemun market?
   B : 네, 거기가 싸거든요. Yes, that place is cheap, you see.

3. A : 왜 혼자 점심을 먹어요? Why are you eating alone?
   B : 친구들이 다 수업에 갔거든요. It's because all my friends went to class.

4. A : 한국말을 잘하시네요! You speak Korean well!
   B : 한국 친구가 많거든요. You see that I have many Korean friends.

5. A : 전 영화 "택시 운전사"를 두 번이나 봤어요.
   I watched the movie "Taxi Driver" even twice.
   B : 그래요? 사실은 저도 세 번이나 봤어요.
   Is that right? In fact, I saw it three times.
   영화가 정말 좋았거든요. [사실은 in fact; -이나 as many as~]
   It was because the movie was really good.

6. A : 음식을 많이 준비했네요?
   You prepared a lot of food!
   B : 네. 오늘 저녁에 민준 씨 생일 파티를 할 거거든요. [Contracted form of 할 것이거든요]
   Yes, as you can see, we'll throw Minjoon's birthday party this evening.

Complete the conversation using ~거든요.

1. 에이미: 내년에는 회사에서 일 안 하실 거예요?
   민준 : 네. ________________________.
   because I will go to graduate school

2. 샤오밍: 그 친구가 자동차를 잘 알아요?
   에이미: 네. ________________________.
   because he is an automobile engineer

3. 제임스: 마이클 씨가 인기가 많네요! [인기가 많다 to be popular]
   준희 : ________________________.
   because he is a good-looking

4. 제시카: 티엔 씨는 영어도 잘하고 베트남어도 잘하네요?

은정 : ________________________________.
because he is a Vietnamese American

5. 민준 : 오늘은 한국 식당에 안 가세요?

미라 : 네, ________________________________.
because I also ate Korean food for dinner yesterday.

Exercise 16

Complete the conversation with ~거든요.

01 에이미: 민준 씨, 대학원에 왜 가세요?

02 민준 : (1) ________________________________.
because I am going to major in management.

03 에이미: 그래요?

04 민준 : 네, 졸업하면 더 좋은 직장을 (2)____________________.
because I can find.

05 에이미: 저는 졸업하고 2-3년은 일할 거예요.
(3) ________________________________.
because I want to work.

06 민준 : 저도 졸업하고 2년 동안 일했어요. 이제는 공부도 하고 싶어요.

Exercise 17

Listen to the conversation between the two friends and fill in the blanks. 54

01 에이미: 민준 씨, 여자 친구 (1)____________________!

02 민준 : 네. 여자 친구는 왜요?

03 에이미: 소개팅 할 수 있는 친구가 (2)____________________.

04 민준 : 그래요? 어떤 친구예요?

05 에이미: (3)________________________이에요. 한국말도 잘 (4)________________.

06 민준 : 그래요? 대학생 (5)________________?

07 에이미: 네. 잘나가는 대학생이에요.

08 민준 : 와~ 혹시 사진 있어요?

III. Culture

Culture of blind dating in Korea: 소개팅 & 선

소개팅 is a blind date between a man and a woman arranged by close friends or family members. Many young Koreans in their 20s and 30s casually go on a blind date after receiving an initial introduction to the person of interest with his or her contact information. What should they talk about during that awkward first date? According to one study, a topic that is more recommended to be brought up during the first blind date is one's interesting travel experience. Interesting experiences tell something concrete about the person thus possibly increase the curiosity of the listener during the conversation. On the other hand, bringing up a favorite movie genre may not be the best choice at the first date because the other person may not share the same interest. Another tip that can lead to a successful blind date is finding a common interest. The research reveals that talking about bad movies or a bad boss actually brings people closer together. Psychologists suggest that bringing up sensitive topics, such as experiences with previous boyfriends or girlfriends, or controversial topics, such as same-sex marriages may increase genuine interest in the speaker. Emotionally sensitive topics are known to bring people closer together, contrast to talking about mundane topics, such as sports or weather.

선 is a more traditional way that Korean men and women are formally introduced, particularly with serious intentions of finding someone who is a "marriage material." Until recently, 선 was called 중매. 중매 has existed since the Joseon dynasty (1392-1920), when men and women were formally introduced with the help of a professional matchmaker, called 중매쟁이. The matchmaker was usually an elder woman in the village who had known every member of the village well for a long time. The modern practice of 선 is close to 소개팅 in its process and has become less formal than its used to be in the old days. Scenes of 선 are shown commonly in many popular Korean TV dramas. On a 선 date, the man and woman usually go to a decent coffee shop or a fancy lounge at a boutique hotel to have coffee and then move to dinner at an upscale restaurant while measuring up whether the other person meets basic marriage requirements. Some people are not shy about bringing up the person's income level, family background, job success, and future goals at this meeting. 선 is, in a way, more of a business style resumé exchange and an interview for marriage. Although this may sound unnatural to some people, there have been many happy marriages in Korea born out of the 중매 or 선 process, and there are a good number of couples who benefit from 선 style dates still today.

IV. Listen & Discuss

Minjoon and Amy are having lunch at their company's cafeteria. Minjoon wants to introduce one of his friends to Amy. Listen to the conversation carefully. Discuss the answers to the following questions with your classmates. Finally, write each answer in a full Korean sentence in the space provided.

1. 에이미 씨한테 한 민준 씨의 제안(suggestion)은 뭐예요?

2. 민준 씨 친구는 어느 나라 사람이에요?

3. 민준 씨 친구는 한국에 얼마 동안 살았어요?

4. 민준 씨 친구 직업은 뭐예요?

5. 에이미 씨는 민준 씨 친구하고 뭘 할 거예요?

Script

Minjoon and Amy are having lunch at the company's cafeteria. Minjoon wants to introduce one of his friends to Amy. Watch the video and guess what is happening in this conversation.

01 민준 : 에이미 씨 남자 친구 없죠!

02 에이미: 네. 근데 왜요?

03 민준 : 제 친구랑 소개팅 하실래요?

04 에이미: 민준 씨 친구면... 한국 사람이에요?

05 민준 : 아뇨. 베트남계 미국인이에요. 근데 한국말을 진짜 잘해요.

06 에이미: 그래요? 어떻게 한국말을 잘해요?[II.1,6]

07 민준 : 한국에서 4년 동안 살았거든요.[II.6]

08 에이미: 그렇구나. 그 친구는 무슨 일 해요?[II.5]

09 민준 : 잘나가는 자동차 엔지니어예요.[II.2,3] 그리고 되게 잘생겼어요.[II.4]

10 에이미: ㅎㅎ 혹시 사진 있어요?

11 민준 : 에이~ 그냥 한번 만나 봐~요!

12 에이미: 음.... 그래요~.

01 Minjoon: Amy, you don't have a boyfriend, do you?

02 Amy : No. But why?

03 Minjoon: Would you like to go on a blind date with my friend?

04 Amy : If he is your friend... is he Korean?

05 Minjoon: No. He is Vietnamese-American. But he speaks Korean really well.

Amy : Really? How come he speaks Korean well?

06 Minjoon: (Because) He lived in Korea for 4 years, you see.

07 Amy : I see. What does your friend do?

08 Minjoon: He is a hotshot automobile engineer. And he is very good-looking.

09 Amy : (smiling) Any chance you have a photo?

10 Minjoon: Well~ you should just try meeting him once ~ !

11 Amy : Hmm··· Okay ~

V. Guided Conversation

With the organization of the model conversation in Listen & Discuss (Script) in mind, practice the modified conversation below with your partner.

A coworker and friend (A) is talking to (B) about a person who is a blind date candidate for (B). Practice the following conversation with your partner, choosing the best option in (   ) to make the conversation flow naturally

01 A: ____________ 씨, ____________ 친구 없죠!
(B's name) (남자; 여자)

02 B: 네.

03 A: ____________ 씨는 어떤 남자/여자를 좋아해요?
(B's name)

04 B: ____________ 는/ㄴ 남자/여자를 좋아해요.
(잘 생기다; 멋있다; 예쁘다; 착하다)

05 A: 그럼, 제 친구랑 소개팅 하실래요?

06 B: ____________ 씨 친구면... ____________ 사람이에요?
(A's name) (nationality of your partner)

07 A: ____________. ____________ 계 미국인이에요.
(Disagree to B.) (different nationality of your partner)

08 근데 한국말을 진짜 잘해요.

09 B: ____________? 어떻게 한국말을 잘 해요?
(show your surprise)

10 A: 한국에서 4년 동안 ____________ 거든요.
(살다; 일하다; 공부하다)

11 B: 그렇구나. 그 친구는 무슨 일 해요?

12 A: 잘나가는 ____________ 예요.
(자동차 엔지니어; 컴퓨터 엔지니어; 회사원; 변호사; 요리사; 학원 강사)

13 그리고 되게 ____________.
(잘 생겼어요; 멋있어요; 예뻐요; 쿨해요; 착해요)

14 B: ㅎㅎ 혹시 사진 있어요?

15 A: 에이~ 그냥 한번 만나 봐~요!

16 B: ____________.
(decide your own answer here to the proposal)

(Switch roles and continue to practice.)

Present the conversation from Step 1 in front of the class. Try not to read it!

Guided Conversation

VI. Spontaneous Conversation

Now is your chance to have real interactions with your classmates in Korean. You can practice speaking with your classmates, writing, and presenting in front of the class!

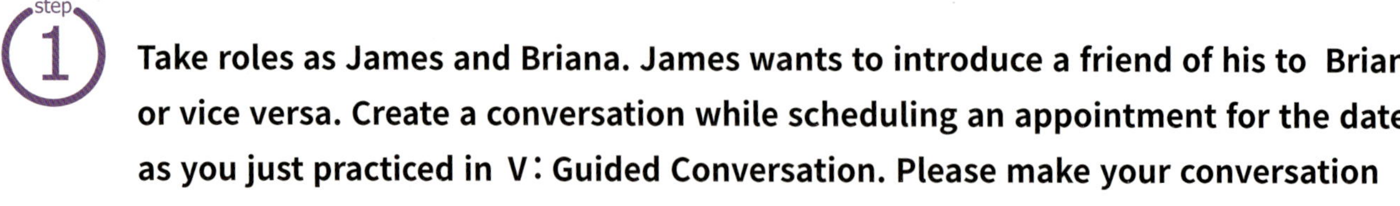

step 1

Take roles as James and Briana. James wants to introduce a friend of his to Briana or vice versa. Create a conversation while scheduling an appointment for the date as you just practiced in V: Guided Conversation. Please make your conversation meaningful by following the guidelines below.

First, before you (as James or Briana) begin the role-play, decide the nationality of your friend whom you want to introduce to your classmate:

중국 한국 미국 말레이시아 베트남 일본 대만 몽골

Choose one: 제가 James/Briana한테 소개할 제 친구는 ___________ 사람이에요.

Second, before moving to Step 2, use the table below to brainstorm details about your friend. You'll use this information for the next set of conversation practice.

	국적 Nationality	**나이** Age	**직업** job	**용모** Appearance	**키** Height; **성격** Personality
Your friend					

step 2

Acting as James and Briana, create a conversation following the directions below.

1. When your classmate asks if you have a boyfriend/girlfriend, show your interest so that your classmate can introduce someone to you.
2. Before accepting your classmate's proposal for a date, discuss several criteria with your classmate that you have in mind, such as occupation, age, appearance, height, nationality, etc.
3. Include ~거든요, ~ 동안 and noun-modifying forms in your conversation.

Write personal details about Briana's or James' friend, based on the above conversation. Write 10 lines in this narrative about the friend.

1.
2.
3.
4.
5.
6.
7.
8.
9.
10.

Based on what you wrote in Step 3, present the narrative you wrote in front of the class. Try not to read from your script!

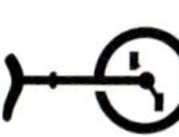

19 시간 있으면 보통 뭐하세요?

What do you usually do when you have time?

Talking about hobbies

Preparation & Practice	I. New Words & Expressions II. Patterns, Expressions & Practice 1. ~다가 — Depicting transition from one event to another 2. 어떤 + NOUN — which ~/what kind of ~; some/any ~ 3. Honorific speech level — The "~습니다" speech style 4. -겠- — must 5. Frequency expressions 6. NOUN 1도 ~고 NOUN 2도 ~고 — to do NOUN 1 and to do NOUN 2 as well III. Culture Popular hobbies in Korea
Conversation Activities	IV. Listen & Discuss V. Guided Conversation VI. Spontaneous Conversation

I. New Words & Expressions

 **Study the words and expressions with the audio.**  56

NOUN

글	writing
레시피	recipe
블로그	blog
사람들	people [사람 *person* + 들 *plural marker*]
스트레스	stress
요리	cooking
요리사	cook; chef
일주일	a week; one week
취미	hobby
파워 블로거	power blogger/influencer
해물 파전	seafood pancake

EXPRESSION

· 스트레스도 풀고 ...
relieving (my) stress ...

· 요리사 해도 되겠어요!
You should become a chef!; You can become a chef!

· 취미로 해요.
(I) do (it) as a hobby.

Form

Dictionary form (Word base + 다)	~아요/~어요 form	~으세요/~세요 form
스트레스를 풀다 to release (one's) stress	스트레스를 풀어요	스트레스를 푸세요

Note 1

In the expression 요리사 해도 되겠어요! (You should become a chef!; You can become a chef!), ~아도/~어도 되겠어요 (I guess you can ~) is the combination of ~아도/~어도 되다 (you can ~), 겠 (must be), and ~어요.

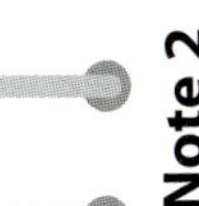

Note 2

You already learned various meanings of -으로/-로 "by ~; in ~; with ~" in Lesson 17 (II.2). For example,

1. 뉴욕에 비행기로 갔어요.	I went to New York by airplane.
2. 볼펜으로 쓰세요.	Please write it with a ball-point pen.
3. 불고기는 소고기로 만들어요.	*Bulgogi* is made from beef.
4. A: hobby가 한국말로 뭐예요?	What is hobby in Korean?
B: 취미예요.	It is 취미.

In this lesson, -으로/-로 is used to mean "as." 취미로 해요 means "I do (it) as a hobby." Here are more examples of -으로/-로 "as."

5. 저는 식당에서 매니저로 일해요.
   I work as a manager at a restaurant.
6. 저는 교환학생으로 서울대학교에 왔어요.
   I came to Seoul National University as an exchange student.

Match each of the words in Column A with the appropriate verb in Column B.

A	B
1. 스트레스를 ·	· a. 만나다
2. 게임을 ·	· b. 풀다
3. 사람들을 ·	· c. 쓰다
4. 블로그를 ·	· d. 하다

Listen to the audio and fill in the blanks. 57

1. A: ________________ 가 뭐예요?
   B: 저는 블로그를 써요.

2. A: 무슨 일 하세요?
   B: 저는 ________________ 예요.

3. A: 블로그 많이 쓰세요?
   B: ________________ 정도 써요.

4. A: ________________ 보통 뭐하세요?
   B: 보통 온라인 게임을 해요.

II. Patterns, Expressions & Practice

1. ~다가 Depicting transition from one event to another

Form ~**다가** is a clausal connective and is used with the base form or the past form of a verb or adjective.

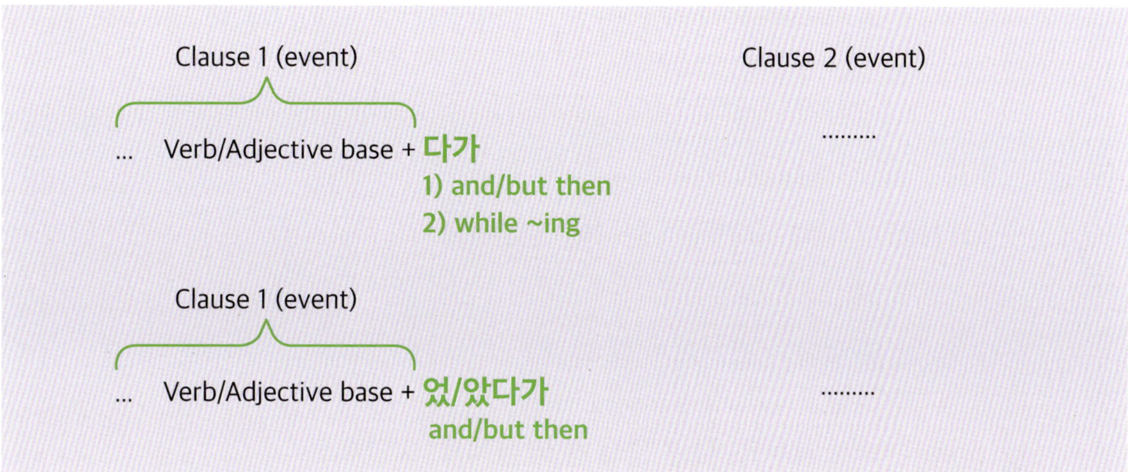

Usage 1. With the base form of a verb or adjective, ~**다가** indicates that while the first event is being carried out, the first event is interrupted and then the second event begins. In this case, ~**다가** is equivalent to "~ **and then** … " or "~ **but then** …."

Clause 1 (event) Clause 2 (event)

... Verb/Adjective base + **다가** ....

1) and/but then

1. A: 날씨가 맑**다가** 갑자기 흐려지네요.
   B: 요즘 날씨가 그래요.
   A: The weather was clear for a while **and then/but then** suddenly gets cloudy.
   B: The weather these days is like that.

2. 비가 오**다가** 갑자기 맑아졌어요.
   Rain came for a while **and then/but then** suddenly it became clear.

3. A: 소개팅에서 그 베트남 친구 만났어요?
   B: 아뇨. 좀 기다리**다가** 그냥 집에 갔어요.
   A: Have you met that Vietnamese friend at the blind dating?
   B: Nope. I waited a while, **and then/but then** just went home.

4. 한국어 숙제하**다가** 영화 봐요.
   I did Korean homework **for a while**, **and then** I am watching a movie.

2. With the base form of a verb or adjective, ~다가 also indicates that the first event is being carried out and while the first event is still continuing, the second event begins to happen. With this usage, it is often the case that the first event and the second event are simultaneously happening at one point. ~다가 is often translated as "in the middle of (while) doing A, B happens."

Clause 1 (event) Clause 2 (event)

... Verb/Adjective base + 다가 ....

2) While ~ing

1. 밥을 먹다가 친구한테서 문자를 받았어요.
   While I was eating, I received a text message from my friend.

2. A: 밥을 먹다가 갑자기 어디 가요?
   While eating, where are you going?
   B: 전화가 와서요. 잠깐 전화 좀 받을게요. 미안해요.
   I got a phone call. So, I will answer the phone for a second. I'm sorry.

3. 스키를 타다가 넘어졌어요.
   While skiing, I fell (on the ground).

4. 클럽에 가다가 길에서 한국어 선생님을 만났어.
   While I was going to the club, I met my Korean teacher on the street.

5. (On the phone)
   A: 지금 뭐 해요?
   What are you doing now?
   B: 온라인 게임을 하다가 배가 고파서 라면 먹어요.
   While playing an online game, I felt hungry, so I am eating ramen.

3. With the past tense form (i.e., 았/었) of a verb or adjective, ~다가 indicates that the first event is completed and then the second event takes place almost immediately in a continuing fashion. It can be translated as "~and/but then …."

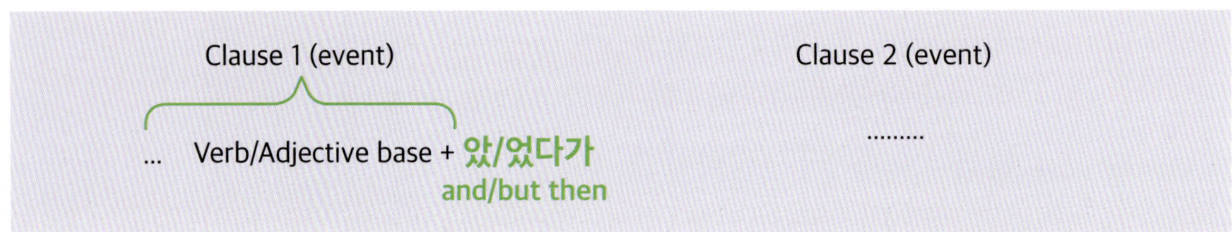

1. 학교에 갔다가 학교 서점에서 책을 샀어요.
   I went to school and (then) at the school bookstore I bought a book.

2. 이 선생님이 교수였다가 이제는 소설가가 되셨어요.
   Professor Yi used to be a university professor but (then) now she has become a novelist.

3. 해물요리를 싫어했다가 요즘은 좋아해요.
   I used to dislike seafood dishes but lately I like them.

4. 그 식당에 갔다가 사람들이 너무 많아서 그냥 나왔어요.
   We went to the restaurant but then there were too many people so we just went out.

Note

Compare ~다가 and ~았다가/~었다가.

1. 우체국에 가다가 수미를 만났어요.
   On my way to the post office, I met Sumi.
2. 우체국에 갔다가 수미를 만났어요.
   I went to the post office and there I met Sumi.

Example 1 indicates that you met Sumi before you arrived at the post office. On the other hand, Example 2 indicates that you met Sumi after you arrived at the post office.

Respond to A, using ~다가 as shown in the English cues.

1. A: 어제 지하철로 집에 갔어요?

   B: 아뇨. ______________________________.
   (I rode the subway, and then rode the bus.)

2. A: 어제 밤에 영화를 다 봤어요?

   B: ______________________________.
   (In the middle of watching the movie, I fell asleep.)

3. A: 제니를 만났어요?

   B: 아뇨. ______________________________.
   (I waited a while, and then I just went home.)

4. A: 숙제 다 했어요?

   B: 아뇨. ______________________________.
   (In the middle of doing homework, I received a phone call.)
   그래서 지금 다시 하고 있어요.

5. A: 지난주에 부모님한테 갔어요?

   B: 아뇨. ______________________________.
   (The weather was clear but then it suddenly snowed a lot.)
   그래서 다음 주에 갈 거예요.

Useful expressions

눈이 오다 to snow [Lit., for snow to come.]
지하철 subway
자다 to sleep (fall asleep)

Exercise 2

Fill in the blanks to complete the conversation.

01 에이미: 혹시 제시카 봤어요?

02 샤오밍: 네. (1)______________________________ 봤어요.
(While going to school yesterday then)

03 에이미: 그랬어요? 제시카 씨는 요즘 뭐 해요?

04 샤오밍: 한국어 스피킹 클럽에서 한국어를 연습해요.

원래 (2)______________________________ 이제는
(He learned Chinese for a while)
한국어를 열심히 배워요.

05 에이미: 그래요? 저도 (3)______________________________
(learned Japanese for a while)
지금은 프랑스어를 배워요. 저는 외국어 배우는 걸 좋아하거든요.

06 샤오밍: 전 요즘 온라인 게임을 해요. 거기서 사람들도 만나고 스트레스도 풀어요.

07 에이미: (4)______________ 재미있는 사람들도 만나요?
(While playing the game)

08 샤오밍: 그럼요!

Listen to the dialogue and fill in the blanks. 

01 민준 : 제시카 씨, 어디 가세요?

02 제시카: (1)____________ 배가 고파서 다시 식당으로 가요.

03 민준 : 아, 벌써 점심 시간이네요. 같이 갈래요?

04 제시카: 네. 근데 민준 씨, 요즘은 시간 있을 때 뭐 해요?

05 민준 : 작년까지 (2)____________ 올해부터는 운동을 더 많이 해요.

06 제시카: 보통 무슨 운동을 해요?

07 민준 : 이번 4월에 보스턴 마라톤에 나갈 거예요. 그래서 마라톤 연습해요.

08 제시카: 와! 대단해요. 저는 작년에는 (3)____________
요즘에는 요리를 많이 해요.

09 민준 : 그래요? 보통 무슨 음식 만들어요?

10 제시카: 스파게티하고, 가끔 돼지 불고기도 만들어요.

11 민준 : 아하! 둘 다 제가 좋아하는 음식이네요!

12 제시카: 하하. 언제 (4)____________ 저한테 문자 해 보세요!

2. 어떤 + NOUN "which~/what kind of ~; some/any ~"

Form 어떤 can't be used alone and must be used before a noun, as shown below.

1. (Questions) 어떤 + NOUN which ~; what kind of ~
2. (Non-questions) 어떤 + NOUN some/any ~

Usage The meaning of 어떤 is different according to the sentence type where it is used.

In questions, 어떤 means "which~" or "what kind of ~."

1. A: 요즘 운동을 많이 해요. I exercise a lot lately.
   B: 어떤 운동(or 것을; 걸; 거) 하세요? What kind of exercise do you do?

2. A: 어떤 거 드실래요? Which one would you like to have?
   B: 녹차로 주세요. Green tea, please.

3. A: 여기 과일 상자가 많네요. 선물로 어떤 게 (or 것이; 과일 상자가) 좋아요?
   There are many fruit boxes. Which one is good for a gift?
   B: 가족 선물로는 사과 상자가 좋아요.
   As for a gift for family, apple boxes are good.

In non-questions, 어떤 means "some/any~."

For example, 어떤 is equivalent to "some" as in "sometime," "someone," or "some + NOUN" expressions. It is also equivalent to "any" as in "anything," "any matter," or "any + NOUN" expressions.

1. 어떤 때는 오전에 운동을 해요. 어떤 때는 저녁에 하고요.
   Sometimes I exercise in the mornings. Sometimes I do in the evenings.

2. 어떤 사람이 제니를 찾아요.
   Someone is looking for Jenny.

3. 집에 어떤 남자가 왔어요.
   Some man came to the house.
   [some + NOUN]

4. 어떤 일이나 잘할 수 있어요.

I can do any work well.
[any+ NOUN]

5. 어떤 것도 문제 없어요.

Anything is possible. [Lit., Anything does not have a problem.]

6. 어떤 여자한테서 전화가 왔어요.

I received a phone call from some woman.
[some + NOUN]

Complete the conversation using 어떤.

1. A: 제 베트남 친구하고 소개팅 할래요?

   B: ________________ 이에요?
   (What type of person is he?)

2. A: 선물로 ____________ 좋을까요?

   B: 여기 이 사과 상자는 어때요?

3. A: ____________하고 데이트 했어요?

   B: 키가 큰 여자하고 데이트 했어요. 전 예쁜 여자가 더 좋은데...

4. A: 다음 학기에 ____________ 을 들을 거예요?

   B: 금요일에 수업이 없는 과목을 들을 거예요.

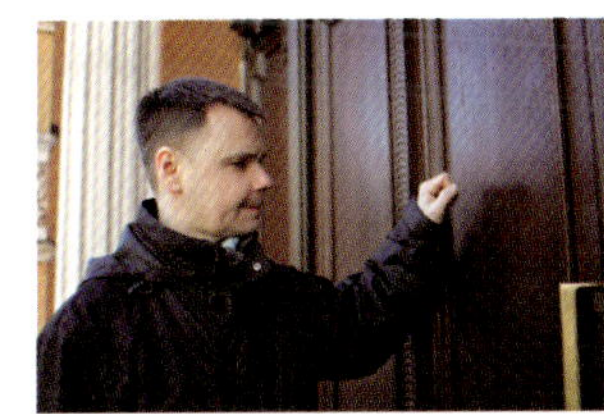

5. A: 누가 왔어요?

   B: ________________ 가 왔어요.
   (Some man came)

Ask appropriate questions, using 어떤.

1. A: ______________________________?

 B: 보통 수영을 많이 해요. 일주일에 세 번쯤 해요.

2. A: ______________________________?

 B: 잘생기고, 착하고, 공부 잘하고, 똑똑하고, 매너도 좋은 남자요.

 A: 하하. 그런 남자가 어디 있어요~

3. A: 취미가 있어요? ______________________________?

 B: 보통 시간이 있으면 온라인 게임을 해요. 가끔 요리도 하고요.

4. A: 아르바이트 하세요?

 B: 네.

 A: ______________________________?

 B: 별카페에서 웨이터로 일해요.

5. A: 그 친구는 ______________________________?

 B: 잘나가는 자동차 엔지니어예요!

Listen to the conversation and fill in the blanks.

59

01 민준 : 전 주말에 시간 있으면 친구들하고 농구를 해요. 에이미 씨는요?

02 에이미: 전 주말에는 요리하는 걸 좋아해요.

03 민준 : 궁금해요! (1)______________ 하세요?

04 에이미: 어제는 파전을 만들었어요. 민준 씨는 (2)______________ 좋아하세요?

05 민준 : 저, 파전 좋아하는데… 전 한국 음식이면 (3)______________ 잘 먹어요.

06 에이미: 하하 그래요? 그럼, 제가 다음에 맛있는 파전 만들어 줄게요.

저도 한국 음식이면 (4)______________ 다 좋아해요.

3. Honorific speech level: The "~습니다" speech style

In Lesson 4 (II.3), you studied one of the two honorific speech styles: the "~아요" speech style (e.g., ~어요/~아요). In the current lesson, we will study the other honorific speech level, which is called the "~습니다" speech style.

Usage

Use the "~습니다" speech style in a situation where the other honorific speech style (i.e., the "~아요" speech style) is not required. There is a tendency to use the "~습니다" style in formal spoken/written discourse (e.g., public speeches/meetings, formal writing), whereas the "~아요" style is used in informal spoken/written discourse (e.g., casual talk, informal writing). You may use the "~습니다" style interchangeably with the "~아요" style in colloquial speech to show respect to the listener.

Types

There are four types of "the ~습니다 speech style" according to the sentence types, as shown in the table below.

Statement	Question	Proposal	Command
~습니다/~ㅂ니다.	~습니까?/~ㅂ니까?	-읍시다/~ㅂ시다.	~으십시오/-십시오. OR ~으시오/-시오.
1. 책을 읽습니다. 2. 친구를 만납니다.	1. 책을 읽습니까? 2. 친구를 만납니까?	1. 책을 읽읍시다. 2. 친구를 만납시다.	1. 책을 읽으시오. 2. 친구를 만나시오.

~으시오/~시오 in commands is rarely used in daily conversation. It is usually used on sign boards for the public or in written (formal) documents.

(For the whole table of speech styles in Korean, see Appendix IV.)

(In statement) You should use the "~습니다/~ㅂ니다" type in statements (not questions). Use the rules below to choose between the two forms.

- ▶ Consonant-ending verb/adjective base + 습니다 : 먹 + 습니다 → 먹습니다
- ▶ Vowel-ending verb/adjective base + ㅂ니다 : 가 + ㅂ니다 → 갑니다
- ▶ 았/었 (past tense), 겠 (L19, Ⅱ. 4) + 습니다 : 먹었 + 습니다 → 먹었습니다
  먹겠 + 습니다 → 겠습니다

Look at the following examples.

1. 요리 블로그를 보다가 에이미 씨 글을 봤습니다.
   [보았 + 습니다 → 봤 + 습니다]
2. 저는 남자 친구가 없습니다.
   [없 + 습니다]
3. 베트남계 미국인인데 한국말을 잘 합니다.
   [하 + ㅂ니다]
4. 여기 식당 순두부는 아주 맛있습니다.
   [맛있 + 습니다]

(In question) You should use the "~습니까?/ㅂ니까?" type when you ask questions. Use the rules below to choose between the two forms.

- ▶ Consonant-ending verb/adjective + 습니까? : 먹 + 습니까? → 먹습니까?
- ▶ Vowel-ending verb/adjective + ㅂ니까? : 가 + ㅂ니까? → 갑니까?
- ▶ 았/었 (past tense), 겠 (L19, Ⅱ. 4) + 습니까? : 먹었 + 습니까? → 먹었습니까?
  먹겠 + 습니까? → 먹겠습니까?

Look at the following examples.

1. A: 안녕하십니까? 김민준입니다.
   [안녕하시 + ㅂ니까]

   B: 처음 뵙겠습니다. 저는 황샤오밍입니다.

2. A: 이번 여름 방학에는 어디 갑니까?
   [가 + ㅂ니까]

   B: 한국에 있는 친구를 만나러 서울에 갑니다.

(In proposal) You should use the "~읍시다/~ㅂ시다" type when you make a proposal. Use the rules below to choose between the two forms.

- ▶ Consonant-ending verb base + 읍시다 : 먹 + 읍시다 → 먹읍시다
- ▶ Vowel-ending verb base + ㅂ시다 : 가 + ㅂ시다 → 갑시다

Look at the following examples.

1. A: 오늘 모임에 같이 갑시다.
   [가 + ㅂ시다]

   B: 네, 좋습니다.

2. (식당에서)

   A: 우리 뭘 먹을까요?

   B: 이 식당에서 잘하는 순두부찌개 먹읍시다.
   [먹 + 읍시다]

(In command) The "~으십시오/~십시오" type and the "~으시오/~시오" type, which are used when giving commands, are not commonly used in daily conversation. You can often find these types on sign boards for the public or in written (formal) documents, etc. "~으십시오/~십시오" sounds less formal than "~으시오/~시오." Use the rules below to choose between the two forms.

- ▶ Verb base (ending in a consonant) + 으십시오/으시오 : 먹 + 으십시오/으시오 → 먹으십시오/으시오
- ▶ Verb base (ending in a vowel) + 십시오/시오 : 가 + 십시오/시오 → 가십시오/시오

Look at the following examples.

1. (On the stairways of a subway)

(뛰지 마 + 시오)

2. (In a computer room)

(음식을 먹지 마 + 시오)

This is a personal diary. Change the "~아요" speech style to the "~습니다" speech style.

지난주 금요일, 저는 민준 씨가 소개해 준 친구를 (1)__________(만났어요). 민준 씨 친구는 베트남계 미국인 (2)__________(이에요). 한국에서 4년 동안 살아서 한국말을 정말 잘 (3)__________(했어요). 그리고 잘나가는 엔지니어이고, 키도 크고 , 얼굴도 (4)__________(잘생겼어요). 다음 주에도 민준 씨 친구를 (5)__________(만나고 싶어요).

This is a job interview. Change the "~아요" speech style to the "~습니다" speech style.

A: 제시카 씨는 언제 (1)__________(졸업하세요)?

B: 내년에 (2)__________(졸업해요).

A: 한국말은 잘 (3)__________(하세요)?

B: 네. 대학교에서 한국학과 국제 관계학을 (4)__________(전공했어요).

A: 그렇군요. 한국에는 얼마 동안 (5)__________(사셨어요)?

B: 6년 동안 (6)__________(살았어요).

4. -겠- "must"

Usage The form "Verb/Adjective + 겠" is used to express a speaker's intention/promise (translated as "will~"), a speaker's formal request (translated as "Would you like~?"), or a speaker's speculation/guess (translated as "must~"). You can distinguish between these various meanings by the context.

In this lesson, we will study 겠 that is used to express a speaker's speculation or guess.

Form Use of 겠 according to speech styles.

Dictionary form (Word base + ~다)	Speech styles			Usage
	아요 style	~아 style	~습니다 style	
Verb/Adjective base +겠다	Verb/Adjective + 겠어요	Verb/ Adjective + 겠어	Verb/ Adjective + 겠습니다	"will/would ~" [Intention] [Formal request] [Speculation]
읽겠다 좋겠다	읽겠어요 좋겠어요	읽겠어 좋겠어	읽겠습니다 좋겠습니다	

Look at the following examples.

1. A: 어제 커피를 많이 마셔서 잠을 못 잤어요.
   B: 그래요? 피곤하겠어요.
   A: I drank a lot of coffee yesterday, so I couldn't sleep.
   B: Oh, really? You must be tired.

2. 제시카 : 저는 정부 장학금을 받아서 이번 여름에 한국에 갑니다.
   민준 : 와~, 정말이에요? 좋겠습니다!
   Jessica : I received a government scholarship, so I am going to Korea this summer.
   Minjoon: Wow, really? You must be happy.

3. 수미 : 이거 내가 만들었는데 맛이 어때? 괜찮아?
   마이클 : 와~ 음식 정말 잘하네. 셰프해도 되겠어.
   Sumi : I made this. How does it taste? Is it okay?
   Micheal : Wow, you cook very well. You can be a chef.

Use ~**으시겠어요**/~**시겠어요** (instead of ~겠어요) which includes ~으시/~시 with ~겠어요 when you talk about seniors or distant equals in your sentence. You can also use ~**으시겠습니다**/~**시겠습니다** interchangeably with ~**으시겠어요**/~**시겠어요**. (For the use of ~으시/~시, refer to Lesson 5 (II.1).)

1. A: 요즘 프로젝트가 많아서 매일 늦게까지 일해요.
   B: 그러세요? 힘드**시겠어요**.
   A: I have many projects these days, so I work until late every day.
   B: Oh, really? It must be hard.

2. A: 그 프로젝트 마감일이 이번 주 금요일입니다. [마감일 due date; deadline]
   B: 아, 그러면 이번 주는 아주 바쁘**시겠습니다**.
   A: The due date of that project is this Friday.
   B: Oh, then you must be very busy this week.

Note 1

You can use **겠** to express your speculation or guess with any verb or adjective tense, as shown in the examples below.

1. A: 어제 에이미 씨하고 같이 한국 식당에서 불고기하고 된장찌개 먹었어요.
   B: 그래요? 맛있**었겠어요**. 어느 식당에 갔어요?

2. A: 지난 주말에 친구들하고 같이 노래방에 갔다왔어요.
   [노래방 karaoke room; 갔다오다 to go and come back]
   B: 노래방이요? 재미있**었겠어요**.

3. A: 어제 한국 영화 클럽 모임이 있었는데 사람들이 많이 왔어요.
   B: 그래요? 제시카 씨도 **왔겠어요**.

Note 2

-**겠**- is also frequently used with the **네요** sentence ending.

피곤하**겠네요**.	Oh, you must be tired.
좋으시**겠네요**.	Oh, you must be happy.
많이 바쁘시**겠네요**.	Oh, you must be very busy.
맛있었**겠네요**.	Oh, it must have been delicious.
재미있으셨**겠네요**.	Oh, it must have been fun.

Complete the dialogues by matching each sentence in column A with the appropriate sentence in column B.

A	B
1. 오늘 하루 종일 너무 바빠서 아침, 점심을 못 먹었어요. ·	· a. 재미있겠어요.
2. 오늘 친구들하고 영화보러 가요. 영화도 보고 저녁도 같이 먹을 거예요. ·	· b. 한국말 잘하겠어요.
3. 제 친구 스티브는 한국에서 8년 살았어요. ·	· c. 배고프겠어요.
4. 다음 주에 시험이 세 개 있어서 주말에 공부할 거예요. ·	· d. 바쁘겠어요.

Give a speculative response to what your friend said by saying "It must have been ~" or "You must have been ~." You may use the following words.

맛있다 to be delicious	재미있다 to be fun
바쁘다 to be busy	기분이 좋다 to feel happy

1. A: 지난 금요일에 한국 영화 클럽 파티가 있어서 거기 갔다왔어요.

   B: ______________________________.

2 A: 지난 학기에 수업도 많이 듣고 인턴 일도 했어요.

   B: ______________________________.

3. A: 지난 학기에 정말 열심히 공부했어요. 다섯 과목 들었는데 올에이(All As)를 받았어요.

   B: ______________________________.

4. A: 지난 토요일에 수미 씨 집에서 여러 나라 음식 파티를 했어요. 한국 음식도 먹고 중국 음식도 먹고 디저트도 먹었어요.

   B: ______________________________.

Give your speculative response to your boss using ~으시겠어요/~시겠어요 or ~으셨겠어요/~셨겠어요. You may use the following words.

아프다	잘하다	재미있다	피곤하다	좋다

1. A: 고등학생 때 수영 선수였어요.

   B: 와~ 그러세요? 수영 ______________________.

2. A: 화장실에서 미끄러졌어요.

   B: 괜찮으세요? ______________________.

3. A: 지난 주말에 LA에 갔다왔어요. LA에 있는 친구하고 같이 한국 노래방에서 놀았어요.

   B: ______________________.

4. A: 일이 많아서 이틀 동안 잠을 못 잤어요.

   B: ______________________.

5. A: 다음 주에 한국으로 출장 가요.

   B: 한국에요? ______________________.

Useful expressions

고등학생 때	at the time when I was a high school student
수영 선수	a swimming athlete
미끄러지다	to slip
놀다	to have fun
이틀	two days
잠을 자다	to sleep
출장 가다	to go on a business trip

5. Frequency expressions

Usage When you answer to a question "How often do you ...? (얼마나 자주 ...?)" or when you express frequency, you can use different frequency words, such as 매일 (everyday), 자주 (often), 종종 (often), 가끔 (occasionally; once in a while), or 때때로 (from time to time).

You can also use "[Time frame]에 [Number of times]" phrase to indicate how often you do something.

Phrase

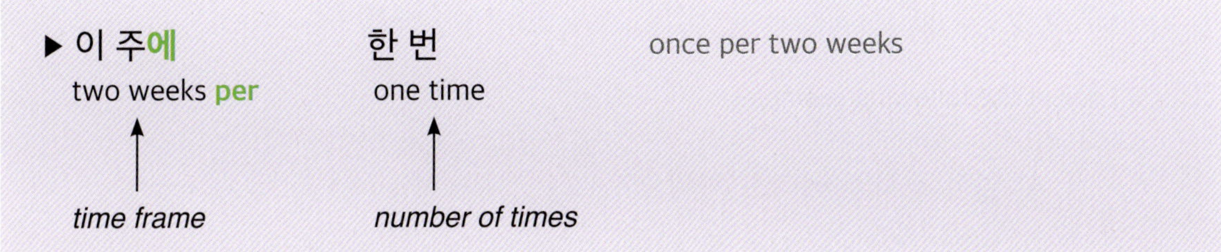

The number of times can be expressed using "Native Korean (NK) numeral + 번(time)."

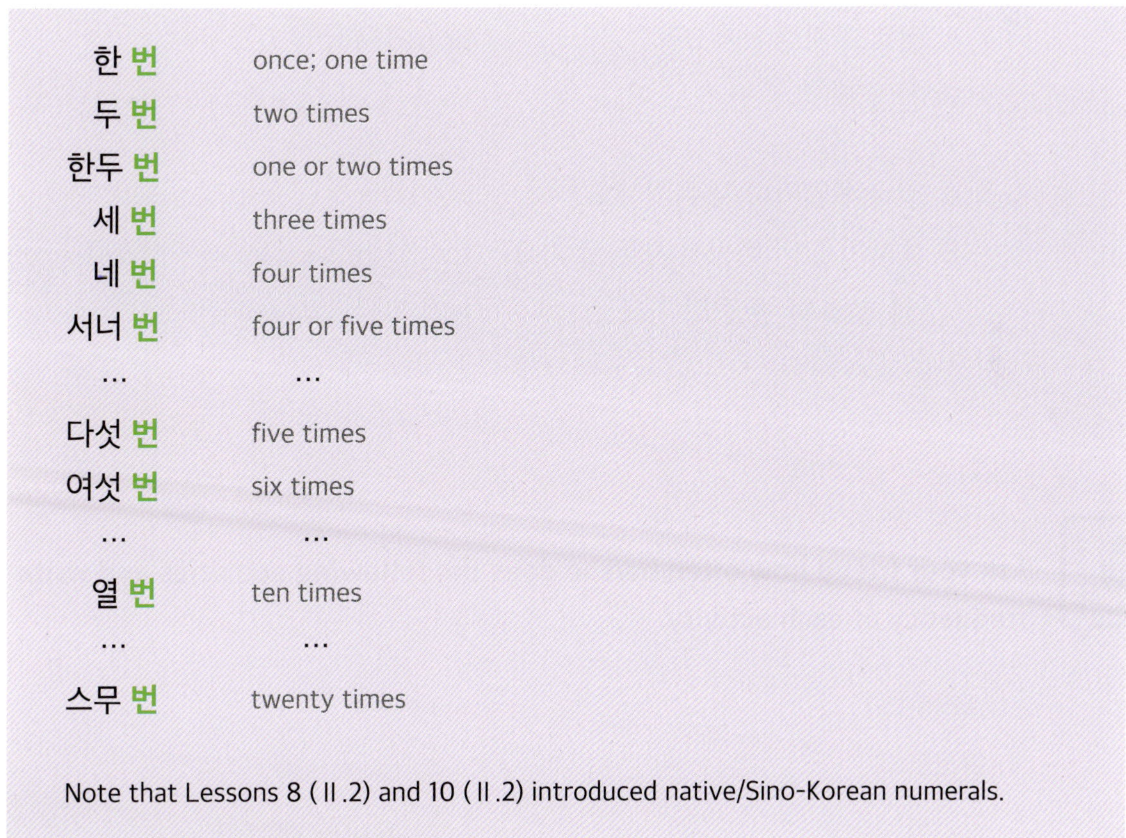

한 번	once; one time
두 번	two times
한두 번	one or two times
세 번	three times
네 번	four times
서너 번	four or five times
…	…
다섯 번	five times
여섯 번	six times
…	…
열 번	ten times
…	…
스무 번	twenty times

Note that Lessons 8 (Ⅱ.2) and 10 (Ⅱ.2) introduced native/Sino-Korean numerals.

Here are common expressions of frequency.

[Time frame]에	[# of times]	
하루에	한 번	once per/a day
일주일에	두 번	twice per/a week
한 달에	세 번	three times per/a month
일 년에	네 번	four times per/a year
일 년에	다섯 번	five times per/a year

Look at the following examples.

1. A: 얼마나 자주 테니스 치세요?	How often do you play tennis?
B: 시간이 없어서 자주 못 쳐요.	I can't play often because I don't have time.
보통 일주일에 한 번쯤 쳐요.	Usually, I play about once a week.
2. A: 블로그 자주 쓰세요?	Do you write blogs often?
B: 한 달에 한두 번 정도 써요.	I write about one or two times a month.
3. A: 한국에 얼마나 자주 가세요?	How often do you go to Korea?
B: 비행기 값이 비싸서 자주 못 가요.	The airfare is expensive, so I can't go often.
삼 년에 한 번 정도 가요.	I go about once every three years.

Useful expressions

쯤	about; around
정도	or so

Ask your friend how often he/she does the following activities and write down the frequency of each activity.

요리하다	to cook
외식하다	to eat outside
영화보다	to watch a movie
미용실에 가다	to go to a hairdresser's
방을 청소하다	to clean the room
부모님께/아버지께/어머니께 전화하다	to call one's parents/father/mother

1. A: 얼마나 자주 요리하세요?

   B: 일주일에 세 번 정도 요리해요.

2. A: ______________________________?

   B: ______________________________.

3. A: ______________________________?

   B: ______________________________.

4. A: ______________________________?

   B: ______________________________.

5. A: ______________________________?

   B: ______________________________.

6. A: ______________________________?

   B: ______________________________.

Exercise 13

Listen to the following conversation between Sumi and Jessica and answer the following questions in Korean. 60

1. 제시카 씨는 얼마나 자주 요가를 해요?

   ______________________________.

2. 수미 씨는 얼마나 자주 조깅해요?

   ______________________________.

3. 수미는 보통 어디에서 조깅해요?

   ______________________________.

6. [NOUN 1]도 ~고 [NOUN 2]도 ~고 "to do NOUN 1 and to do NOUN 2 as well"

Usage "[NOUN 1]도 ~고 [NOUN 2]도 ~고" means "to do both [NOUN 1] and [NOUN 2]" or "to do [NOUN 1] and to do [NOUN 2] as well."

Form Use 요 (i.e., the "~아요" speech style) after ~고 to show respect to the listener.

▶ … [NOUN 1]도 Verb/Adjective고 [NOUN 2]도 Verb/Adjective고요.

1. A: 오늘 바쁘세요?
   B: 네, 조금 바빠요. 숙제도 있고 아르바이트도 있고요.
   [Noun 1 도 Verb 고] [Noun 1 도 Verb 고]
2. A: 내일 한국 영화 클럽 미팅에 사람들이 많이 와요?
   B: 네. 제시카도 오고 스티브도 오고요.
   [Noun 1 도 Verb 고] [Noun 1 도 Verb 고]

In colloquial speech, this expression can be followed by "그래요" ("I do so") or 그랬어요 ("I did so").

3. A: 주말에 보통 뭐하세요?
   B: 집 청소도 하고 숙제도 하고 그래요.
   I clean my home and do homework as well. That's what I do.
4. A: 여름방학 동안 뭐 했어요?
   B: 공부도 하고 여행도 하고 그랬어요.
   I studied and traveled as well. That's what I did.
5. 주말에 친구들도 만나고 영화도 보고 그래요.
   I meet friends and watch movies on weekends as well. That's what I do.
6. A: 한국에 있는 동안 어디 어디 가 봤어요?
   B: 인천에도 가고 전주에도 가고 그랬어요.
   I went to Incheon and went to Jeonju as well. That's what I did.

Note 1 [NOUN 1]도 ~고 [NOUN 2]도 ~아요/~어요 is also used.

1. A: 어떤 영화 좋아하세요?
   B: 액션 영화도 좋아하고 코미디 영화도 좋아해요.

2. A: 주말에 보통 뭐하세요?

   B: 공부도 하고 친구도 만나요.

3. 마이클은 한국말도 잘하고 러시아어도 잘해요.

4. 작년 여름에 LA에도 가고 시애틀에도 갔어요. (treated as one single event)
   [Verb base + 고] [Verb + 았]

   작년 여름에 LA에도 갔고 시애틀에도 갔어요. (treated as two separate events)
   [Verb 았 + 고] [Verb + 았]

Respond to the following questions using "-도 ~고 -도 ~고요."

1. A: 요리 자주 하세요?

   B: 일주일에 두세 번 해요. 한국 음식도 하고 중국 음식도 하고요.
   (한국 음식을 하다, 중국 음식을 하다)

2. A: 한국 영화 클럽에서는 뭐 해요?

   B: 여러 가지 해요. ______________________.
   (영화를 보다, 한국말을 연습하다)

3. A: 주말에 뭐 했어요?

   B: 이것저것 했어요. ______________________.
   (설거지를 하다, 빨래를 하다)

4. A: 어떤 음식 좋아하세요?

   B: 아무 거나 다 좋아해요. ______________________.
   (햄버거를 좋아하다, 피자를 좋아하다)

5. A: 시간 있으면 뭐 하세요?

   B: 저는 보통 운동을 해요. ______________________.
   (조깅을 하다, 테니스를 치다)

Useful expressions

여러 가지	various things
이것저것	this (thing) and that (thing)
설거지	dishwashing
설거지를 하다	to do dishwashing
빨래	laundry
빨래를 하다	to do laundry
아무 거나 다	anything [아무 거나 anything; 다 all]

Look at the following table of weekend activities. Tell what each person often does on weekends using -도 ~고 -도 ~고 그래요.

이름	Weekend activities
제인	아르바이트를 하다; 운동을 하다; 쇼핑을 하다
존	조깅을 하다; 온라인 게임을 하다
준호	빨래를 하다; 방 청소를 하다 to clean the room
영미	친구들을 만나다; 숙제를 하다; 드라마를 보다
샤오밍	요리를 하다; 블로그를 쓰다

1. 제인은 주말에 아르바이트도 하고 운동도 하고 쇼핑도 하고 그래요.
2. 존은 주말에 ______________________.
3. 준호는 주말에 ______________________.
4. 영미는 주말에 ______________________.
5. 샤오밍은 주말에 ______________________.

Listen to the conversation between Minjoon and Amy and answer the questions using -도 ~고 -도 ~고 그랬어요, or -도 ~고 -도 ~았어요/~었어요. 61

1. 지난 여름 방학에 에이미 씨는 뭐 했어요?

______________________.

2. 에이미 씨는 어느 도시에 갔어요? [어느 도시 which city]

______________________.

3. 에이미 씨는 LA에서 뭐 했어요?

______________________.

4. 민준 씨는 여름에 뭐 했어요?

______________________.

III. Culture

Popular hobbies in Korea

According to a poll by Gallup Korea in 2014, Koreans enjoy different hobbies depending on their age group. Due to the geographical landscape of Korea, which is characterized by numerous mountain ranges occupying about 70% of the country, Koreans have traditionally enjoyed hiking and mountain climbing as their most beloved hobby. This is still true of people in their 40s and 50s. Today, Koreans in their 30s enjoy more diversified hobbies, such as listening to music, exercising, reading, and playing online games. Some enjoy cooking, collecting character figures, or traveling. Younger generations in their 20s enjoy more digital-oriented hobbies, such as playing online games, or listening to music from the Internet.

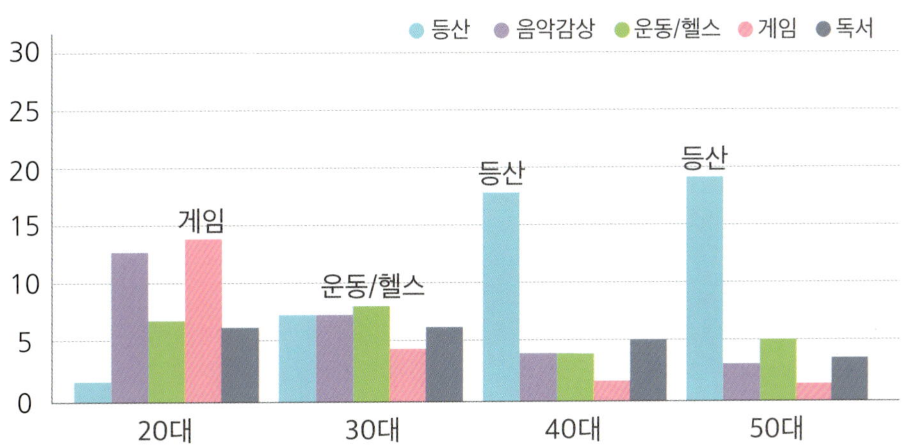

In 2016, Job Korea conducted a survey about the top five hobbies among the working age group in Korea. The survey revealed that the most popular hobbies are exercise (35.3%), followed by movies or TV dramas (28.6%), traveling (13.5%), famous restaurant tours (12.2%), and reading (10.5%).

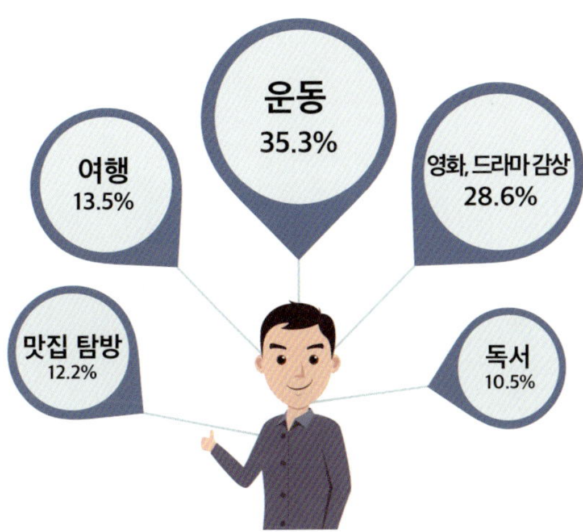

味 미 taste

A sapling (未) that is still growing is thin and fragile. This character means to use one's tongue (口) to distinguish very thin and fragile (未) differences in taste.

Character	Pronunciation	Meaning
味	미 [mi]	taste

Breakdown

味	口	구	mouth
味	未	미	not

Footnote
"未" - A shorter horizontal line (一) is added to the top of "木" to emphasize that the growth is not yet finished. The tree is, therefore, not great in size, but rather small and still growing.

취미 chwi-mi	趣味	intention/go toward + taste = hobby
의미 ui-mi	意味	meaning + taste = meaning
무의미 mu-ui-mi	無意味	none + meaning = meaningless
조미료 jo-mi-ryo	調味料	adjust + taste + ingredient = seasoning
미각 mi-gak	味覺	taste + realize = palate, taste

Source: Your First Hanja Guide
Written by TalkToMeInKorean, KONG & PARK.
Learn Essential Chinese Characters Used in the Korean Language

IV. Listen & Discuss

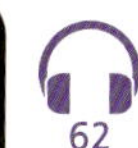

Xiaoming's hobby is playing online games and Amy's hobby is blogging about her cooking. Amy is a power blogger. Listen to the conversation carefully. Discuss the answers to the following questions with your classmates. Finally, write each answer in a full Korean sentence in the space provided.

1. 샤오밍 씨는 어제 인터넷에서 무엇을 봤습니까?

2. 샤오밍 씨는 에이미 씨의 어떤 레시피를 칭찬했습니까? [칭찬하다 to praise]

3. 에이미 씨의 취미는 무엇입니까?

4. 에이미 씨는 얼마나 자주 블로그를 씁니까?

5. 샤오밍 씨의 취미는 무엇입니까?

6. 샤오밍 씨는 왜 게임을 합니까?

Script

Xiaoming's hobby is playing online games, and Amy's hobby is blogging about her cooking. Amy is a power blogger.

01 샤오밍: 어제 요리 블로그를 보다가 에이미 씨 글을 봤어요. [II.1]

02 에이미: 어, 어떤 거요? [II.2]

03 샤오밍: 해물 파전 레시피요.
에이미 씨, 요리사 해도 되겠어요! [II.4]

04 에이미: 에이, 아니에요. 그냥 취미로 해요.

05 샤오밍: 블로그 많이 쓰세요?

06 에이미: 네. 일주일에 한 번 정도 써요. [II.5] 제가 요리를 좋아해서요.

07 샤오밍: 와~ 파워 블로거시네요. 하하.

08 에이미: 샤오밍 씨는 시간 있으면 보통 뭐하세요?

09 샤오밍: 보통 온라인 게임을 해요.
스트레스도 풀고, 사람들도 만나고요. [II.6]

01 Xiaoming: While I was reading the cooking blogs yesterday, I saw your writing, Amy.

02 Amy : Oh, which one?

03 Xiaoming: It was the seafood pancake recipe.
Amy, you should become a chef!

04 Amy : No, it can't be. I am doing that just as a hobby.

05 Xiaoming: Do you write a lot of blogs?

06 Amy : Yes. I write about once a week. Because I like cooking.

07 Xiaoming: Wow~ You are a power blogger. Haha.

08 Amy : What do you usually do when you have time, Xiaoming?

09 Xiaoming: I usually play online games.
(It's good for) relieving stress and meeting people.

V. Guided Conversation

With the organization of the model conversation in Listen & Discuss (Script) in mind, practice the modified conversation below with your partner.

Two friends are talking about their hobbies. Practice the following conversation with your partner, choosing the best option from (   ) to make the conversation flow naturally.

01 A: 어제 ________ 블로그를 보다가 ________ 씨 글을 봤어요.
(다이어트; 미용; …) (your partner's name)

02 B: 어, 어떤 거요?

03 A: ________ (이)요.
(다이어트 음식; 좋은 화장품; …)

04 ________ 씨, ________ 해도 되겠어요!
(B's name) (영양사; 미용 관리사; …)

05 B: 에이, 아니에요. 그냥 취미로 해요.

06 A: 블로그 많이 쓰세요?

07 B: 네. ________ 써요. 제가 ________ 을/를 좋아해서요.
(매일; 일주일에 두 번; 주말마다; 수요일마다) (다이어트 연구; 미용 연구)

08 A: 와~ 파워 블로거시네요. 하하.

09 B: ________ 씨는 시간 있으면 보통 뭐하세요?
(A's name)

10 A: 보통 ________ 을/를 해요.
(your choice of hobby)
________, ________.
(Reason 1 of doing this hobby: use ~도~고) (Reason 2 of doing this hobby: use ~도~고)

Useful expressions

미용	beauty
스타크래프트	Starcraft (online game)
영양사	nutritionist
미용 관리사	beautician
연구	research

(Switch roles and continue to practice.)

Present the conversation from Step 1 in front of the class. Try not to read it!

Guided Conversation

VI. Spontaneous Conversation

Now is your chance to have real interactions with your classmates in Korean. You can practice speaking with your classmates, writing, and presenting in front of the class!

Create a conversation about each one's hobbies, following the guidelines below. First, choose each person's hobby before starting conversation.

Hobby choices

미용 게임 요리 음악 영화 한국 드라마 책 읽기 등산 여행
운동 (축구, 농구, 골프, 스포츠 댄스, 힙합 댄스, 마라톤) 한국 문화 블로깅 ...

Your hobby : ______________________

Your partner's hobby: ______________________ (Ask your partner about this.)

Second, talk about each other's hobbies, including the information below. (You do not need to follow the order of the questions below.)

1. How long your partner has had the favorite hobby.
2. What kinds of activities your partner do for the hobby.
3. How often your partner engages in the hobby. (Use frequency expressions in your question and answer.)
4. Where your partner engages in the hobby.
5. Why your partner practices the hobby or what reward(s) he/she received from it.
6. With whom your partner enjoys the hobby.

Fill in the table with the information about your partner's hobby based on your conversation above.

Partner's name	
Hobby	
Length of the hobby	
Activities for the hobby	

Frequency of the hobby	
Place the hobby occurs	
Reason for having the hobby	
Co-participants in the hobby	
Other information	

Write a narrative about your partner's hobby based on the table above.

Based on what you wrote in Step 2, present the narrative you wrote in front of the class. Try not to read from your script!

20 지난번 소개팅은 어땠어요?

How was the blind date last time?

Explaining the situation and making an offer

Preparation & Practice	I. New Words & Expressions II. Patterns, Expressions & Practice 1. 주다, 주시다, 드리다 — to give 2. ~아 주다/~어 주다 — to do (something) for (someone) ~아 주시다/~어 주시다 ~아 드리다/~어 드리다 3. ~기로 하다 — to decide to ~ 4. -을/-를 하다 — (for someone) to do (something) -이/-가 되다 — (for something) to be done 5. 지난/이번/다음 + NOUN — last/this/next ~ III. Culture Popular dating places and activities in Korea
Conversation Activities	IV. Listen & Discuss V. Guided Conversation VI. Spontaneous Conversation

I. New Words & Expressions

 **Study the words and expressions with the audio.**  63

NOUN

베트남	Vietnam
별	star
별카페	Star Cafe
서로	each other
소개팅	blind date

VERB

기다리다	to wait
망가지다	to break down; to be out of order; to be destroyed
망하다	to be messed up

ADJECTIVE

아쉽다	to be a shame

ADVERB

참	(1) by the way; (2) really, very

EXPRESSION

· ~말이에요	I mean ~
·어땠어요?	How was (it)?
·연락을 하다	to contact [someone]; to contact [some place]
· 지난번	last time

Form

Dictionary form (Word base + 다)	~아요/~어요 form	~으세요/~세요 form
망하다	망해요	--
기다리다	기다려요	기다리세요
망가지다	망가져요	--
연락(이) 되다	연락이 돼요	--
연락(을) 하다	연락을 해요	연락을 하세요
아쉽다	아쉬워요	--
소개(를) 하다	소개를 해요	소개를 하세요

Note 1

You may use **참** "by the way" when some idea suddenly occurs to you. By using **참**, the topic of the conversation can be shifted.

민준 : 에이미 씨, 요즘 바쁘세요?
에이미: 네, 좀 바빠요.
민준 : **참**, 제시카 씨는 요즘 어떻게 지내세요?

Note 2

~ **말이에요** "I mean ~" is used to confirm what the speaker just said or meant. Refer to "II. New Words & Expressions (Lesson 15)" for more examples of **말이에요**.

Note 3

망했다 is the past tense form of **망하다** "to be messed up." ~이/~가 망하다 literally means "(for something) to go fail." **망했다** can be translated in various ways depending on the context, including "to be messed up," "to be ruined," "to fail," or "to do terribly."

Note 4

시간 "time; hour" can be used as a counter indicating a duration of time. **시** "o'clock," on the other hand, is a counter indicating the exact point in time. For example, 한 **시간** means "one hour," whereas 한 **시** means "one o'clock."

한 **시간**	one hour	한 **시**	one o'clock
두 **시간**	two hours	두 **시**	two o'clock
세 **시간**	three hours	세 **시**	three o'clock
네 **시간**	four hours	네 **시**	four o'clock
다섯 **시간**	five hours	다섯 **시**	five o'clock
열 **시간**	ten hours	열 **시**	ten o'clock
스무 **시간**	twenty hours	열두 **시**	twelve o'clock

Note 5

아쉬워요 "That's a shame" or **아쉽네요** "Oh, that's a shame" is used when you wish that a situation were different or when you feel the situation is disappointing/ unfortunate.

Listen to the audio and fill in the blanks.  64

1. 제가 ________ 별카페에서 기다렸는데, 그 친구는 ________ 별카페서 기다렸어요.

2. ____________동안 서로 기다리다가 그냥 집에 갔어요.

3. 핸드폰이 망가져서 연락을 ____________.

4. 그 친구 ____________ 다시 만나기로 했어요.

Exercise 2

Listen to the audio and fill in the blanks. 65

1. A: 지난번 소개팅은 ________________? 그 베트남 친구 ________________.

   B: 망했어요!

2. A: 어떻게 알았어요?

   B: 민준 씨 ______________________________.

3. A: 연락이 안 됐어요?

   B: 네. 핸드폰이 망가져서 연락을 못 했어요.

   A: ____________________________________.

4. A: 제가 다른 사람 ________________________________?

   B: 아뇨. 괜찮아요.

II. Patterns, Expressions & Practice

1. 주다, 주시다, 드리다 "to give"

Form The table shows three forms of verbs which you can use to describe a giver's action of giving in your sentences. The parentheses show different speech styles of the verb.(See Appendix V. for speech styles.)

Non-honorific form	(subject) Honorific form	Humble form
주다 (줘요) (줍니다)	주시다 (주세요) (주십니다)	드리다 (드려요) (드립니다)

Note 1 When you choose one over the other verbs in your sentence, you should also consider using the correct markers for the giver and the recipient. The following table shows four types of markers that are used along with the "giving" verbs.

	Non-honorific	Honorific
Giver (Subject maker)	-이/-가	-께서
Recipient marker	-한테/-에게	-께

Note 2 Here are some useful sentence patterns that are often used in daily conversation.

1. (-한테/-에게/-께) (-을/-를) 보내다 to send (something to someone)
2. (-한테/-에게/-께) 전화(를) 하다 to give a call (to someone)
3. (-한테/-에게/-께) 얘기(를) 하다 to tell a story (to someone)
4. (-한테/-에게/-께) 선물(을) 하다/주다 to give a gift (to someone)
5. (-한테/-에게/-께) 편지(를) 하다/쓰다 to write a letter (to someone)

Usage When you (as speaker) describe one's action of giving to another, you should first consider the social relationship (e.g., social power, social rank, age) between the giver and the recipient and then their relationship with you. Then, use the correct giver/subject marker (이/가 vs. 께서), the correct recipient marker (한테/에게 vs. 께), and the correct verb (주다 vs. 주시다 vs. 드리다) in your sentence.

Using the family tree below, understand how to use the correct "giver" marker, "recipient" marker, and "giving" verb in your sentence.

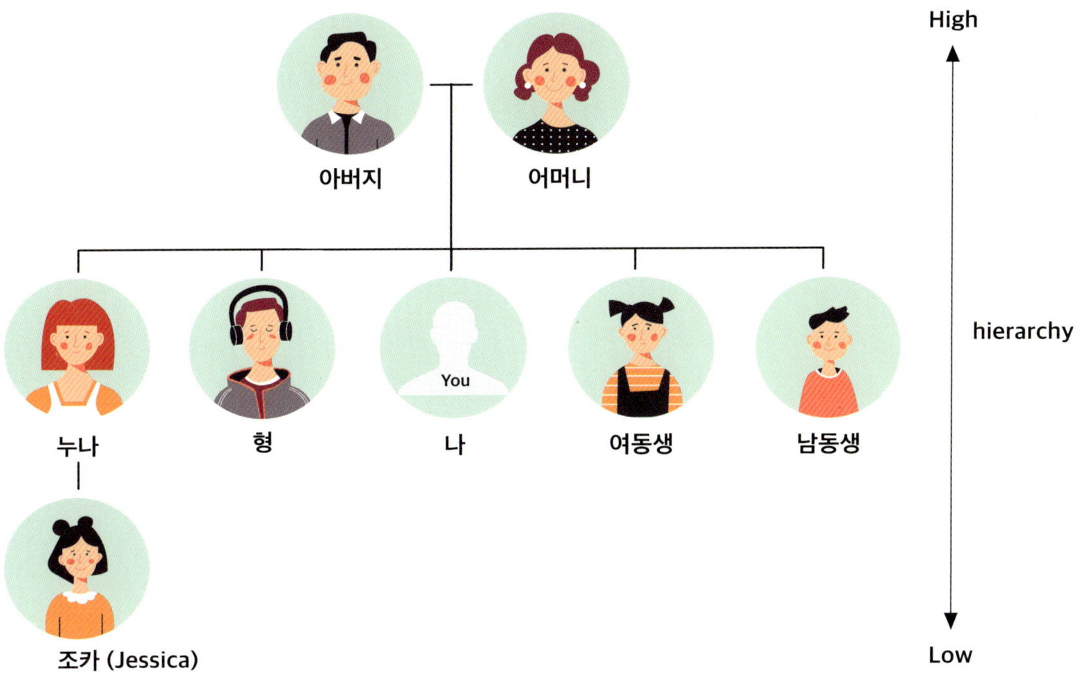

Situation 1

- Mark the Giver with -이/-가 if "Speaker (you) ≧ Giver (in hierarchy)."
- Mark the Recipient with -한테/-에게 if "Giver ≧ Recipient (in hierarchy)."
- Use 주다 if "Giver ≧ Recipient (in hierarchy)."

1a.

나 (Speaker): 누나가 남동생한테 선물을 줘요/줍니다.

My older sister gives a gift to my younger brother.

1b.

나 (Speaker): 누나가 조카한테 선물을 줘요/줍니다.

My older sister gives a gift to my niece (Jessica, her daughter).

Situation 2

- Mark the Giver with -께서 if "Speaker (you) < Giver (in hierarchy)."
- Mark the Recipient with -한테/-에게 if "Giver ≧ Recipient (in hierarchy)."
- Use 주시다 if "Giver > Recipient (in hierarchy)."

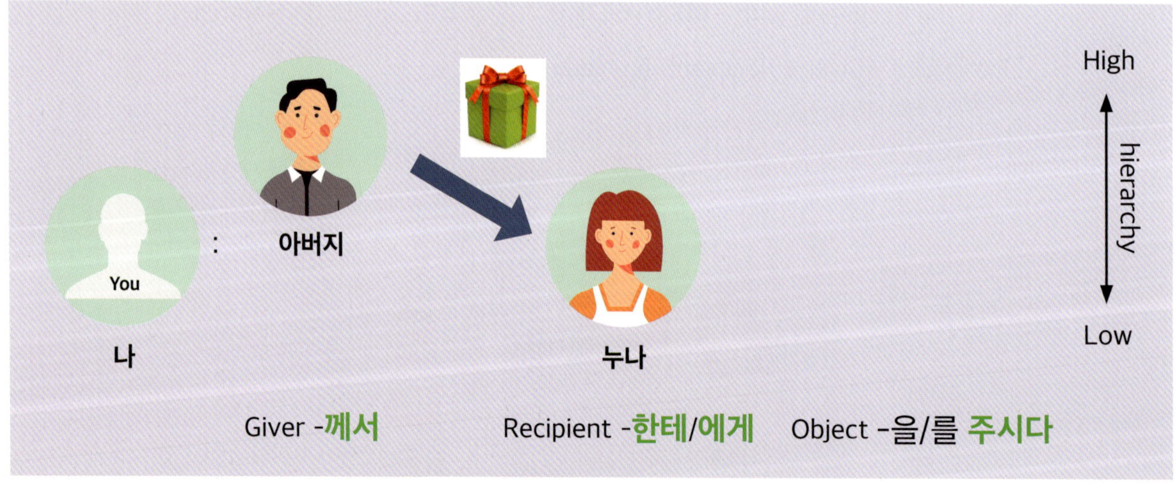

나 (speaker): 아버지께서 누나한테 선물을 주세요/주십니다.

My father gives a gift to my older sister.

Situation 3

- Mark the Giver with -이/-가 if "Speaker (you) ≧ Giver (in hierarchy)."
- Mark the Recipient with -께 if "Giver < Recipient (in hierarchy)."
- Use 드리다 if "Giver < Recipient (in hierarchy)."

나 (Speaker): 누나가 아버지께 선물을 드려요/드립니다.

My older sister gives a gift to my father.

Note 1

Unlike honorific verbs (e.g., 주세요, 물으세요, 보세요) in which -으시/-시 is always inserted, humble verbs have different forms from those of the plain counterparts. Here is a list of the most frequently used humble verbs.

Plain	Honorific	Humble	Example
주다	주시다	드리다	마크가 김 선생님께 카드를 드렸어요. Mark gave a card to Mr. Kim.
묻다	물으시다	여쭙다/여쭈다	질문이 있는데 선생님께 여쭈어도 될까요? I have a question; can I ask you, teacher?
말하다	말씀 하시다	말씀드리다	마크가 사장님께 말씀드렸어요. Mark told (it) to the boss.

Circle the verb that best corresponds to the picture.

1.

민수가 할머니께 꽃을 (줘요/주세요/드려요).

Patterns, Expressions & Practice

2. 

민수가 영주한테 꽃을 (줘요/주세요/드려요).

3. 

영주가 김 선생님께 꽃을 (줘요/주세요/드려요).

4. 

할머니께서 영주한테 꽃을 (줘요/주세요/드려요).

Choose the most appropriate expressions from the parentheses.

1. 혜정: 건우 씨, 이번 어머니 날에 어머니께 무슨 선물 ______________________?
(줄 거예요? /주실 거예요? /드릴 거예요?)

건우: 저는 카드하고 꽃을 ______________________.
(줄 거예요 /주실 거예요 /드릴 거예요)

2. 현우: 서현 씨, 어제 생일이었죠? 생일 선물 많이 받았어요?

서현: 어머니께서 기프트카드를 ______________________.
(줬어요/주셨어요/드렸어요)

그리고 동생이 티셔츠를 ______________________.
(줬어요/주셨어요/드렸어요)

3. 지연: 내일이 에이미 씨 생일인데 무슨 선물 ______________________?
(줄까요? /주실까요?/드릴까요?)

민준: 커피숍 기프트카드 어때요? 에이미 씨가 커피숍에 자주 가잖아요.

Listen to the audio and circle the picture that best corresponds to the audio.

1. a.  b. 

2. a.  b. 

3. a.  b. 

4. a.  b. 

2. ~아 주다/~어 주다 "to do (something) for (someone)"
~아 주시다/~어 주시다
~아 드리다/~어 드리다

Form In the construction of "Verb base + 아/어 주다," "주다" does not carry the meaning of "to give." Instead, the meaning of 주다 becomes diluted and it merely adds the sense of "someone does something for another's benefit" to the meaning of the verb base (i.e., the main verb).

▶ Verb base (ending in 아 or 오) + 아 주다/주시다/드리다

: 찾 + 아 주다 → 찾아 주다/찾아 주시다/찾아 드리다

▶ Verb base (not ending in 아 or 오) + 어 주다/주시다/드리다

: 만들 + 어 주다 → 만들어 주다/만들어 주시다/만들어 드리다

The table shows three forms of verbs that you can use to describe a person's action in your sentences (i.e., doing something for someone). The parentheses show different speech styles.

Plain form	Honorific form	Humble form
~아 주다/~어 주다 (~아 줘요/~어 줘요) (~아 줍니다/~어 줍니다)	~아 주시다/~어 주시다 (~아 주세요/~어 주세요) (~아 주십니다/~어 주십니다)	~아 드리다/~어 드리다 (~아 드려요/~어 드려요) (~아 드립니다/~어 드립니다)

Usage Apply the same rules for ~주다, ~주시다, or ~드리다 when you choose among ~아/어 주다, ~아/어 주시다, and ~아/어 드리다.

Situation 1

나 (Speaker): 누나가 남동생한테 선물을 사 줘요/사 줍니다.

My older sister buys a gift for my younger brother.

Look at the following example.

01 엄마: 점심에 뭘 만들어 줄까? [← (내가) 점심에 (너한테) 무엇을 만들어 줄까?]
02 민준: 불고기 요리해 주세요.

Mother : What should I make you for lunch?
Minjoon: Please cook some *bulgogi*.

In Line 01, the speaker (엄마) is the giver in the sentence. Thus, she uses the plain form ~어 주다 to describe her own action.

Situation 2

Look at the following example.

1. 어머니**께서** 남동생**한테** 불고기를 만들**어 주셨어요**.

   My mother cooked *bulgogi* for my younger brother.

2. 엄마: 점심에 뭘 만들어 줄까?

   민준: 불고기 요리**해 주세요**. [←어머니, (어머니**께서**) (저**한테**) 불고기를 요리 해 **주세**요.]

   Mother : What should I make you for lunch?
   Minjoon: Please cook some *bulgogi*.

3. (At an airport front desk)

   A: 손님, 성함을 말씀**해 주세요**. Sir, please tell us your name.
   B: 스티브 김입니다. It's Steve Kim.

4. (Family talk)

   엄마 : 이 책을 아이들한테 좀 읽**어 주세요**.
   할머니: 그럼, 읽어 줘**야지**~

   Mother : Please read this book to our children.
   Grandmother: Sure! I must read it (for them).

5. (At a restaurant)

   웨이터: 손님, 뭘 **드릴까요**?
   제시카: (referring to Amy) 오늘이 이 친구 생일이에요. 맛있게 잘 **해 주세요**!

Waiter : How may I serve you?

Jessica: Today is this friend's birthday. Please treat us well! (lit.: Please cook deliciously well for us!)

Situation 3

나 (Speaker): 누나가 아버지께 선물을 사 드려요/사 드립니다.

My older sister buys a gift for my father.

Look at the following examples.

1. 옷 가게 점원: 뭘 도와 드릴까요?
   올리비아 : 청바지 좀 보여 주세요.
   Clerk : How may I help you?
   Olivia: Please show me some blue jeans.

2. 서준 : (looking at the heavy luggage) 할머니, 좀 도와 드릴까요?
   할머니: 아이구, 고마워요!
   Seojoon : Ma'am, may I help you?
   Grandmother: Oh my, thank you!

3. 조이 : 다른 사람 소개해 드릴까요?
   제니 : 좋은 사람 있어요?
   조이 : 네. 사진 보여 드릴까요?
   [보이+어 드릴까요 → 보여 드릴까요]
   Zoe : Would you like me to introduce you to a different person?
   Jenny : Yes, do you have a good person?
   Zoe : Yes. Would you like me to show you a photo?

4. 제이미 : 해물 파전 만들**어 드릴까요**?
리밍 : 좋죠~!
Jamie : Should I make you a seafood pancake?
Liming : Sure thing~!

5. 왕타오 : 다음 주에 한국에 가요.
지 민 : 아, 그래요? 그럼 여행 한국어 좀 가르**쳐 드릴까요**?
Wangtao: I'm going to Korea next week. [가르치+**어 드릴까요** → 가르**쳐 드릴까요**]
Jimin : Is that right? Then should I teach you a bit of travel Korean?

6. 베키 : 아, 정말 배고프네요!
석진 : 샌드위치 좀 만들**어 드릴까요**?

Fill in the blanks to show your intention to volunteer for the activities.

1. 어머니: 된장찌개 좀 ________________________? (끓이다 to boil or cook)
   아들 : 네~

2. (Between friends)
   A: 여기 프린터에 종이가 없네요. [종이 paper]
   B: 지금 학교에 가는데 제가 종이를 ________________________? (사다)

3. A: (at the department store) 손님, 뭘 ________________________? (돕다)
   B: 저 스웨터 좀 보여주세요.

4. A: 이 색깔 샘플이 있어요?
   B: 네. 여기 있어요. ________________________? (보이다)

5. (Between friends)
   A: 오늘 한국 음식이 먹고 싶어요.
   B: 오후에 시간 있어요. 한국 음식 ________________________? (요리하다)

Make a request to each person using the ~어 주다/~아 주다 pattern.

1. 엄마: 뭘 좀 만들어 줄까?

   딸: 김치 볶음밥 ______________________.
   (만들다)

2. A: (taxi driver) 어디로 갈까요?

   B: 광화문으로 ______________________.
   (가다)

3. A: 모자는 무슨 색으로 살까요?

   B: 빨간색으로 ______________________.
   (사다)

4. A: 119입니다. 무슨 일이세요?

   B: 빨리 좀 ______________________!
   (오다)

5. 민준: 제시카 씨, 뭐 해요?

   제시카: 아, 민준 씨. 한국말 잘하시죠? 이 말 연습 좀 ______________________.
   (돕다)

Listen to the audio and fill in the blands. 

(한국 식당에서)

01 점원: 손님, 뭘 ______________________?

02 민준: 여기 떡볶이 맛있어요?

03 점원: 네. 근처에선 유명해요. 얼마나 ______________________?

04 민준: 저는 ______________________.

05 점원: 네, 알겠습니다. 다른 건 뭐 필요하세요?

06 민준: 아, 그리고 물 좀 ______________________?

07 점원: 네, ______________________.

Useful expressions

갖다 주다 to bring (something) to (someone)

3. ~기로 하다 to decide to ~

Form Attach ~기로 하다 to the verb base.

▶ Verb base + 기로 하다 to decide to ~; to be supposed to ~

Look at the following examples. Also pay attention to the various speech styles of ~기로 하다.

1. (The ~아요 speech style)
   A: 제니 씨를 언제 만나기로 했어요?
   When were you supposed to meet Jenny?
   B: 오늘 오후 4시에요.

2. (The ~아 speech style)
   A: 우리 다음에 언제 만날까?
   B: 내일 만날까?
   A: 그래. 내일 오전 괜찮아. 그럼 그때 서로 문자 하기로 하자.

3. (The ~아 speech style)
   A: 오늘 저녁은 뭘 먹을까?
   B: 룸메이트하고 불닭을 만들어 먹기로 했어. 같이 먹을래?
   A: 음~ 다이어트 하기로 했는데... 내일부터 하지 뭐!

4. (The ~아 speech style)
   A: 금요일에 친구들하고 무슨 영화를 볼 거야?
   B: 한국 영화를 보기로 했어.

5. (The ~습니다 speech style)
   A: 민준 씨한테 선물로 뭘 할 겁니까?
   B: 핸드폰 케이스를 사기로 했습니다.

6. (The ~아 speech style)
   A: 이번 방학 때 뭐 할 거야?
   B: 자동차 회사에서 인턴십을 하기로 했어.

Patterns, Expressions & Practice

Exercise 7

Respond to the questions using ~기로 하다 using the information given.

1. A: 내일 무슨 공부하기로 했어요?

   B: ________________________________.
   (한국어 공부)

2. A: 이번 주에 누구를 만날 거예요?

   B: ________________________________.
   (제시카)

3. A: 생일에 뭘 먹을까?

   B: ________________________________.
   (순두부 + 불닭)

4. A: 주말에 뭘 볼까?

   B: ________________________________.
   (한국 드라마)

5. A: 여름에 뭘 하기로 했어요?

   B: ________________________________.
   (인턴쉽)

Exercise 8

Ask questions in Korean using the information given in the parentheses.

1. A: 점심 뭐 먹기로 했어요?
   (What did you decide to eat for lunch?)

   B: 부대찌개요!

2. A: ________________________________?
   (Where did you decide to go in the summer?)

   B: 시카고에 계신 부모님 집에 갈 거예요.

3. A: ________________________________?
   (When did you decide to meet the project group tomorrow?)

   B: 10시부터 두 시간 만나기로 했어.

4. A: ________________________________?
   (What did you decide to make for tomorrow's breakfast?)

   B: 토스트하고 베이컨이요.

5. A: ____?
(Which country's food should we buy on Minjoon's birthday?)
B: 민준 씨가 한국 음식하고 중국 음식을 잘 먹잖아요. 그 두 나라 음식을 사죠?

Listen to the audio and fill in the blanks. 

01 민준 : 이번 크리스마스에 (1)____________________?

02 에이미: 부모님 집에 (2)____________________. 민준 씨는요?

03 민준 : 저는 친구들하고 같이 저녁 (3)____________________.

미국 친구 제임스가 저를 초대했어요.

04 에이미: 잘 됐네요. 부모님 선물을 사야 되는데…

05 민준 : 뭘 (4)____________________?

06 에이미: 아직 잘 모르겠어요.

4. -을/-를 하다 (for someone) to do (something)
-이/-가 되다 (for something) to be done

하다 means "to do" and 되다 means "to be done." -을/-를 하다 literally means "(for someone) to do (something)" and -이/-가 되다 literally means "(for something) to be done" or "(for something) to occur."

Form

▶ NOUN+ 을/를 하다 (for someone) to do + NOUN [Active construction]

▶ NOUN+ 이/가 되다 for NOUN to be done (by someone) [Passive construction]

- The object marker "을/를" in the active construction is replaced with the subject marker "이/가" in the passive construction.

Note For many verbs ending in 하다, you can change them from the active meaning to the passive meaning simply by replacing 하다 with 되다.

Active verb with ~하다		Active verb with ~되다	
걱정(을) 하다	to worry	걱정(이) 되다	to be worried
기대(를) 하다	to expect	기대(가) 되다	to be expected
시작(을) 하다	to start (something)	시작(이) 되다	(for something) to start
사용(을) 하다	to use	사용(이) 되다	to be used
완성(을) 하다	to complete	완성(이) 되다	to be completed
이해(를) 하다	to understand	이해(가) 되다	to be understood
연락(을) 하다	to contact	연락(이) 되다	to be contacted
준비(를) 하다	to prepare	준비(가) 되다	to be prepared
해결(을) 하다	to solve	해결(이) 되다	to be solved

Look at the following examples.

1. 이해를 해요. [NOUN를]	I understood (it).	[Lit., I do understanding.]
이해가 돼요. [NOUN가]	It is understood (by me).	[Lit., Understanding is done.]
2. 준비를 했어요. [NOUN를]	I prepared (it).	[Lit., I did preparation]
준비가 됐어요. [NOUN가]	(It) is prepared (by me).	[Lit., Preparation was done.]

Choose a word with the appropriate subject or object marker.

1. 제시카한테 ______________ 됐어요?
   (연락을/연락이)

2. 바빠서 에이미한테 ______________ 못 했어요.
   (연락을/연락이)

3. 내일 피크닉이 있는데 내일 ______________ 걱정돼요.
   (날씨를/날씨가)

4. ______________ 준비 됐어. 빨리 와.
   (저녁을/저녁이)

5. 10분 후에 ______________ 시작합니다. 준비하세요.
   (미팅을/미팅이)

Fill in the blanks with either a subject marker or an object marker.

1. A: 저는 마이클_____ 이해해요.
   B: 그래요? 저는 마이클_____ 이해 안 돼요.

2. A: 몇 시에 미팅_____ 시작해요?
   B: 한 시에 미팅_____ 시작돼요.

3. A: 파티 준비_____ 다 했어요?
   B: 네. 준비_____ 다 됐어요.

4. A: 에이미한테 연락_____ 했어?
   B: 전화했는데 연락_____ 안 돼.

5. 지난/이번/다음 + NOUN last/this/next ~

Usage The expressions 지난 + NOUN, 이번 + NOUN, and 다음 + NOUN refer to the past, present, future time, respectively. Let's look at some frequent examples of these expressions.

last + NOUN	this + NOUN	next + NOUN
지난번 last time	이번 this time	다음번 next time
지난 주말 last weekend	이번 주말 this weekend	다음 주말 next weekend
지난 달 last month	이번 달 this month	다음 달 next month
지난 해 last year	이번 해 this year	다음 해 next year
지난주 수요일 last Wednesday	이번 주 수요일 this Wednesday	다음 주 수요일 next Wednesday
지난 시간 last time	이번 시간 this time	다음 시간 next time
지난 학기 last semester	이번 학기 this semester	다음 학기 next semester

Patterns, Expressions & Practice

Look at the following examples.

1. A: **지난** 한국어 시간에 뭐 배웠어요?
   B: 가족하고 시간 표현이요. [표현 expressions]
   다음 시간에는 전공에 관한 표현을 배워요. [-에 관한 concerning]

2. A: 언제 그 식당에 갔어요?
   B: **지난**주 화요일에요. 음식들이 다 괜찮았어요. 우리 **다음**번에 같이 갈래요?

3. A: 다음 주말에 뭐 할 거예요?
   B: **이번** 주말 내내 에세이를 썼는데도 다 못 해서 **다음** 토요일에도 에세이를 써야 해요.
   [~아야/어야 하다 to have to ~]

4. A: 이제 1월 1일이네요! **이번** 해 무슨 좋은 계획이 있어요? [계획 plans]
   B: 다이어트요! **지난** 해에도 다이어트였는데… ㅎㅎ **이번**에는 잘 해야죠!

5. A: **다음** 미팅에는 뭘 준비할까요?
   B: **이번**에는 쿠키하고 한국차를 준비해요. **지난** 미팅에서는 케이크를 먹었잖아요.

Complete each conversation with the appropriate expressions from the box.

이번 수요일	지난 해	이번 학기	지난번	이번 겨울
지난 주말	지난 수요일	이번 해	이번 토요일	

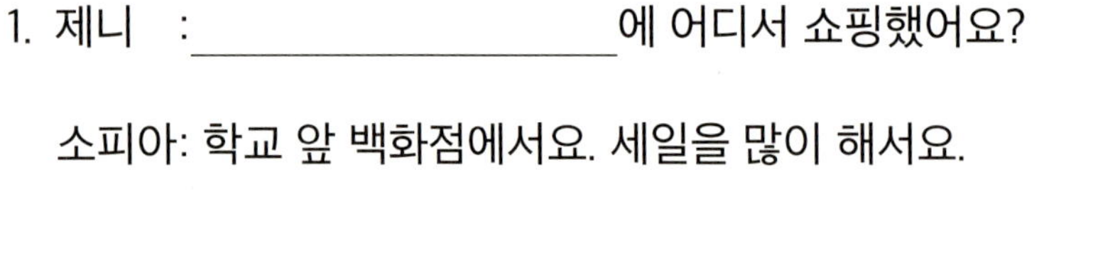

1. 제니 : ________________에 어디서 쇼핑했어요?
   소피아: 학교 앞 백화점에서요. 세일을 많이 해서요.

2. 제니 : 우리 다음 미팅이 언제 있죠?
   리 밍 : 다음 미팅은 ________________ 이에요.
   ________________에는 미팅을 수요일에만 할 거예요.

3. 왕타오 : ________________에 리우페이 씨 블로그를 봤어요.

언제부터 요리를 했어요?

리우페이: ____________________부터 시작했어요.

이번 해에는 너무 추워서 집에서 요리만 했어요.

4. 현우 : ________________에 뭐 좋은 계획 있어요?

왕타오: ________________에는 운동을 좀 할 거예요.

수요일하고 금요일에 수영을 할 계획이에요.

5. 릴리: ____________________에는 전공 수업이 너무 많아서 한국어 수업을 못 들어요.

지호: 아, 그럼 주말 한국어 말하기 클럽에 오실 거예요?

릴리: 네. 그럴 계획이에요. ______________________에 미팅이 몇 시죠?

Exercise 13

Create sentences to complete each dialogue by following the English cues.

1. A: 다음 프로젝트 미팅이 언제 있죠?

B: ____________________________________.
(The next meeting is on Monday.)

2. 제시카: 그 베트남 남자 친구는 언제 만나요?

에이미: 아, ____________________________________.
(It is this Saturday. Why?)

3. 제시카: ____________________________________?
(Do you cook next week?)

민준 : 네. 한국어 클럽에서 할 거예요. 오세요!

4. 마이클: 언제부터 한국어를 배웠어요?

제임스: ______________________________.
(I learned it from last year.)

______________________________에도 배울 거예요.
(I'll also learn it this year.)

여자 친구가 한국 사람이라서요.

5. 에이미: ____________________에는 왜 못 왔어요?

제시카: 미안해요. 지난 수요일에는 피아노 레슨이 있었어요.

근데 다음 한국 영화 클럽 미팅은 언제죠?

에이미: ________________는 수요일이 아니고 목요일이에요.

Exercise 14

Listen to the conversation between the two friends on campus and fill in the blanks. 69

제시카: (1) 다음 학기에 한국어 배워요?
샤오밍: 네, 그럴 거예요. 제시카 씨는요?
제시카: 전공 공부가 어려워서 (2)____________________에는 아마 못 배울 거예요.
그래서 전 (3)____________________에 배울 거예요.
샤오밍: 네. 그럼 그동안 한국 영화나 드라마 많이 보세요.
전 (4)____________________에 한국어 2를 배워요.
근데 제시카 씨는 에이미 씨하고 언제 만나요?
제시카: (5)____________________오후에 만날 거예요. 그 때 둘 다 시간이 돼요.
샤오밍: 지금 에이미 씨하고 프로젝트를 같이 하는데
우리는 (6)____________________에 만나요.
제시카: 다들 정말 바쁘네요!
샤오밍: 네, (7)____________________가 끝나면 언제 한번 다 같이 점심 먹어요!

III. Culture

Popular dating places and activities in Korea

In Korea, the most common way to find a date is by being introduced to someone by your friends. The most common place to have a first meeting is probably at a cafe. There are a lot of cafes in Korea, on every corner and street. South Koreans are said to be among the top consumers of coffee in the world.

There are many other places where you can hang out with your date or friends. If you like outdoor activities, you may go for a hike or stroll. About 70 % of the land in Korea is mountainous, so you can easily find trails and mountains in your neighborhood.

Other popular places include places with a great view or scenery, *noraebang* (singing room), amusement parks, and movie theatres.

Here are some of the famous dating places in Seoul.

IV. Listen & Discuss

Jessica and Amy are talking about the last blind date that Amy went. Listen to the conversation carefully. Discuss the answers to the following questions with your classmates. Then write each answer in a full Korean sentence in the space provided.

1. 에이미 씨는 소개팅에서 누구를 만나기로 했습니까?

2. 제시카 씨는 어떻게 에이미 씨의 데이트를 알았습니까?

3. 에이미 씨가 기다린 데이트 장소는 어디였습니까?

4. 에이미 씨는 만나기로 한 사람을 얼마 동안 기다렸습니까?

5. 에이미 씨는 만나기로 한 사람한테 왜 연락을 못 했습니까?

6. 에이미 씨는 이번 주말에 무엇을 합니까?

Script

☞ **Jessica and Amy are talking about the blind date that Amy went last time.**

01 제시카: 참! 지난번 소개팅은 어땠어요? 그 베트남 친구 말이에요.

02 에이미: 망했어요! 근데, 어떻게 알았어요?

03 제시카: 민준 씨한테서 들었어요.

04 에이미: 제가 학교 앞 별카페에서 기다렸는데, 그 친구는 학교 뒤 별카페에서 기다렸어요.

05 제시카: 어, 그래서요?

06 에이미: 한 시간 동안 서로 기다리다가 그냥 집에 갔어요.

07 제시카: 연락이 안 됐어요?[II.5]

08 에이미: 네. 핸드폰이 망가져서 연락을 못 했어요.

09 제시카: 아쉽네요. 제가 다른 사람 소개해 드릴까요?[II.1,2]

10 에이미: 아뇨, 괜찮아요. 그 친구 이번 주말에 다시 만나기로 했어요.[II.3,5]

01 Jessica: Oh! How was the blind date last time?
I'm talking about the Vietnamese guy.

02 Amy : It was a disaster! Wait, how did you know?

03 Jessica: I heard it from Minjoon.

04 Amy : I waited at the Star Cafe in front of the school but he waited at the Star Cafe behind the school.

05 Jessica: Well, so?

06 Amy : We waited for each other for an hour, and then we both just went home.

07 Jessica: Weren't you able to contact each other?

08 Amy : My cell phone was broken, so I couldn't contact him.

09 Jessica: That's too bad. Should I introduce you to a different person?

10 Amy : No, that's all right. We decided to meet again this weekend.

V. Guided Conversation

With the organization of the model conversation in Listen & Discuss (Script) in mind, practice the modified conversation below with your partner.

Two friends (A and B) are talking about a date that B had last weekend. Practice the following conversation with your partner, choosing the best option from ( ) to make the conversation flow naturally.

01 A: ________ (참; 아; 저), 지난번 소개팅은 어땠어요? 그 ________ (베트남; 미국; 중국; 한국) 친구 말이에요.

02 B: 망했어요! 근데, 어떻게 알았어요?

03 A: ________ (another friend's name) 씨한테서 들었어요. 그런데 왜 망쳤어요?

04 B: 네. ________ (say a reason for being messed up: misunderstanding meeting places).

05 A: 그랬어요? 그럼 서로 못 만났겠어요.

06 B: 네. 맞아요. ________ (30분; 40분; 한 시간; …) 동안 서로 기다리다가 그냥 집에 갔어요.

07 A: 연락이 안 됐어요?

08 B: 네. ________ (배터리가 없어서; 핸드폰이 없어서; 핸드폰이 망가져서) 연락을 못 했어요.

09 A: 아쉽네요. 제가 ________ (제 친구; 제가 아는 사람; 다른 사람) 소개해 드릴까요?

10 B: 아뇨, 괜찮아요. 그 친구 이번 ________ (수요일; 금요일; 토요일; 일요일; 주말) 에 다시 만나기로 했어요.

(Switch roles and continue to practice.)

Present the conversation from Step 1 in front of the class. Try not to read it!

VI. Spontaneous Conversation

Now is your chance to have real interactions with your classmates in Korean. You can practice speaking with your classmates, writing, and presenting in front of the class!

Switching roles, create a new conversation with your classmate by following the directions below.

1. Classmate A's role

Share what happened at the time of your blind date, which you had last week, with your classmate by choosing one of the situations (A, B, or C) in the table below.

	Situation A	Situation B	Situation C
Time of your original blind date	3pm, last Wednesday	1pm, last Friday	6pm, last Saturday
Where you and your partner were supposed to meet for the blind date	the statue in front of Humanities building (인문대 앞 동상)	Inside of the Good Morning coffee shop	In front of the school bookstore (학교 서점)
Where you mistakenly waited for your partner	In front of the school main gate (학교 정문)	Inside of the Northern Light coffee shop	Inside of the school bookstore
Why you couldn't/didn't contact your partner	You lost your phone.	You fell asleep.	You decided to wait until your partner showed up.
Time of your rescheduled blind date	3pm, this Wednesday	1pm, this Friday	6pm, this Saturday

2. Classmate B's role

In this task, you are mainly asking questions to your classmate about their blind date. Initiate the conversation by asking your classmate how his or her blind date was last week. Then continue to ask questions by following the similar turns in the Guided Conversation in order to have your conversation move naturally according to Situation A, B, or C.

Write a narrative about the experience of your past blind date, based on the conversation you had with your classmate. Try to include ~아/~어 주다, ~기로 하다, -을/-를 하다, -이/-가 되다, and 지난/이번/다음 ~ in your narrative.

Based on what you wrote in Step 2, present the narrative you wrote in front of the class. Try not to read from your script!

Answer Keys
&
Appendices

Answer keys

Lesson 11

New Words & Expressions (p.13)

Exercise 1

1. 수업 2. 끝나요 3. 다시 4. 나중에

Exercise 2

1. 몇 시예요? 2. 이따가 봐요. 3. 인제 갈게요.; 어, 그럼 어떡하지?

Patterns, Expressions & Practice (p.15)

Exercise 1

1. B: 열 시 십 분이에요. 2. B: 열한 시 오십 오 분이에요.
3. B: 일곱 시예요. 4. B: 다섯 시 오 분이에요.

Exercise 2

2. 오전 아홉 시 삼십 분이에요.
3. 오후 열두 시 십 분이에요.
4. 오후 두 시 십오 분이에요.

Exercise 3

1. 아홉 시 사십오 분(9:45)이에요. 2. 열 시 (10:00)에 있어요.
3. 열한 시 삼십 분 (11:30)에 끝나요.
4. 네 시 삼십 분(4:30)에 가요.

Exercise 4

1. 맛없어서요. 2. 비싸서요. 3. 바빠서요. 4. 있어서요.

Exercise 5

1. 아파서/수업이 없어서
2. 비가 와서
3. 늦어서
4. 숙제가 많아서
5. 배가 불러서

Exercise 6

1. b 2. a 3. d 4. c 5. e

Exercise 7

Answers may vary.

Exercise 8

1. 이번 주 토요일이에요. (It is on this Saturday.)
2. 저녁 일곱 시에 있어요. (It is at 7:00 p.m.)
3. 못 가요. 아르바이트가 있어서요.
(She can't go. Because she has a part-time job.)
4. 못 가요. 요즘 일이 많아서 바빠서요.
(He can't go. Because he is a little busy because he has a lot of work these days.)

Exercise 9

1. 에 2. 에서 3.에서; 에서 4. 에; 에 5.에; 에 6. 에서; 에서

Exercise 10

1. 한국에/한국에서 2. 서울에서 3. 서울에
4. 서울에서; 영어를

Exercise 11

Answers may vary.

Listen & Discuss (p.29)

1. 지금 한 시 사십오 분이에요.
2. 두 시에 수업이 있어요.
3. 네 시에 끝나요.
4. 아뇨, 없어요.
5. 네 시 반쯤에 만나요.
6. 제시카 씨가 샤오밍 씨한테 문자를 보내요.

Spontaneous Conversation : Sample answers (p.32)

Step 2

Sample conversation

01 A: 지금 몇 시예요?
02 B: 9:50 분이요.
03 A: 어, 그럼 저는 인제 갈게요. 10시에 한국어 수업이 있어서요.
04 B: 아, 그래요? 그럼 우리 언제 만나요?
05 A: 11시는 어때요?
06 B: 제가 11시부터 11시 50분까지 한국영화클럽 모임이 있어요.
07 혹시 12시는 어때요?
08 A: 12시부터 12:40분까지 다른 친구와 약속이 있어요.
09 1시쯤은 시간 돼요?
*시간이 되다 (for time) to be available
10 B: 미안해요. 제가 그 때는 한국 식당에서 일을 해요.
11 우리 그냥 저녁 7시쯤 여기서 다시 만날까요?
12 A: 네, 좋아요. 제가 나중에 문자할게요.
13 B: 네~ 그럼 나중에 봐요.

(Translation)

01 A: What time is it now?
02 B: It's 9:50.
03 A: Um, then I will go now. It's because I have a Korean class at 10 o'clock.
04 B: Oh, is that so? Then when do we meet?
05 A: How about 11am?
06 B: I have a Korean Movie Club meeting from 11am until 11:50am.
07 How about 12pm by any chance?
08 A: I have a meeting with another friend from 12pm until 12:40pm.
09 Are you available around 1pm?
10 B: I am sorry. I work at a Korean restaurant at that time.
11 Then shall we just meet here again around 7pm?
12 A: Sure, that sounds good. I will text you later.
13 B: Sure~ see you later, then.

Lesson 12

New Words & Expressions (p.35)

Exercise 1

1. 김밥 2. 양파 3. 마트 4. 인터넷

Exercise 2

1. 좀 드세요. 2. 맛있네요. 3. 떡, 고추장, 양파 4. 어디서

Patterns, Expressions & Practice (p.38)

Exercise 1

2. 했어요?; 쇼핑했어요. 3. 왔어요. 4. 먹었어요.
5. 졸업했어요. 6. 샀어요 7. 배웠어요?

Exercise 2

1. 봤어요, 했어요 2. 했어요; 먹었어요 3. 갔어요, 만났어요
4. 잤어요, 청소했어요.

Exercise 3

1. 갔어요 2. 들었어요; 재미있었어요 3. 좋았어요. 4. 먹었어요.

Exercise 4

2. 라면 3. 한국학 4. 커피 5. 사진 6. 물 7. 한국어

Exercise 5

2. 제가/ 저는 텔레비전을 봐요.
3. 민준씨는/민준씨가 김밥을 아주 좋아해요.
4. 제임스가/제임스는 한국에서 영어를 가르쳐요.

Exercise 6

1. 에이미가 커피를 마셨어요.
2. 민준이 저녁을 먹었어요.
3. 제시카가 김밥을 만들었어요.
4. 샤오밍이 영화를 봤어요.

Exercise 7

1. 지금 제니는 한국어를 배워요. 2. 저는 어제 백화점에서 옷을 샀어요. 3. 지금 마이클은 피자를 주문했어요. 4. 저는 지난 주말에 친구를 만났어요.

Exercise 8

Answers may vary.
1. 농구를 좋아해요 (농구: basketball) 2. 경제학 수업을 들었어요. 3. 저는 동양학을 전공했어요. 4. 저는 스파게티를 잘해요. 5. 저는 친구하고 영화를 봤어요. 6. 저는 베이글을 먹었어요.

Exercise 9

1. 소피아하고 린다를 2. 생물학을 3. 생물학하고 한국학을
4. 한국 영화와 드라마를 5. 한국 문화를

Exercise 10

1. 크네요 2. 좋네요 3. 맛있네요 4. 없네요; 갔네요

Exercise 11

Answers may vary.
1. 비싸네요/좀 비싸네요. 2. 예쁘네요/괜찮네요/좋네요.
3. 맛있네요/정말 맛있네요 4. 싸네요/아주 싸네요.

Exercise 12

Answers may vary.
2. 맛있네요 3. 시험이 많네요/바쁘네요.
4. 싸네요. 5. 멋있네요/예쁘네요.

Listen & Discuss (p.51)

1. 아뇨. 한국마트에서 샀어요.
2. 떡볶이에요.
3. 떡하고, 설탕하고, 고추장하고 양파예요.
4. 인터넷 블로그에서 배웠어요.

Spontaneous Conversation : Sample answers (p.54)

Step 1

01 A: 제가 (된장찌개; 순두부찌개; 비빔밥; 해물파전; …)을/를 만들었어요. 여기 맛 좀 보세요.
02 B: 음~ 맛있네요! 여기 뭐가 들어갔어요?
03 A: (ingredient 1하고 ingredient 2하고 … 아참 그리고 last ingredient)이/가 들어갔어요.
04 B: 어디서 배웠어요?
05 A: (인터넷 블로그에서; 제 엄마한테서; …) 배웠어요.
06 B: 대단하네요!
07 여기 (된장찌개; 순두부찌개; 비빔밥; 해물파전; …) 맛 좀 보세요.
08 A: 어, (B's name) 씨가 만들었어요?
09 B: 아뇨. 한국마트에서 샀어요.
10 A: 음~ 맛있네요!

(Translation)
01 A: I made (된장찌개; 순두부찌개; 비빔밥; 해물파전; …). Please have some.
02 B: Mnm ~ It's delicious! What did you put in here? [Literally, What entered here?]
03 A: I put (ingredient 1, ingredient 2 …) Oh yeah and (last ingredient).
04 B: Where did you learn the recipe?
05 A: I learned it (from blogs on the Internet; from my mom; …).
06 B: Wow~ incredible!
07 Here I have (된장찌개; 순두부찌개; 비빔밥; 해물파전; …). Please have some.
08 A: Oh, did you make it?
09 B: Nope, I bought it at a Korean mart.
10 A: Mm~ It's delicious!

Step 2

(Narrative about my friend's dish 해물 파전)
제 친구는 해물 파전을 만들었어요. 해물 파전에 밀가루, 해물 그리고 파가 들어 갔어요. 제 친구는 인터넷 블로그에서 해물 파전을 배웠어요. 그런데 해물 파전이 정말 맛있었어요. 제 친구는 정말 대단해요!

(Translation)
My friend cooked seafood scallion pancakes. He/She put flour, seafood, and scallions in it. He/She learned the recipe from blogs on the Internet. By the way, the seafood pancakes were very delicious. He/She is really incredible!

Lesson 13

New Words & Expressions (p.57)

Exercise 1

1. 빨리 2. 벌써 3. 비밀 4. 아직

Exercise 2

1. 목요일이에요 2. 맞아요. 3. 그러게요. 4. 왜 그래요?

Patterns, Expressions & Practice (p.60)

Exercise 1

2. B: 다섯 살이에요.

3. B: 네 살이에요.
4. B: 스물한 살이에요.
5. B: 쉰셋이세요.
6. B: 여든넷이세요.

Exercise 2

1. 스물 다섯(25)이에요. 2. 스물 일곱(27)이에요.
3. 스물 일곱(27)이에요. 4. 서른 둘(32)이에요.

Exercise 3

2. A: 스티브 씨, 생일이 몇 월 며칠이에요?
   B: 팔 월 십사 일이에요.
3. A: 샤나 씨, 생일이 몇 월 며칠이에요?
   B: 유 월 팔 일이에요.
4. A: 샤오밍 씨, 생일이 몇 월 며칠이에요?
   B: 시 월 이 일이에요.
5. A: 제시카 씨, 생일이 몇 월 며칠이에요?
   B: 십이 월 이십일 일이에요.

Exercise 4

2. A: 한글날은 몇 월 며칠이에요?
   B: 한글날은 시 월 구 일이에요.
3. A:어린이날은 몇 월 며칠이에요?
   B:어린이날은 오 월 오 일이에요.
4. A: 부처님 오신 날은 몇 월 며칠이에요?
   B:부처님 오신 날은 음력 사 월 팔 일이에요.
5. A: 추석은 몇 월 며칠이에요?
   B:추석은 음력 팔 월 십오 일이에요.
6. A: 크리스마스은 몇 월 며칠이에요?
   B: 크리스마스는 십이 월 이십오 일이에요.

Exercise 5

1. 이 월 팔 일이에요. 2. 이 월 십구 일이에요.
3. 오 월 이십 일이에요.

Exercise 6

1. 대학생으로 보여요/고등학생으로 보여요.
2. 회색으로 보여요/검은색으로 보여요.
3. 40대로 보여요/50대로 보여요.
4. 여자 아이로 보여요/남자 아이로 보여요.

Exercise 7

Answers may vary. Examples:

1. 대학생으로 보여요 2. 초등학생으로 보여요.
3. 직장인으로 보여요 4. 중학생으로 보여요./고등학생으로 보여요.

Exercise 8

1. 중국 사람이에요. 2. 40대로 보여요.
3. 아뇨. 대학생처럼 보여요. 4. 서울에서 찍었어요.

Exercise 9

1. 바빠 보여요. 2. 좋아 보여요. 3. 슬퍼 보여요.
4. 화나 보여요.

Exercise 10

1. 커 보여요. 2. 맛있어 보여요. 3. 어려워 보여요/복잡해 보여요. 4. 비싸 보여요/멋있어 보여요.

Listen & Discuss (p.73)

1. 십이 월 이십일 일 목요일이에요.
2. 스물 넷이에요/스물 다섯 살이에요.
3. 시간 참 빨리 가네요.
4. 고등학생으로 보여요.

Spontaneous Conversation : Sample answers (p.76)

Step 1

Answer sample

Step 1

(B is looking at A's family photo.)

01 A: 아버지께서는 연세가 어떻게 되세요?
02 B: 쉰 둘이세요.
03 A: 참 젊어 보이세요. 생신은 언제예요?
04 B: 8월 2일이에요.
05 A: 이건 제 가족 사진이에요.
06 B: 이 분이 어머니세요?
07 A: 네.
08 B: 어머니께서는 연세가 어떻게 되세요?
09 A: 오십 대세요.
10 B: 정말요? 사십 대로 보여요!
11 A: ㅎㅎ 네 좀 젊어 보이세요.
(Continue to talk about other family members.)

(Translation)

01 A: May I ask how old your father is?
02 B: He is 52 years old.
03 A: He looks really young. What is his birthday?
04 B: It's August 2.
05 A: This is my family photo.
06 B: Is this your mother?
07 A: Yes.
08 B: May I ask how old your mother is?
09 A: She is in her fifties.
10 B: She looks in her forties!
11 A: hh in fact she looks a little younger.
(Continue to talk about other family members.)

Step 2

B씨 아버지는 연세가 쉰 둘이세요. 그런데 젊어 보이세요. 생신은 팔 월 이 일이에요.

(The following is about other family members.) B 씨 언니는 대학생이에요. 나이는 스물세 살이에요. 그런데 고등학생처럼 보여요. 생일은 칠 월 육 일이에요. 그리고 동생은 고등학생이에요. 열여섯 살이에요. 생일은 십일 월 이십육 일이에요.

(Translation)

B's father is 52 years old. But he looks in his 40s. His birthday is August 2. (The following is about other family members.) B's older sister is a university student. She is 23 years old. But she looks like a high school student. Her birthday is July 6. And B's younger sibling is a high school student. He/she is 16 years old. His/her birthday is December 26.

Lesson 14

New Words & Expressions (p.79)

Exercise 1

1. 추워요. 2. 더워요. 3. 따뜻해져요.

Exercise 2

1. 원래 이렇게 2. 언제쯤 3. 뭐라구요? 4. 그냥 표현이

Patterns, Expressions & Practice (p.82)

Exercise 1

1. 7월이면 2. 여섯 시면 3. 세 시간이면 4. 토요일이면

Exercise 2

1. 있으면; 없으면 2. 마시면 3. 타면 4. 좋으면; 오면

Exercise 3

1. 보통 토요일에 운동해요. 2. 농구해요.
3. 한국 드라마 보고 온라인 게임도 해요.

Exercise 4

1. 맑아요. 2. 추워요. 3. 비가 와요. 4. 더워요.
5. 바람이 불어요.

Exercise 5

2. 영도에서 오 도예요. 흐리고 맑아요.
3. 영하 오 도에서 영하 삼 도예요. 흐리고 맑아요.
4. 영상 육 도에서 영상 십 도예요. 흐리고 비가 와요.
5. 영하 사 도에서 영상 오 도예요. 맑아요.

Exercise 6

1. 시카고예요.
2. 춥고 눈이 많이 와요. 그리고 바람이 많이 불어요.
3. 삼 년 동안 살았어요. 4. 안 추워요. 따뜻해요.
5. 부산이에요. 6. 추워요. 그런데 보통 눈은 안 와요.

Exercise 7

2. 날씨가 따뜻해졌어요.
3. 날씨가 서늘해졌어요.
4. 날씨가 더워졌어요.
5. 날씨가 맑아졌어요.

Exercise 8

2. 맛있어졌어요/좋아졌어요. 3. 비싸졌어요.
4. 좋아졌어요. 5. 많아졌어요.

Exercise 9

1. 날씨가 많이 따뜻해졌어요.
2. 요즘 일이 많아서 많이 바빠졌어요.
3. 일이 많아졌어요.

Exercise 10

1. 배고파 죽겠어요.
2. 바빠 죽겠어요.
3. 힘들어 죽겠어요/무거워 죽겠어요
4. 배불러 죽겠어요.
5 졸려 죽겠어요/피곤해 죽겠어요.
6. 시끄러워 죽겠어요.

Listen & Discuss (p.93)

1. 14(십사)도예요.
2. 네, 올해가 유난히 추워요.
3. 5(오)월이면 따뜻해져요.
4. 아주 더워요.

Spontaneous Conversation : Sample answers (p.97)

Step 1

01 A: 헉! 오늘 정말 덥네요
02 B: 네, 진짜 더워요! 오늘 아침이 99도예요.
03 A: 텍사스는 원래 이렇게 더워요?
04 B: 네, 올 여름이 유난히 더 덥네요.
05 A: 그래요? 그럼 언제쯤 시원해져요?
06 B: 음... 11월이면 시원해져요.
07 A: 서울은 9월이면 벌써 시원해요.
08 텍사스 겨울은 보통 몇 도까지 내려가요?
09 B: 1월에는 36도까지 내려가요.
10 A: 아 그래요? 몰랐어요
11 B: 서울은 겨울에 많이 추워요?
12 A: 네, 1월이 정말 추워요. 20도까지 내려가요.
13 B: 겨울은 길어요?
14 A: 네. 11월에서 3월까지 겨울이에요.
15 너무 길고 추워서 텍사스 사람은 서울에서 추워 죽어요!
16 B: 네? 뭐라구요? 죽어요?!
17 A: 하하. 그냥 표현이 그래요.

(Translation)

01 A: Ah, today is really hot.
02 B: Yes, it's really hot! It's 99 degrees this morning.
03 A: Is Texas always this hot?
04 B: Yeah. This year is particularly hotter.
05 A: Really? Approximately when does it become cooler, then?
06 B: Um··· It becomes cooler by November.
07 A: In Seoul, by September, it is already cool.
08 How low does the temperature go down in winter in general?
09 B: It goes down to 36 degrees in January.
10 A: Is that right? I didn't know.
11 B: Is winter in Seoul very cold?
12 A: Yes. January is really cold. It goes down to 20 degrees.
13 B: Is winter long?
14 A: Yes. Winter is from November until March.
15 Because it is so long and cold, Texans can get killed from the cold in Seoul!
16 B: What? What did you say? Die?
17 A: Haha. It is just an expression.

Step 2

B의 고향은 텍사스예요. 텍사스는 여름에 진짜 더워요. 11월이면 시원해져요. 겨울에는 1월에 57도까지 내려가요. A의 고향은 서울이에요. 서울은 9월이면 시원해져요. 서울은 1월에는 20도까지 내려가요. 서울의 겨울이 길고 추워요. 너무 추워서 텍사스 사람은 서울에서 추워 죽어요!

(Translation)

B's hometown is Texas. Texas is really hot in summer. It becomes cooler by November. In winter, in January, the temperature goes down to 57 degrees. A's hometown is Seoul. It becomes cooler by September. The temperature goes down to 20 degrees in January in Seoul. The winter in Seoul is long and cold. It's so cold that Texans can get killed in Seoul!

Lesson 15

New Words & Expressions (p.101)

Exercise 1

1. 점심 먹으러 2. 먹을까요? 3. 가 봤어요?

Exercise 2

1. 말이에요? 2. 아직 3. 뭐가 맛있어요? 4. 안 비싸요?

Patterns, Expressions & Practice (p.105)

Exercise 1

1. 네 2. 아니요/아뇨 3. 네 4. 아니요/아뇨

Exercise 2

2. 네. 못해요. 3. 네. 없어요. 4. 아니요. 좋아해요.
5. 아니요. 들어요.

Exercise 3

(Answers may vary.)
2. 학교 체육관에 가요. 3. 보통 백화점에 가요. 4. AMC 영화관에 가요. 5. 공원에 가요. 6. 코리아 하우스에 가요.

Exercise 4

2. 쇼핑하러 백화점에 가요.
3. 영어 가르치러 한국에 가요.
4. 친구 만나러 카페에 가요.
5. 저녁을 먹으러 친구집에 가요.

Exercise 5

2. 서울에서 영어를 가르치러 가요.
3. 여행도 하고 쇼핑도 하러 가요.
4. 친구가 대전에 살아서 친구를 만나러 가요.
5. 부산대학교에서 한국 역사 수업을 들으러 가요.

Exercise 6

2. 잡채 먹어 봤어요?
3. 된장찌개 먹어 봤어요?
4. 육개장 먹어 봤어요?
5. 불닭 먹어 봤어요?

Exercise 7

Conversation 1
1. a, c 2. b
Conversation 2
3. a 4. c, d, e

Exercise 8

2. f 3. c 4. a 5. d 6. e

Exercise 9

1. 차는 마시는데
2. 이번 주말에는 바쁜데
3. 이 선글라스가 예쁜데
4. 한국 사람인데
5. 생선은 좋아하는데

Exercise 10

1. 가는데 2. 좋은데 3. 인데 4. 맛있는데 5. 왔는데

Listen & Discuss (p.117)

1. 코리아 하우스예요.
2. 비빔밥하고 불닭이요.
3. 순두부를 좋아해요.
4. 8불에서 12불 정도 해요.

Spontaneous Conversation : Sample answers (p.121)

Step 3
오늘 저녁 먹으러 서울 가든에 가 봤어요. 친구는 짜장면을 주문했어요. 짜장면은 10불이었어요. 저는 양념치킨을 좋아하는데, 친구가 육개장을 권했어요. 그래서, 육개장을 주문했는데, 맛이 없었어요. 좀 매웠어요. 가격은 12불 정도 했어요. 서울 가든에 가면, 육개장은 주문하지 마세요. 짜장면은 맛있었어요. 서울 가든에서는 짜장면을 주문하세요.

(Translation)
I went to Seoul Garden to eat dinner. My friend ordered Jjajangmyeon (black bean noodles). Jjajangmyeon was 10 dollars. I like seasoned fried chicken, but my friend recommended a spicy shredded beef soup. So I ordered the spicy shredded beef soup, but the taste was not good. It was a bit spicy. The price was about 12 dollars. Don't order the spicy shredded beef soup if you go to Seoul Garden. Jjajangmyeon was delicious. At Seoul Garden, (I'd recommend) you should order Jjajangmyeon.

Lesson 16

New Words & Expressions (p.125)

Exercise 1

1. 생일 2. 선물 3. 핸드폰 케이스

Exercise 2

1. 축하해요. 2. 들었어요. 3. 고마워요. 4. 그럼요.

Patterns, Expressions & Practice (p.127)

Exercise 1

1. 께 2. 한테서/한테(from) 3. 한테서/한테 (from)
4. 께 5. 한테서/한테(from) 6. 한테

Exercise 2

1. 께; 한테 2. 를 3. 하고 4. 에서 5. 에 6. 한테서 7. 한테

Exercise 3

1. 께 2. 한테 3. 한테서 4. 한테 5. 한테 6. 께

Exercise 4

2. b 3. a 4. c. 5. e

Exercise 5

Answers may vary. These are sample answers.
2. 어제는 바빴지만, 오늘은 시간이 많아요
3. 그 친구를 자주 만났지만, 지금은 자주 못 만나요.
4. 창문을 열었지만, 아직도 더워요.

Exercise 6

1. 오래됐지만, 2. 크고 좋았지만, 3. 없었지만,
4. 맛있었지만, 5. 불편했지만,

Exercise 7

1. 구경해 보세요. 2. 먹어 보세요. 3. 들어 보세요.
4. 가 보세요. 5. 배워 보세요. 6. 사귀어 보세요.

Exercise 8

2. 들어 보세요. 3. 입어 보세요. 4. 이 헤드폰 한 번 써 보세요.; 음악을/노래를 한 번 들어보세요. 5. 열어 보세요.

Exercise 9

1. 전화해 보세요 2. 가 보세요. 3. 부탁해 보세요. 4. 물어 보세요. 5. 신청해 보세요 6. 참가해 보세요

Exercise 10

1. 먹어봐도 돼요? 2. 만들어 봐도 돼요? 3. 열어 봐도 돼요? 4. 들어 봐도 돼요? 5. 입어 봐도 돼요?

Exercise 11

Answers may vary.
Example: 리사와 에이미는 한국어 클럽 미팅에 같이 갈 거예요.

Exercise 12

2. 화장실에 가도 돼요? 3. 여기 앉아 봐도 돼요?
4. 내일 드려도 돼요?

Exercise 13

03 (나는), (갈게), (있어서.)
04 (그래?)
05 (봐)
06 (나는), (끝나.), (너는?)
07 (나는), (없어.), (만날까?)
08 (응), (그래.), (내가), (문자할게)
09 (응), (봐.)

Exercise 14

02 (만들었어?)
03 (아니), (샀어.)
04 (들어 있어.)
05 (난), (만들었어), (봐.)
06 (맛있네!!), (들어갔어?)
07 (양파.)
08 (그래), (배웠어?)
09 (블로그에서.)
10 (대단해!)

Exercise 15

01 제시카: 배 안 고파? 우리 점심 먹으러 가~
02 샤오밍: 그래. 이 근처 한국 식당에 가 봤어?
03 제시카: "코리아 하우스" 말이야?
04 샤오밍: 응.
05 제시카: 아니. 아직 안 가 봤어.
06 샤오밍: 거기 음식 괜찮은데 거기서 먹을까?
07 제시카: 거긴 뭐가 맛있어?
08 샤오밍: 비빔밥하고 불닭이 맛있어.
09 제시카: 음... 난 순두부 좋아하는데...
10 샤오밍: 어, 순두부도 있어!
11 제시카: 안 비싸?
12 샤오밍: 응. 8불에서 12불 정도 해.
13 제시카: 좋아! 그럼, 거기 가.

Listen & Discuss (p.149)

1. 민준 씨 생일이에요.
2. 샤오밍한테 들었어요.
3. 핸드폰 케이스를 줬어요.
4. 네. 마침 민준 씨가 필요했어요.

Spontaneous Conversation : Sample answers(p.153)

Step 1

01 A: 졸업 축하해요!
02 B: 고마워요.
03 A: 이거 별 거 아니지만….졸업 선물이에요.
04 B: 와~ 고마워요! 열어 봐도 돼요?
05 A: 네. 열어 보세요.
06 B: 와! 넥타이네요! 아주 마음에 들어요.
07 A: 잘 됐네요. 고르기 힘들었는데.
08 B: 저녁 먹으러 서울식당에 가는데 같이 가요.
09 A: 서울식당이요?
10 B: 네. 가봤어요?
11 A: 네. 한번 가봤어요.
12 B: 무슨 음식 좋아하세요?
13 A: 저는 돌솥비빔밥이요.
14 B: 그럼 같이 가요. 제가 저녁 살게요.

(Translation)
01 A: Congratulations on your graduation!
02 B: Thank you.
03 A: It's not anything special, but…it is a graduation gift (for you).
04 B: Wow, thank you! May I open it now?
05 A: Sure. Please open it.
06 B: Wow! It is a necktie! I like it very much.
07 A: Great that you like it. It was hard to choose.
08 B: I am going to Seoul Restaurant to have dinner. Please join me.
09 A: Seoul Restaurant?
10 B: Yes. Have you been there?
11 A: Yes, I've been there once.
12 B: What kind of food do you like?
13 A: I like dolsot-bibimbap.
14 B: Then, let's go together. I'll buy you dinner.

Step 2

오늘은 친구 B의 졸업이었어요. 저는 친구한테 졸업 선물을 줬어요. 넥타이를 줬는데 친구가 그 넥타이를 아주 좋아했어요. 우리는 같이 저녁을 먹으러 서울 식당에 갔어요. 저는 돌솥비빔밥을 좋아해서 돌솥비빔밥을 먹었어요. 친구는 육개장을 먹었어요. 우리는 함께 즐거운 시간을 보냈어요.

(Translation)
It was my friend B's graduation day today. I gave a graduation gift to him. I gave him a necktie and he liked it very much. We went to Seoul Restaurant to have dinner together. I like dolsot-bibimbap (hot stone bibimbap), so I ordered it. My friend had yukgaejang (spicy shredded beef soup). We had a good time together.

Lesson 17

New Words & Expressions (p.157)

Exercise 1

2. e 3. a 4. b 5. c

Exercise 2

1. 언제 졸업하세요? 2. 아니에요. 3. 한국말로 4. 대학원에

Patterns, Expressions & Practice (p.159)

Exercise 1

1. 뉴욕에 갈 거예요; 재미있을 거예요; 만날 거예요. 2. 뭐 하실 거예요?; 찾을 거예요; 일할 거예요? 3. 배울 거예요?; 필요할 거예요. 4. 갈 거예요; 전화할 거예요. 5. 어디에 갈 거야?; 먹을 거야; 누가 올 거야?

Exercise 2

1. 영화 볼 거예요?; 갈 거예요; 살 거예요. 2. 기자 할 거예요; 찾을 거예요 3. 아직 잘 못할 거예요 4. 많을 거야; 그럴 거야 5. 할 거야?; 먹을 거야

Exercise 3

1. 뭐 할 거예요? 2. 숙제 할 3. 못 갈 거예요. 4. 다 갈 거예요.

Exercise 4

2. 바쁘죠? 3. 가죠? 4. 재미있었죠? 5. 이죠? 6. 끝났죠?

Exercise 5

1. 하죠. 2. 많죠. 3. 물론이죠. 4. 먹죠.

Exercise 6

2. 야채하고 계란으로 만들어요.
3. 배추로 만들어요.
4. 소고기로 만들어요.
5. 김하고 야채하고 밥으로 만들어요.

Exercise 7

1. 대학원 2. 석사학위 3. 언론학 4. 국제 관계학

Exercise 8

1. 자전거로 2. 비행기로 3. KTX로 4. 지하철로

Exercise 9

1. F 2. T 3. T 4. T

Exercise 10

Answers may vary.

Exercise 11

Answers may vary.

Exercise 12

1. 쓰려고 해요/쓰려고 배워요 2. 배우려고 3. 가려고 해요
4. 여행하려고 해요.

Exercise 13

04 (1) 여행하려고 06 (2) 공부하려고요.
08 (3) 아르바이트를 하려고요. 10 (4) 찾으려고 해요.

Exercise 14

2. A: 제임스는 왜 인터넷에서 검색해요?
   B: 제임스는 아르바이트를 하려고 인터넷에서 검색해요.
3. A: 소라는 왜 소개팅을 해요?
   B: 소라는 남자 친구를 찾으려고 소개팅을 해요.
4. A: 준은 왜 한국 영화 클럽을 찾아요?
   B: 준은 한국어를 공부하려고 한국 영화 클럽을 찾아요.
5. A: 미라는 왜 어머니한테서 요리를 배워요?
   B: 미라는 한국 음식을 요리하려고 어머니한테서 요리를 배워요.
6. A: 지성은 왜 달리기를 연습해요?
   B: 지성은 마라톤을 뛰려고 달리기를 연습해요.

Exercise 15

1. c 2. e 3. a 4. b 5. d 6. F

Exercise 16

1. c 2. a 3. d 4. b

Exercise 17

Answers may vary.
1. 시험을 못 봤어요.
2. 학교에 갔어요.
3. 중국어를 잘 못 해요.
4. 아직 아파요.

Listen & Discuss (p.181)

1. 한국말 참 잘하시네요!
2. 내년에 졸업할 거예요.; 1년 더 일할 거예요.
3. 기자를 할 거예요.
4. 기자요/기자예요.
5. 경영학을 전공하려고 해요.

Spontaneous Conversation : Sample answers (p.184)

Step 1

(Interview with Classmate 1)

01 A: 마이클 씨는 언제 졸업하세요?
02 B: 내년에 졸업해요.
03 A: 졸업하고 뭐 하실 거예요?
04 B: 한국에 가려고 해요.
05 A: 한국에서 뭐 하실 거예요?
06 B: 한국어를 더 배우려고 해요. 아직 잘 못해서요. 그리고 한국에서 영어를 가르치려고 해요.

(Interview with Classmate 2)

01 A: 제니퍼 씨는 언제 졸업하세요?
02 B: 이번 여름에 졸업해요.
03 A: 졸업하고 뭐 하실 거예요?
04 B: 글로벌 회사에서 일하려고 해요. 회사에서 좀 더 일하고 대학원에 갈 거예요.
05 A: 대학원에서 무슨 공부할 거예요?
06 B: MBA하려고 해요.

Step 2

마이클 씨는 내년에 졸업해요. 졸업하고 한국에 가려고 해요. 한국에서 한국어를 더 배우려고 해요. 한국어를 아직 잘 못해서요. 그리고 한국에서 영어를 가르치려고 해요.
제니퍼 씨는 이번 여름에 졸업해요. 졸업하고 글로벌 회사에서 일하려고 해요. 회사에서 좀 더 일하고 대학원에 갈 거예요. 대학원에서 MBA를 하려고 해요.

(Translation)

Michael is graduating next year. He intends to go to Korea after graduation. He intends to learn Korean more in Korea because he feels his Korean is not good enough. And he plans to teach English in Korea.
Jeniffer is graduating this summer. She intends to work for a global company. She is going to go to a graduate school after working for a while. She intends to do an MBA.

Lesson 18

New Words & Expressions (p.187)

Exercise 1

1. d 2. c 3.a 4. b

Exercise 2

1. 남자 친구 2. 4년 동안 3. 잘나가는; 잘생겼어요
4. 만나 봐요.

Patterns, Expressions & Practice (p.190)

Exercise 1

1. 그동안 2. 1년 동안 3. 겨울 동안; 2주 동안
4. 여름 동안 5. 가는 동안; 오는 동안

Exercise 2

For a month	한 달 동안	During class time	수업 시간 동안
For three months	세 달 동안	During the lunch hour	점심 시간 동안
During this year	올해 한 해 동안	During the meeting time	미팅 시간 동안
During that (time); meanwhile	그동안	While dating	데이트 하는 동안

Exercise 3

(1) 언제 (2) 7월이랑 8월 두 달 동안 (3) 8월 동안 (4) 겨울 동안

Exercise 4

2. 이 식당에는 {마이클이 좋아하는} 한국 음식이 없어요.
3. 저기 {제시카 씨 옆에 얘기하는} 사람은 누구예요?
4. 저는 어제 저녁에 학교 뒤 식당에서 { 제 룸메이트를 좋아하는} 여학생을 만났어요.
5. 오늘 오후에는 {내가 잘 아는} 친구를 커피숍에서 만난다.

Exercise 5

2. 음악을 듣는 사람은 제인이에요.
3. 아이스크림을 먹는 사람은 다이아나예요.
4. 소파에서 자는 사람은 수미예요.
5. 사진을 찍는 사람은 마이클이에요.
6. 수영(을) 하는 사람은 제임스예요.

Exercise 6

1. 받은 2. 살 3. 간 4. 간 5. 갈 (neutral future)/가는 (definite future) 6. 시작할 (neutral future)/시작하는 (definite future) 7. 끝날 (neutral future)/끝나는 (definite future)

Exercise 7

2. 한국어를 가르치시는 교수님이세요.
3. 생물학을 공부하는 학생이에요.
4. 학생들이 공부하는 도서관이에요.
5. 이번학기에 한국어 수업을 듣는 사람들이에요.

Exercise 8

1. 어려운/어렵던 2. 싼 3. 추운 4. 맛있는 5. 따뜻한
6. 가까운; 드시는 7. 유명하던

Exercise 9

1. 뚱뚱해요. 2. 말랐어요. 3. 고양이가 귀여워요.
4. 고양이가 예뻐요.

Exercise 10

1. 진수예요. 2. 마크예요. 3. 소연이에요. 4. 지영이에요.

Exercise 11

1. c 2. b 3. a 4. d

Exercise 12

1. 그 소파 얼마예요? 2. 이 떡 좀 드실래요?; 이 떡 좀 드세요.
3. 저 시계 누구 거예요?; 저 시계 누구 시계예요?
4. 그 컴퓨터 5. 그 가방 어디서 샀어요?

Exercise 13

1. 그 앱은 안 비싸요. 2. 이 태블릿 pc 어제 샀어요.
3. 그 클럽에 자주 가세요? 4. 그 대학 어때요?
5. 그 쿠키를 만들었어요?

Exercise 14

02 여기 03 이 05 저 06 저 07 저 08 여기요

Exercise 15

1. 대학원에 갈 거거든요. 2. 자동차 엔지니어거든요.
3. 잘생겼거든요. 4. 베트남계 미국인이거든요.
5. 어제 저녁에도 한국 음식을 먹었거든요.

Exercise 16

02 (1) 경영학을 전공할 거 거든요. 04 (2) 찾을 수 있거든요.
05 (3) 일하고 싶거든요

Exercise 17

01 (1) 없죠! 03 (2) 있거든요. 05 (3) 한국계 미국인
05 (4) 하거든요. 06 (5) 이죠?

Listen & Discuss (P.213)

Answers may vary.

1. (민준 씨) 친구하고 소개팅 하는 거예요.
2. 베트남계 미국인이에요.
3. 4년 동안 살았어요.
4. 자동차 엔지니어예요.
5. 민준 씨 친구하고 소개팅 할 거예요.

Spontaneous Conversation : Sample answers (p.216)

Step 1

제(Briana)가 제임스한테 소개할 제 친구는 중국 사람이에요.

Your friend				
국적 Nationality	나이 Age	직업 Job	용모 Appearance	키 Height; 성격Personality
중국사람	25 (스물 다섯 살)	대학원생	예뻐요 멋있어요	키가 커요/작아요. 성격이 좋아요.

Step 2

01 Briana: 제임스 씨, 여자 친구 있어요?
02 James: 없어요. 왜요?
03 Briana: 제 친구 왕팡이랑 소개팅 하실래요?
04 James: 왕팡이요? 중국 사람이에요?
05 Briana: 네, 중국 사람이에요.
06 James: 왕팡은 영어 잘해요? 저는 중국말을 못 하거든요.
07 Briana: 네, 영어 잘해요. 미국에서 5년 동안 살았거든요.
08 James: 왕팡은 무슨 일 해요?

09 Briana: 지금 대학원생이에요.
10 James: 아, 그래요? 무슨 공부해요?
11 Briana: 경제학 공부해요.
12 James: 성격은 어때요?
13 Briana: 성격도 아주 좋아요.
14 James: 몇 살이에요?
15 Briana: 25 살이에요. 그리고 키가 크고 되게 멋있어요.
16 James: ㅎㅎ 그래요? 음…좋아요.

Step 3
(As James, you write about Briana's friend.)
브리아나 씨 친구 이름은 왕팡이에요. 왕팡 씨는 중국 사람이에요. 그런데 영어를 잘해요. 왕팡 씨는 미국에서 5년 동안 살았어요. 왕팡 씨는 지금 대학원생이에요. 경제학을 공부해요. 왕팡 씨는 성격이 아주 좋아요. 지금 25살이고, 키도 크고, 아주 멋있어요.

(Translation)
Briana's friend's name is Wang Fang. Wang Fang is Chinese. But she speaks English well. Wang Fang lived in the US for 5 years. Wang Fang is a graduate student now. She is studying economics. Wang Fang has a good personality. She is 25 years old now, tall, and very stylish.

Lesson 19

New Words & Expressions (p.219)

Exercise 1
1. b 2. d 3. a 4. c

Exercise 2
1. 취미 2. 요리사 3. 일주일에 한 번 4. 시간 있으면

Patterns, Expressions & Practice (p.221)

Exercise 1
1. 지하철을 탔다가 버스를 타고 갔어요. 2. 영화를 보다가 잤어요. 3. 기다리다가 그냥 집에 갔어요. 4. 숙제를 하다가 전화를 받았어요. 5. 날씨가 좋았다가 갑자기 눈이 많이 왔어요.

Exercise 2
02 (1) 어제 학교에 가다(가) 04 (2) 중국어를 배우다가
05 (3) 일본어를 배우다가 07 (4) 게임을 하다(가)

Exercise 3
02 (1) 기숙사 방에 가다가 05 (2) 온라인 게임을 많이 하다가
08 (3)운동을 많이 하다가 12 (4) 운동하다가 배고프면

Exercise 4
1. 어떤 사람 2. 어떤 게 3. 어떤 여자
4. 어떤 과목 5. 어떤 남자

Exercise 5
Answers may vary.
1. 어떤 운동 많이 하세요? 2. 어떤 남자가 좋아요?
3. 어떤 거 좋아하세요? 4. 어떤 일 하세요? 5. 어떤 친구예요?

Exercise 6
03 (1) 어떤 요리를 04 (2) 어떤 음식을
05 (3) 어떤 음식이나 06 (4) 어떤 거나

Exercise 7
(1) 만났습니다. (2) 입니다. (3) 했습니다. (4) 생겼습니다.
(5) 만나고 싶습니다.

Exercise 8
(1) 졸업하십니까? [졸업하 + 시 + ㅂ니까?] (2) 졸업합니다.
(3) 하십니까? [하+시+ㅂ니까?] (4) 전공했습니다.
(5) 사셨습니까? [사+시+었+습니까? → 사 + 셨 +습니까?]
(6) 살았습니다.

Exercise 9
1. c 2. a 3. b 4. d

Exercise 10
1. 재미있었겠어요/재미있으셨겠어요. 2. 바빴겠어요/바쁘셨겠어요. 3. 기분이 좋았겠어요/기분이 좋으셨겠어요. 4. 맛있었겠어요.

Exercise 11
1. 하시겠어요/잘하셨겠어요. 2. 아프시겠어요.
3. 재미있으셨겠어요. 4. 피곤하시겠어요. 5. 좋으시겠어요.

Exercise 12
Answers for B may vary.
2. A: 얼마나 자주 외식하세요?
3. A: 얼마나 자주 영화보세요?
4. A: 얼마나 자주 미용실에 가세요?
5. A: 얼마나 자주 방을 청소하세요?
6. A: 얼마나 자주 부모님께 전화하세요?

Exercise 13
1. 보통 한 달에 두 번 정도 요가를 해요.
2. 일주일에 세번해요. 3. 집 근처에서 해요.

Exercise 14
2. 영화도 보고 한국말도 연습하고요.
3. 설거지도 하고 빨래도 하고요.
4. 햄버거도 좋아하고 피자도 좋아하고요.
5. 조깅도 하고 테니스도 치고요.

Exercise 15
2. 조깅도 하고 온라인 게임도 하고 그래요.
3. 빨래도 하고 방청소도 하고 그래요.
4. 친구들도 만나고 숙제도 하고 드라마도 보고 그래요.
5. 요리도 하고 블로그도 쓰고 그래요.

Exercise 16
1. 여행도 하고 운동도 하고 그랬어요/여행도 하고 운동도 했어요.
2. LA에도 가고 시카고에도 가고 그랬어요/LA에도 가고 시카고에도 갔어요.
3. 한국 식당에도 가고 LA에 있는 친구도 만나고 그랬어요.
4. 서울에서 공부도 하고 아르바이트도 하고 그랬어요/서울에서 공부도 하고 아르바이트도 했어요.

Listen & Discuss (p.245)

1. 에이미 씨 요리블로그에서 에이미 씨 글을 봤습니다.
2. 해물 파전 레시피를 칭찬합니다.
3. 블로그 쓰는 것입니다/겁니다.
4. 일주일에 한 번 정도 씁니다.
5. 온라인 게임을 하는 것입니다/온라인 게임입니다.
6. 스트레스도 풀고 사람들도 만나기 위해 게임을 합니다.

Spontaneous Conversation : Sample answers (p.248)

Step 1

Your hobby: 여행

Your partner's hobby: 음악

(You are Speaker A, your friend is Speaker B "제니퍼".)

01 A: 취미가 뭐예요?
02 B: 음악이에요. 저는 시간 있으면 보통 음악을 들어요.
03 A: 아, 그래요? 어떤 음악을 들으세요?
04 B: 요즘은 K-pop을 들어요.
05 A: 자주 들으세요?
06 B: 네, 거의 매일 들어요. 그리고 K-pop 클럽에도 가요.
07 A: K-pop 클럽은 자주 가세요?
08 B: 한 달에 한 번 정도 가요.
09 A: K-pop 클럽 멤버들은 어디서 만나요?
10 B: 캠퍼스 카페에서 만나요.
11 A: 멤버들이 많이 와요?
12 B: 10명 정도 와요.

Step 2

Partner's name	제니퍼
Hobby	음악
Length of the hobby	3년
Activities for the bobby	K-pop을 듣다; K-pop 클럽에 가요.
Frequency of the hobby	K-pop을 거의 매일 들어요; 한 달에 한 번 정도; K-pop 클럽에 가요
Place the hobby occurs	K-pop 클럽은 캠퍼스 카페에서 만나요
Reason for having the hobby	한국 문화를 좋아해요; 한국이를 배울 수 있어요
Co-participants in the hobby	K-pop 클럽 멤버들은 10명 정도 와요.
Other information	

Step 3

제니퍼 씨의 취미는 음악이에요. 제니퍼 씨는 시간이 있으면 보통 음악을 들어요. 요즘은 K-pop을 들어요. 거의 매일 들어요. 제니퍼 씨는 K-pop 클럽에도 가요. 한 달에 한 번 정도 가요. K-pop 클럽은 캠퍼스 카페에서 만나는데 10명 정도 와요.

(Translation)

Jennifer's hobby is music. When she has time, she usually listens to music. She listens to K-pop these days. She listens to it almost every day. Jennifer goes to a K-pop club, too. She goes there about once a month. The K-pop club is held at a campus café. About 10 members come to the club meeting.

Lesson 20

New Words & Expressions (p.251)

Exercise 1

1. 학교 앞; 학교 뒤 2. 한 시간 3. 못 했어요 4. 이번 주말에

Exercise 2

1. 어땠어요?; 말이에요. 2. 한테서 들었어요 3. 아쉽네요
4. 소개해 드릴까요?

Patterns, Expressions & Practice (p.254)

Exercise 1

1. 드려요. 2. 줘요. 3. 드려요. 4.주세요.

Exercise 2

1. 드릴 거예요?; 드릴 거예요. 2. 주셨어요; 줬어요.
3. 줄까요?

Exercise 3

1. b 2. a 3. b 4. a

Exercise 4

1. 끓여 줄까? 2. 사 줄까요? 3. 도와 드릴까요?
4. 보여 드릴까요? 5. 요리해 줄까요?

Exercise 5

1. 만들어 주세요 2. 가 주세요 3. 사 주세요.
4. 와 주세요. 5. 도와 주세요

Exercise 6

01 도와 드릴까요? 02 맵게 해 드릴까요? 03 좀 맵게 해 주세요. 04 갖다 주실래요? 05 바로 갖다 드릴게요.

Exercise 7

1. 한국어 공부하기로 했어요. 2. 제시카를 만나기로 했어요.
3. 순두부하고 불닭을 먹기로 했어.
4. 한국 드라마를 보기로 해. 5. 인턴쉽을 하기로 했어요.

Exercise 8

2. 여름에 어디에 가기로 했어요?
3. 내일 프로젝트 그룹을 언제 만나기로 했어?
4. 내일 아침에 뭘 만들기로 했어요?
5. 민준 씨 생일에 어느 나라 음식을 사기로 할까요?

Exercise 9

01 (1) 뭐 하기로 했어요? 02 (2) 가기로 했어요.
03 (3) 먹기로 했어요. 05 (4) 사기로 했어요?

Exercise 10

1. 연락이 2. 연락을 3. 날씨가 4. 저녁이 5. 미팅을

Exercise 11

1. 을; 이 2. 을; 이 3.를; 가 4. 을; 이

Exercise 12

1. 지난 주말 2. 이번 수요일; 이번 학기 3. 지난번; 이번 겨울
4. 이번 해; 이번 해 5. 이번 학기; 이번 토요일

Exercise 13

1. 다음 미팅은 월요일이에요. 2. 이번 주 토요일에요. 왜요?
3. 다음 주에 한국 음식 요리해요? 4. 지난 해부터 배웠어요.; 이번 해/올해 5. 지난 수요일; 다음 주

Exercise 14

2. 다음 학기 3. 다음 해 4. 이번 학기
5. 다음 화요일 6. 다음 목요일 7. 이번 학기

Listen & Discuss (p.275)

1. 베트남 친구를 만나기로 했습니다.
2. 민준 씨한테서 들었습니다.
3. 학교 앞 별카페였습니다.
4. 한 시간 동안 기다렸습니다.
5. 핸드폰이 망가져서 연락을 못 했습니다.
6. 베트남 친구를 다시 만나기로 했습니다.

Spontaneous Conversation : Sample answers (p.278)

Step 1

1. Classmate A's role

01 A: 지난주에 소개팅을 하기로 했는데 그 친구를 못 만났어요.
02 B: 어, 왜요?
03 A: 지난 수요일 오후 3시에 인문대 앞 동상에서 만나기로 했는데요.
04 B: 네
05 A: 제가 깜박하고 학교정문 앞에서 기다렸어요.
06 B: 어, 그래서요?
07 A: 서로 기다리다가 그냥 집에 갔어요.
08 B: 연락이 안 됐어요?
09 A: 네, 제가 핸드폰을 잃어버려서 연락이 안 됐어요.
10 B: 그럼, 다시 만나기로 했어요?
11 A: 네, 이번 주 수요일 3시에 다시 만나기로 했어요.
* ~을/~를 깜박하다 to completely slip one's mind; ~을/~를 잃어버리다 to lose

2. Classmate B's role

01 B: 지난번 소개팅은 어땠어요?
02 A: 그 중국 친구 말이에요?
03 B: 네.
04 A: 지난 토요일 오후 6시에 학교 서점에서 만나기로 했는데…
05 B: 네.
06 A: 저는 학교 서점 앞에서 기다리고 그 친구는 학교서점 안에서 기다렸어요.
07 B: 어, 그래서요?
08 A: 저는 오래 기다리다가 그냥 집에 갔어요.
09 B: 아쉽네요. 그래서 아직 그 친구를 못 만났어요?
10 A: 네. 근데 이번 주 토요일 6시에 다시 만나기로 했어요.

Step 2

지난주에 소개팅을 하기로 했는데 그 친구를 못 만났어요. 그 친구를 지난 수요일 3시에 인문대 앞 동상에서 만나기로 했어요. 그런데 제가 깜박하고 학교정문 앞에서 기다렸어요. 우리는 서로 기다리다가 그냥 집에 갔어요. 그 친구가 저한테 전화했는데 제가 핸드폰을 잃어버려서 연락이 안 됐어요. 그 친구한테 정말 미안했어요. 그 친구하고 이번 주 수요일에 다시 만나기로 했어요. 제가 그 친구한테 저녁을 사 주기로 했어요.

(Translation)

I was supposed to have a blind date last week, but I couldn't meet that friend. I was supposed to meet him/her at the statue in front of the Humanities college. But I forgot about it and waited in front of the school main gate. We waited for each other and then just went home. He/She called me, but I couldn't answer because I lost my cell phone. I was very sorry. I'm meeting him/her again this Wednesday. I decided to buy him/her dinner.

Listening scripts (of Section I, II, IV)

Lesson 11

I. New Words & Expressions (p.13)

Exercise 1

Listen to the audio and fill in the blanks.

1. 저는 오늘 수업 없어요.
2. 저는 오늘 수업이 4시에 끝나요.
3. 저녁에 다시 봐요.
4. 제가 나중에 문자할게요.

Exercise 2

Listen to the audio and fill in the blanks.

1. A: 지금 몇 시예요?
   B: 1시 45분이요.
2. A: 4시 반쯤 여기서 만날까요?
   B: 네. 그럼 이따가 봐요.
3. A: 저는 인제 갈게요. 2시에 수업이 있어서요.
   B: 아, 그래요? 어, 그럼 어떡하지?

II. Patterns, Expressions & Practice (P.15)

Exercise 3

Listen to the dialogue between the two people and answer the questions in Korean.

Woman: 지금 몇 시예요?
Minjoon: 아홉 시 사십 오 분이에요.
Woman: 미팅이 몇 시에 있어요?
Minjoon: 열 시에 있어요.
Woman: 미팅이 몇 시에 끝나요?
Minjoon: 열한 시 삼십 분에 끝나요.
Minjoon: 에이미 씨는 오늘 몇 시에 집에 가세요?
Woman: 저는 네 시 삼십 분에 가요.

Exercise 8

Listen to the conversation between Minjoon and Amy and answer the questions in Korean.

01 민준 : 에이미 씨, 이번 한국영화클럽 미팅에 가세요?
02 에이미: 미팅이 언제예요?
03 민준 : 이번 주 토요일이요.
04 에이미: 토요일 몇 시요?
05 민준 : 저녁 일곱 시요.
06 에이미: 어... 저는 못 가요. 아르바이트가 있어서요.
07 민준 : 아~ 그래요? 저도 못 가요.
08 에이미: 민준 씨는 왜 못 가세요?
09 민준 : 요즘 일이 많아서 좀 바빠요.

Exercise 10

Listen to the conversation between Amy and Minjoon and fill in the blanks below in Korean.

01 에이미: 민준 씨 동생도 미국에 살아요?
02 민준 : 아니요. 동생은 한국에 있어요.
03 에이미: 대학생이에요?
04 민준 : 네. 서울에서 대학교에 다녀요.
05 에이미: 아, 그래요? 우리 언니도 서울에 있어요.
06 민준 : 아, 그래요? 서울에서 뭐해요?
07 에이미: 서울에서 영어 가르쳐요.

IV. Listen & Discuss (P.29)

Jessica and Xiaoming are talking about a group project together. Listen to the conversation carefully. Discuss the answers to the following questions with your classmates. Then write the answer in a full Korean sentence in the space provided.

01 제시카: 지금 몇 시예요?
02 샤오밍: 1시 45분이요.
03 제시카: 어, 그럼 저는 인제 갈게요. 2시에 수업이 있어서요.
04 샤오밍: 아, 그래요? 어... 그럼 어떡하지?
05 제시카: 음. 저녁에 다시 봐요.
저는 수업이 4시에 끝나요. 샤오밍 씨는요?
06 샤오밍: 전 오늘 수업 없어요. 그럼, 4시 반쯤에 여기서 다시 만날까요?
07 제시카: 네, 그래요. 그럼, 제가 나중에 문자할게요.
08 샤오밍: 네~ 그럼 이따가 봐요.

Lesson 12

I. New Words & Expressions (p.35)

Exercise 1

Listen to the audio and fill in the blanks.

1. Sound: 김밥 2. Sound : 양파 3. Sound: 마트
4. Sound: 인터넷

Exercise 2

Listen to the audio and fill in the blanks.

1. A: 김밥 좀 드세요.
   B: 어, 제시카 씨가 만들었어요?
2. A: 전 떡볶이를 만들었어요. 맛 좀 보세요.
   B: 음~ 맛있네요.
3. A: 여기 뭐 들어갔어요?
   B: 떡하고 고추장하고 양파요.
4. A: 어디서 배웠어요?
   B: 인터넷에서요.

II. Patterns, Expressions & Practice (P.38)

Exercise 3

Jessica went to Korea last summer. Listen to her narration about her trip to Korea and fill in the blanks.

저는 작년 여름에 한국에 갔어요. 서울에 있었어요. 대학교에서 한국어 수업을 들었어요. 수업이 재미있었어요. 그리고 한국어 선생님도 아주 좋았어요. 학교에서 한국 친구들을 많이 사귀었어요. 서울에서 한국 음식을 많이 먹었어요.

Exercise 6

Listen to the audio and write what you hear.

1. 에이미가 커피를 마셔요.
2. 민준이 저녁을 먹어요.
3. 제시카가 김밥을 만들었어요.
4. 샤오밍이 영화를 봐요.

Exercise 9

Listen to Jessica's narration about her friends and fill in the blanks.

저는 오늘 오후에 소피아하고 린다를 만나요. 소피아는 제 룸메이트예요. 생물학을 전공해요. 이번 학기에 생물학하고 한국어를 들어요. 린다는 한국영화클럽에서 만났어요. 한국 영화와 드라마를 좋아해요. 린다는 이번학기에 한국문화를 들어요.

Exercise 12

Listen to the audio and provide your own response using -네요. You may use the words in the box below.

1. 이거 제 어동생 사진이에요.
2. 이거 떡볶이예요. 좀 드세요.
3. 오늘 시험이 4개 있어요.
4. 제 아파트 렌트가 300불이에요.
5. 이 한복 어때요?

IV. Listen & Discuss (P.51)

A group of students learning Korean are having a potluck party in a dorm kitchen. Listen to the conversation carefully. Discuss the answers to the following questions with your classmates. Then, write each answer in a full Korean sentence in the space provided.

01 제시카: 김밥 좀 드세요.
02 샤오밍: 어, 제시카 씨가 만들었어요?
03 제시카: 아뇨. ㅎㅎ 한국 마트에서 아침에 샀어요.
밥하고 고기, 시금치, 당근이 들어 있어요.
04 샤오밍: 아~. 전 떡볶이를 만들었어요. 여기 맛 좀 보세요.
05 제시카: (after trying) 음~ 맛있네요! 여기는 뭐가 들어갔어요?
06 샤오밍: 떡하고, 설탕하고, 고추장하고... 아 참 그리고 양파요.
07 제시카: 아, 그래요. 떡볶이는 어디서 배웠어요?
08 샤오밍: 인터넷 블로그에서요.
09 제시카: 우와~ 대단해요!

Lesson 13

I. New Words & Expressions (p.57)

Exercise 1

Listen to the audio and fill in the blanks.

1. 시간 참 빨리 가네요.
2. 벌써 12월이 다 갔어요.
3. 제 나이는 비밀이에요.
4. 지영 씨 아직 고등학생으로 보여요.

Exercise 2

Listen to the audio and fill in the blanks.

1. A: 오늘이 수요일이에요, 목요일이에요?
B: 목요일이요.
2. A: 오늘 30일이에요?
B: 네. 맞아요.
3. A: 시간 참 빨리 가네요! 벌써 12월이 다 갔어요!
B: 그러게요.
4. A: 지영 씨 아직 고등학생으로 보여요!
B: 에이~ 정말 왜 그래요?

II. Patterns, Expressions & Practice (P.60)

Exercise 2

Amy and Minjoon are talking about people's ages. Listen to the conversation and write the age of each person in the blanks.

01 에이미: 민준 씨, 혹시 수미 씨 나이 아세요? 수미 씨는 나이가 어떻게 돼요?
02 민준 : 스물 다섯 살이에요. 저하고 동갑이에요.
03 에이미: 아, 그래요?
04 민준 : 제시카 씨도 스물 다섯이죠?
05 에이미: 아뇨. 제시카 씨는 스물 일곱 살이에요.
06 민준 : 아~ 네. 저희 형도 스물 일곱 살이에요.
07 에이미: 아, 그래요? 저는 오빠가 있는데...제 오빠는 서른 둘이에요.

Exercise 5

Listen to the conversation between James and Michelle and answer the questions in Korean.

01 제임스: 미셸 씨, 오늘이 몇 월 며칠이에요?
02 미셸 : 이월 팔 일이요.
03 제임스: 미셸 씨, 생일이 이 월이죠?
04 미셸 : 네.
05 제임스: 미셸 씨는 생일이 언제예요?
06 미셸 : 이 월 십구 일이요. 제임스 씨는요?
07 제임스: 저는 오 월 이십 일이에요.

Exercise 8

Listen to the audio and answer the following questions in Korean.

1. 에이미: 소피아 씨는 한국 사람같이 보여요.
민준 : 한국 사람 아니에요?
에이미: 아니에요. 중국 사람이에요.
2. 김 선생님은 40대인데 30대로 보여요.
3. 마크 씨는 고등학생인데 대학생처럼 보여요.
4. A: 이거 서울 사진이에요?
B: 네.
A: 근데 미국같이 보여요.

IV. Listen & Discuss (P.73)

Minjoon and his American colleague Shana are chatting at a coffee shop after a regular meeting of the Korean Conversation Club. Shana is 30 years old. Listen to the conversation carefully. Discuss the answers to the following questions with your classmates. Then, write

each answer in a full Korean sentence in the space provided.
01 샤나: 오늘이 수요일이에요, 목요일이에요?
02 민준: 목요일이요.
03 샤나: 그럼, 오늘 21일이에요?
04 민준: 네, 맞아요.
05 샤나: 어휴~ 그럼 내일까지 보고서를 끝내야 되네요.
06 민준: 네. 시간 참 빨리 가네요.
07 샤나: 그러게요. 벌써 12월이 다 갔어요!
08 민준: 이제 저는 스물 다섯이 돼요.
09 샤나: 그래요? 음..., 제 나이는 ㅎㅎ 비밀이에요~
10 민준: 샤나 씨 아직 고등학생으로 보여요!
11 샤나: 에이~ ㅎㅎ 정말 왜 그래요?

Lesson 14

I. New Words & Expressions (p.79)

Exercise 1

Listen to the audio and fill in the blanks.
1. 오늘 진짜 추워요. 오늘 아침이 14도예요.
2. 한국은 여름에 많이 더워요?
3. 5월이면 따뜻해져요.

Exercise 2

Listen to the audio and fill in the blanks.
1. A: 뉴욕은 원래 이렇게 추워요?
   B: 네. 올해가 유난히 더 춥네요.
2. A: 언제쯤 따뜻해져요?
   B: 5월이면 따뜻해져요.
3. A: 한국은 여름에 더워 죽어요.
   B: 네? 뭐라구요?
4. A: 죽어요?
   B: 하하. 그냥 표현이 그래요.

II. Patterns, Expressions & Practice (P.82)

Exercise 3

Listen to the conversation between Amy and Minjoon and answer the questions in Korean.
에이미: 민준 씨, 주말에 보통 뭐하세요?
민준 : 저는 토요일이면 보통 운동 해요.
에이미: 무슨 운동 하세요?
민준 : 농구해요. 에이미 씨는 시간 있으면 보통 뭐하세요?
에이미: 저는 시간 있으면 한국 드라마 봐요. 그리고 온라인 게임도 해요.
민준 : 어, 그래요? 저도 온라인 게임 좋아해요.

Exercise 6

Listen to the conversation about winter weather in Chicago, Hawaii, and Busan and answer the following questions in Korean.
민수 : 제시카 씨, 고향이 시카고죠? 시카고 겨울 날씨 어때요?
제시카: 시카고는 겨울에 춥고 눈이 많이 와요. 그리고 바람이 많이 불어요.
민수 : 아 그래요? 제시카 씨, 하와이에서도 살았죠?
제시카: 네. 3년 살았어요.
민수 : 하와이는 겨울에 날씨가 어때요?
제시카: 겨울에 안 추워요. 따뜻해요. 민수 씨 고향은 서울이에요?
민수 : 아뇨. 부산이에요.
제시카: 부산은 겨울에 날씨가 어때요? 추워요?
민수 : 네. 추워요. 그런데 보통 눈은 안 와요.

Exercise 9

Listen to the conversation between Amy and Minjoon and answer the questions in Korean.
민준 : 에이미 씨. 오늘 날씨 좋죠?
에이미: 네. 날씨가 많이 따뜻해졌어요.
민준 : 에이미 씨는 요즘 일이 어때요?
에이미: 요즘 일이 많아요. 그래서 많이 바빠졌어요.
민준 : 그래요? 저도 요즘 일이 많아졌어요.

IV. Listen & Discuss (P.93)

Minjoon and Amy are at the office talking about the recent weather in New York. Listen to the conversation carefully. Discuss the answers to the following questions with your classmates. Then, write each answer in a full Korean sentence in the space provided.
01 민준 : 으~, 오늘 정말 춥네요.
02 에이미: 네, 진짜 추워요! 오늘 아침이 14도예요.
03 민준 : 뉴욕은 원래 이렇게 추워요?
04 에이미: 네, 올해가 유난히 더 춥네요.
05 민준 : 그래요? 그럼 언제쯤 따뜻해져요?
06 에이미: 음... 5월이면 따뜻해져요.
07 민준 : 와~ 한국은 5월이면 벌써 더워요.
08 에이미: 아 그래요? 몰랐어요. 한국은 여름에 많이 더워요?
09 민준 : 네, 정말 디워요. 더워 죽어요!
10 에이미: 네? 뭐라구요? 죽어요?!
11 민준 : 하하. 그냥 표현이 그래요.

Lesson 15

I. New Words & Expressions (p.101)

Exercise 1

Listen to the audio and fill in the blanks.
1. 배 안 고파요? 우리 점심 먹으러 가요.
2. 거기 음식 괜찮은데 거기서 먹을까요?
3. 이 근처 한국 식당에 가 봤어요?

Exercise 2

Listen to the audio and fill in the blanks.
1. A: 이 근처 한국 식당에 가 봤어요?
   B: '코리아 하우스' 말이에요?
   A: 네.
2. A: 코리아 하우스 가 봤어요?
   B: 아직 안 가봤어요.
3. A: 거긴 뭐가 맛있어요?

B: 비빔밥하고 불닭이 맛있어요.
4. A: 거기 안 비싸요?
B: 네. 8불에서 12불 정도 해요.

II. Patterns, Expressions & Practice (P.105)

Exercise 7

Listen to the conversation between Minjoon and Jessica and answer the following questions.

<Conversation 1>
01 민준 : 제시카 씨, 한국 음식 먹어 봤어요?
02 제시카: 네, 먹어 봤어요.
03 민준 : 무슨 음식 먹어 봤어요?
04 제시카: 불고기하고 만두 먹어 봤어요.
05 민준 : 갈비는 먹어 봤어요?
06 제시카: 아니요, 아직 안 먹어 봤어요.
07 민준 : 갈비 한번 먹어 보세요. 진짜 맛있어요.
08 제시카: 아, 그래요?

<Conversation 2>
01 제시카: 민준 씨, 유럽에 가 봤어요?
02 민준 : 네. 유럽 여행해 봤어요.
03 제시카: 유럽 어디어디 가 봤어요?
04 민준 : 영국하고 프랑스하고 이탈리아에 가 봤어요.
05 제시카: 그럼 로마에도 가 봤어요?
06 민준 : 아니요. 밀라노에만 가 봤어요. 그리고 파리하고 런던에 가 봤어요.

IV. Listen & Discuss (P.117)

Jessica and her friend Xiaoming are talking about what to eat for lunch. Listen to the conversation carefully. Discuss the answers to the following questions with your classmates. Then, write each answer in a full Korean sentence in the space provided.

01 제시카: 배 안 고파요? 우리 점심 먹으러 가요.
02 샤오밍: 그래요. 이 근처 한국 식당에 가 봤어요?
03 제시카: "코리아 하우스" 말이에요?
04 샤오밍: 네.
05 제시카: 아뇨. 아직 안 가 봤어요.
06 샤오밍: 거기 음식 괜찮은데 거기서 먹을까요?
07 제시카: 거긴 뭐가 맛있어요?
08 샤오밍: 비빔밥하고 불닭이 맛있어요.
09 제시카: 음... 전 순두부 좋아하는데...
10 샤오밍: 어, 순두부도 있어요!
11 제시카: 안 비싸요?
12 샤오밍: 네. 8불에서 12불 정도 해요.
13 제시카: 좋아요! 그럼, 거기 가요.

Lesson 16

I. New Words & Expressions (p.125)

Exercise 1

Listen to the audio and fill in the blanks.

1. 생일 2. 선물 3. 핸드폰 케이스

Exercise 2

Listen to the audio and fill in the blanks.

1. A: 생일 축하해요!
B: 제 생일 어떻게 알았어요?
2. A: 제 생일 어떻게 알았어요?
B: 샤오밍한테 들었어요.
3. A: 이거 선물이에요.
B: 와~ 고마워요.
4. A: 지금 열어 봐도 돼요?
B: 그럼요.

II. Patterns, Expressions & Practice (P.127)

Exercise 3

Listen to the audio and fill in the blanks.

1. 오늘 수업 시간에 선생님께 질문을 드렸어요.
2. 어제 친구가 저한테 전화를 했어요.
3. 샤오밍한테서 생일 선물을 받았어요!
4. 언니한테 할머니 소식을 들었어요.
5. 민준 씨한테 무슨 선물을 줄까요?
6. 이거 할아버지께 드리는 선물이에요.

Exercise 11

Listen to the audio and write what Lisa and Amy will do together next week.

리사 : 한국어 클럽 미팅이 몇 시에 있어요?
에이미: 수요일 저녁 5시에 있어요.
리사 : 영어해도 돼요?
에이미: 아니요. 한국어만 돼요.
리사 : 아, 그래요?
에이미: 네. 그리고 같이 차도 마셔요.
리사 : 좋은데요? 저도 가도 돼요?
에이미: 그럼요! 다음 주에 같이 가요!

IV. Listen & Discuss (P.149)

Amy is speaking to Minjoon in the company's break room. They both work as interns. Listen to the conversation carefully. Discuss the answers to the following questions with your classmates. Then, write each answer in a full Korean sentence in the space provided.

01 에이미: 생일 축하해요!
02 민준 : 어! 제 생일 어떻게 알았어요?
03 에이미: 샤오밍한테 들었어요.
이거 별 거 아니지만⋯ 선물이에요.
05 민준 : 와~ 고마워요! 지금 열어 봐도 돼요?
06 에이미: 그럼요~. 열어 보세요.
07 민준 : 우와! 핸드폰 케이스네요!
마침 필요했는데. 잘 쓸게요!
09 에이미: 잘 됐네요. 고르기 힘들었는데.

Lesson 17

I . New Words & Expressions (p.157)

Exercise 2

Listen to the audio and fill in the blanks.

1. A: 전 내년에 졸업하는데...제시카 씨는 언제 졸업하세요?
   B: 저도 내년에요.
2. A: 한국말 참 잘하시네요!
   B: 아니에요. 아직 잘 못해요.
3. A: Journalist 한국말로 뭐예요?
   B: 기자예요.
4. A: 민준 씨는 뭐 하실 거예요?
   B: 저는 1년 더 일하고 대학원에 갈 거예요.

II . Patterns, Expressions & Practice (P.159)

Exercise 3

Listen to the conversation between two friends and fill in the blanks.

민준 : 내일 뭐 할 거예요?
제시카: 숙제 할 거예요. 이번 주에 숙제가 너무 많아요.
민준 : 저녁에 시간 있어요? 내일 저녁에 에이미 씨 생일 파티가 있어요.
제시카: 어머 그래요? 저는 시간이 없어서 아마 못 갈 거예요.
민준 : 숙제 빨리 하고 생일 파티에 가요. 다른 친구들도 다 갈 거예요.
제시카: 알겠어요. 빨리 해 볼게요.

Exercise 7

Listen to the audio and provide the corresponding Korean words for the English words from the conversation.

제시카: 민준 씨, graduate school 한국말로 뭐예요?
민준 : 대학원이에요.
제시카: Master's degree는 한국말로 뭐예요?
민준 : 석사학위예요.
제시카 씨, 언론학은 영어로 뭐예요?
제시카: Journalism이에요.
민준 : 국제 관계학은 영어로 뭐예요?
제시카: International Studies예요.

Exercise 9

Listen to the narration by Steve, and mark the following statements as T(True)or F(False).

저는 한국말은 잘하지만 일본말은 못해요.
저는 농구를 잘 못해요. 그런데 테니스는 잘해요.
저는 요리를 자주 해요. 스파게티를 잘 만들어요. 그런데 한국 음식은 못해요.

Exercise 13

Listen to the audio and fill in the blanks with the appropriate information.

01 제임스: 준희 씨, 2월에 졸업이죠?
02 준희 : 네. 벌써 그렇게 됐네요.
03 제임스: 졸업하고 좋은 계획 있어요?
04 준희 : 네. 한달 동안 여자 친구하고 유럽을 여행하려고 해요. 프랑스, 독일, 이탈리아, 그리스에 가 볼 거예요.
05 제임스: 와, 좋은데요. 외국어 잘하세요?
06 준희 : 조금요. 고등학교에서 프랑스 말을 배웠는데, 다음 주부터 다시 공부하려고요.
07 제임스: 그래요. 돈은 있어요?
08 준희 : 네. 조금 있지만 많이는 없어요. 그래서 카페에서 아르바이트를 하려고요.
09 제임스: 여자 친구도 일해요?
10 준희: 여자 친구도 아르바이트를 찾으려고 해요.

Exercise 16

Listen to the audio and circle the picture that best discribes what you hear.

1. 저녁을 먹었는데도 배가 고파요.
2. 피곤한데도 숙제를 했어요.
3. 한국 사람이 아닌데도 한국 말을 아주 잘해요.
4. 어젯밤에 많이 잤는데도 피곤하고 졸려요.

IV. Listen & Discuss (P.181)

Minjoon and Jessica are chatting at a coffee shop after a Korean Conversation Club meeting. Listen to the conversation carefully. Discuss the answers to the following questions with your classmates. Finally, write each answer <u>in a full Korean sentence</u> in the space provided.

01 민준 : 전 내년에 졸업하는데... 제시카 씨는 언제 졸업하세요?
02 제시카: 저도 내년에요.
03 민준 : 졸업하고 뭐 하실 거예요?
04 제시카: Journalist요. 근데 journalist는 한국말로 "기자"죠?
05 민준 : 네, 기자요. 제시카 씨, "기자"도 아시고... 한국말 참 잘하시네요!
06 제시카: 아니에요. 아직 잘 못해요. 민준 씨는 뭐 하실 거예요?
07 민준 : 저는 1년 더 일하고 대학원에 갈 거예요.
08 제시카: 아~ 뭐 전공하실 거예요?
09 민준 : 경영학 전공하려고 해요. 회사를 다녔는데도 아직 공부가 더 필요해서요.

Lesson 18

I . New Words & Expressions (p.187)

Exercise 2

Listen to the audio and fill in the blanks.

1. A: 에이미 씨, 남자 친구 있어요?
   B: 아니요. 없어요.
2. A: 어떻게 한국말을 잘해요?
   B: 한국에서 4년 동안 살았거든요.
3. A: 그 친구는 무슨 일 해요?
   B: 잘 나가는 자동차 엔지니어예요. 그리고 되게 잘생겼어요.
4. A: 혹시 그 친구 사진 있어요?

B: 에이~ 그냥 한 번 만나봐요.

II. Patterns, Expressions & Practice (P.190)

Exercise 3

Listen to the conversation and fill in the blanks with the time expressions.

브라이언: 에이미 씨는 한국에 언제 있었어요?
에이미 : 7월이랑 8월 두 달 동안 있었어요.
브라이언: 언제가 제일 더웠어요?
에이미 : 8월 동안이요.
브라이언: 전 겨울 동안 한국에 있었어요. 근데 그때 정말 추웠어요.

Exercise 11

Listen to the audio and circle the picture that best corresponds to what you hear.

1. 마이클은 키가 작아요. 그리고 아주 말랐어요.
2. 제인은 머리가 길어요. 키가 보통이에요.
3. 영호는 잘 생겼어요. 머리가 짧아요. 키가 커요.
4. 리나는 귀여워요. 그리고 날씬해요. 머리가 길어요.

Exercise 14

Listen to the conversation taking place at a baseball game and fill in the blanks.

에이미: 와, 사람이 많네요!
민준 : 네, 여기 앉으세요.
에이미: 이 의자에요?
민준 : 네. 언제 왔어요?
에이미: 지금 왔어요. 저 사람은 누구예요?
민준 : 핫도그 파는 사람이에요. 저 핫도그 좀 드실래요?
에이미: 네, 배고파요. 제가 저 핫도그 사 드릴게요.
민준 : 좋죠~! 여기요~!

Exercise 17

Listen to the conversation between the two friends and fill in the blanks.

에이미: 민준 씨, 여자 친구 없죠!
민준 : 네. 여자 친구는 왜요?
에이미: 소개팅 할 수 있는 친구가 있거든요.
민준 : 그래요? 어떤 친구예요?
에이미: 한국계 미국인이에요. 한국말도 잘하거든요.
민준 : 그래요? 대학생이죠?
에이미: 네. 잘 나가는 대학생이에요.
민준 : 와~ 혹시 사진 있어요?

IV. Listen & Discuss (P.213)

Minjoon and Amy are having lunch at their company's cafeteria. Minjoon wants to introduce one of his friends to Amy. Listen to the conversation carefully. Discuss the answers to the following questions with your classmates. Finally, write each answer in a full Korean sentence in the space provided.

01 민준 : 에이미 씨 남자 친구 없죠!
02 에이미: 네. 근데 왜요?
03 민준 : 제 친구랑 소개팅 하실래요?
04 에이미: 민준 씨 친구면... 한국 사람이에요?
05 민준 : 아뇨. 베트남계 미국인이에요. 근데 한국말을 진짜 잘 해요.
06 에이미: 그래요? 어떻게 한국말을 잘 해요?
07 민준 : 한국에서 4년 동안 살았거든요.
08 에이미: 그렇구나. 그 친구는 무슨 일 해요?
09 민준 : 잘 나가는 자동차 엔지니어예요. 그리고 되게 잘 생겼어요.
10 에이미: ㅎㅎ 혹시 사진 있어요?
11 민준 : 에이~ 그냥 한 번 만나 봐~요!
12 에이미: 음... 그래요~.

Lesson 19

I. New Words & Expressions (p.219)

Exercise 2

Listen to the audio and fill in the blanks.

1. A: 취미가 뭐예요?
   B: 저는 블로그를 써요.
2. A: 무슨 일 하세요?
   B: 저는 요리사예요.
3. A: 블로그 많이 쓰세요?
   B: 일주일에 한 번 정도 써요.
4. A: 시간 있으면 보통 뭐하세요?
   B: 보통 온라인 게임을 해요.

II. Patterns, Expressions & Practice (P.221)

Exercise 3

Listen to the dialogue and fill in the blanks.

민준 : 제시카 씨, 어디 가세요?
제시카: 기숙사 방으로 가다가 배가 고파서 다시 식당으로 가요.
민준 : 아, 벌써 점심 시간이네요. 같이 갈래요?
제시카: 네. 근데 민준 씨 요즘은 시간 있을 때 뭐 해요?
민준 : 작년까지 온라인 게임을 많이 하다가 올해부터는 운동을 더 많이 해요.
제시카: 보통 무슨 운동을 해요?
민준 : 이번 4월에 보스턴 마라톤에 나갈 거예요. 그래서 마라톤 연습해요.
제시카: 와! 대단해요. 저는 작년에는 운동을 많이 하다가 요즘에는 요리를 많이 해요.
민준 : 그래요? 보통 무슨 음식 만들어요?
제시카: 스파게티하고, 가끔 돼지 불고기도 만들어요.
민준 : 아하! 둘 다 제가 좋아하는 음식이네요!
제시카: 하하. 언제 운동하다가 배고프면 저한테 문자 해 보세요!

Exercise 6

Listen to the conversation and fill in the blanks.

민준 : 전 주말에 시간 있으면 친구들하고 농구를 해요. 에이

미 씨는요?
에이미: 전 주말에는 요리하는 걸 좋아해요.
민준 : 궁금해요! 어떤 요리를 하세요?
에이미: 어제는 파전을 만들었어요. 민준 씨는 어떤 음식을 좋아하세요?
민준 : 저, 파전 좋아하는데… 전 한국 음식이면 어떤 음식이나 잘 먹어요.
에이미: 하하 그래요? 그럼, 제가 다음에 맛있는 파전 만들어 줄게요. 저도 한국 음식이면 어떤 거나 다 좋아해요.

Exercise 13

Listen to the following conversation between Sumi and Jessica and answer the following questions in Korean.
수미 : 제시카 씨, 취미 있으세요? 시간 있으면 보통 뭐하세요?
제시카: 시간이 있으면 요가를 해요.
수미 : 그래요? 얼마나 자주 요가하세요?
제시카: 바빠서 자주 못 해요. 한 달에 두 번 정도 해요. 수미 씨는 무슨 운동을 좋아하세요?
수미 : 저는 보통 조깅을 해요. 보통 일주일에 세 번 해요.
수미 : 그래요? 어디서 조깅하세요?
제시카: 집 근처에서 조깅해요.

Exercise 16

Listen to the conversation between Minjoon and Amy and answer the questions using -도 ~고 -도 ~고 그랬어요, or -도 ~고 -도 ~았어요/~었어요.
민준 : 지난 여름 방학에 뭐 했어요?
에이미: 이것저것 했어요. 여행도 하고 운동도 하고요.
민준 : 어디 여행했어요?
에이미: LA에도 가고 시카고에도 갔어요.
민준 : 그래요? 재미있었겠네요. LA에서는 뭐 했어요?
에이미: 한국 식당에도 가고 LA에 있는 친구도 만나고 그랬어요. 민준 씨는 여름에 뭐 했어요?
민준 : 저는 서울에 있었어요. 공부도 하고 아르바이트도 하고 그랬어요.

IV. Listen & Discuss (P.245)

Xiaoming's hobby is playing online games and Amy's hobby is blogging about her cooking methods. Amy is a power blogger. Listen to the conversation carefully. Discuss the answers to the following questions with your classmates. Finally, write each answer in a full Korean sentence in the space provided.
샤오밍: 어제 요리 블로그를 보다가 에이미 씨 글을 봤어요.
에이미: 어, 어떤 거요?
샤오밍: 해물 파전 레시피요.
에이미 씨, 요리사 해도 되겠어요!
에이미: 에이, 아니에요. 그냥 취미로 해요.
샤오밍: 블로그 많이 쓰세요?
에이미: 네. 일주일에 한 번 정도 써요.제가 요리를 좋아해서요.
샤오밍: 와~ 파워 블로거시네요. 하하.
에이미: 샤오밍 씨는 시간 있으면 보통 뭐하세요?
샤오밍: 보통 온라인 게임을 해요.
스트레스도 풀고, 사람들도 만나고요.

Lesson 20

I. New Words & Expressions (p.251)

Exercise 1

Listen to the audio and fill in the blanks.
1. 제가 학교 앞 별카페에서 기다렸는데, 그 친구는 학교 뒤 별카페서 기다렸어요.
2. 한 시간 동안 서로 기다리다가 그냥 집에 갔어요.
3. 핸드폰이 망가져서 연락을 못 했어요.
4. 그 친구 이번 주말에 다시 만나기로 했어요.

Exercise 2

Listen to the audio and fill in the blanks.
1. A: 지난번 소개팅은 어땠어요? 그 베트남 친구 말이에요.
B: 망했어요!
2. A: 어떻게 알았어요?
B: 민준 씨한테서 들었어요.
3. A: 연락이 안 됐어요?
B: 네. 핸드폰이 망가져서 연락을 못 했어요.
A: 아쉽네요.
4. A: 제가 다른 사람 소개해 드릴까요?
B: 아뇨. 괜찮아요.

II. Patterns, Expressions & Practice (P.254)

Exercise 3

Listen to the audio and circle the picture that best corresponds to the audio.
1. 사장님께서 마크한테 선물을 주셨어요.
2. 에이미가 김 선생님께 책을 드렸어요.
3. 아버지께서 저한테 돈을 주셨어요.
4. 제시카가 사장님께 카드를 드렸어요.

Exercise 6

Listen to the audio and fill in the blanks.
점원: 손님, 뭘 도와 드릴까요?
민준: 여기 떡볶이 맛있어요?
점원: 네. 근처에선 유명해요. 얼마나 맵게 해 드릴까요?
민준: 저는 좀 맵게 해 주세요.
점원: 네, 알겠습니다. 다른 건 뭐 필요하세요?
민준: 아, 그리고 물 좀 갖다 주실래요?
점원: 네, 바로 갖다 드릴게요.

Exercise 9

Listen to the audio and fill in the blanks.
민준 : 이번 크리스마스에 뭐 하기로 했어요?
에이미: 부모님 집에 가기로 했어요. 민준 씨는요?
민준 : 저는 친구들하고 같이 저녁 먹기로 했어요. 미국 친구 제임스가 저를 초대했어요.
에이미: 잘 됐네요. 부모님 선물을 사야 되는데…
민준 : 뭘 사기로 했어요?

에이미: 아직 잘 모르겠어요.

Exercise 14

Listen to the conversation between the two friends on campus and fill in the blanks.

제시카: 다음 학기에 한국어 배워요?
샤오밍: 네, 그럴 거예요. 제시카 씨는요?
제시카: 전공 공부가 어려워서 다음 학기에는 아마 못 배울 거예요. 그래서 전 다음 해에 배울 거예요.
샤오밍: 네. 그럼 그동안 한국 영화나 드라마 많이 보세요. 전 이번 학기에 한국어 2를 배워요. 근데 제시카 씨는 에이미 씨하고 언제 만나요?
제시카: 다음 화요일 오후에 만날 거예요. 그 때 둘 다 시간이 돼요.
샤오밍: 지금 에이미 씨하고 프로젝트를 같이 하는데 우리는 다음 목요일에 만나요.
제시카: 다들 정말 바쁘네요!
샤오밍: 네, 이번 학기가 끝나면 언제 한번 다 같이 점심 먹어요!

IV. Listen & Discuss (P.275)

Jessica and Amy are talking about the last blind date that Amy went. Listen to the conversation carefully. Discuss the answers to the following questions with your classmates. Then write each answer in a full Korean sentence in the space provided.

01 제시카: 참! 지난번 소개팅은 어땠어요? 그 베트남 친구 말이에요.
02 에이미: 망했어요! 근데, 어떻게 알았어요?
03 제시카: 민준 씨한테서 들었어요.
04 에이미: 제가 학교 앞 별카페에서 기다렸는데, 그 친구는 학교 뒤 별카페서 기다렸어요.
05 제시카: 어, 그래서요?
06 에이미: 한 시간 동안 서로 기다리다가 그냥 집에 갔어요.
07 제시카: 연락이 안 됐어요?
08 에이미: 네. 핸드폰이 망가져서 연락을 못 했어요.
09 제시카: 아쉽네요. 제가 다른 사람 소개해 드릴까요?
10 에이미: 아뇨, 괜찮아요. 그 친구 이번 주말에 다시 만나기로 했어요.

Appendix I : Vocabulary (Korean - English)

Korean	English	Page
[time] 부터	from [time]	162
-가까이에	close to ~	133
~고 싶다	to want to~	136, 201
-까지	until	97
-도	also	157
-도 하고 -도 하다	to do ~ and also do ~	109
말이다	to mean	101
말이에요	I mean~	251
아직	yet	157
-에 가 봤다	to have been to ~	101
-에 관심이 있다	to be interested in ~	23
-에 따르면	according to ~	117
-에 참가하다	to participate in ~	136
-에서	at ~	35
-을/를 사귀다	to make a friend	201
-을/를 사면서	in buying	149
-의	of	97
-이나	as many as~	209
-이랑/-랑	with ~; ~ and	187
~지만	~ but; although ~	125
-하고 동갑이다	the same age	62
-한테	to [person]	125
-한테(서)	from [person]	125
10개월 [십 개월]	10 months	183
12월	December	56, 58, 59
14도	fourteen degrees	79
1개월 [일 개월]	1 month	183
1시45분	one o'clock forty-five munutes	13
2개월 [이 개월]	2 months	183
6개월 [육 개월]	6 months	183
KTX를 타다	to take the KTX	83

ㄱ

Korean	English	Page
가격	price	120, 154
가깝다	to be close	113
가다	to go	38, 41, 112, 136, 137, 159, 165, 193
가르치다	to teach	27
가방	bag	48, 202, 206
가수이다	to be a singer	113, 132
가을	fall	84, 92, 97, 98
가족	family	226
간장	soy sauce	49
간호사	nurse	40
갈비	ribs	111, 147
갈비구이	grilled ribs with sweet soy sauce	115
갈비찜	steamed ribs with sweet soy sauce	115
감기에 걸리다	to catch a cold	22
갔다 오다	to go and come back	140
갔어요	went	38
갖다 주다	to bring to	264
같이	together	134
개띠	dog zodiac	71
개월	counter for a number of months	183
거기	there; that place	24, 101, 112, 118, 120, 206
거기서	at there	101
거긴	as for that place	101, 104
걱정(을) 하다	to worry	268
걱정(이) 되다	to be worried	268
걷다	to walk	159, 194
검색하다	search	174
검은색	black color	66
게임	game	243, 245, 248
겨울	winter	80, 84, 87, 92, 97, 98
경기	economic conditions	88
경영학	studies of business management	158, 182
경제	economics	23
계란	eggs	54, 167, 190
계란프라이	fried eggs	54
계획	plan	161, 162, 172, 174, 271
고기	meat	34, 35, 52, 145
고등학생	high school student	56, 57, 58, 59, 66, 67, 68, 74, 76
고등학생때	at the time when I was a high school student	236
고양이	cat	204
고장나다	to break down; to become out of order	136
고추장	gochujang	34, 35, 49, 52, 54, 145, 167
고치다	to fix	136
고향	hometown	40, 87, 98
골프	golf	170, 171, 248
공부	study	176
공부하다	to study	39, 112, 193, 197
공원	a public park	196
과목	subject	22, 227, 235
과일	fruit	226
과장님	section chief	143
광화문	Gwanghwamun Gate	264
괜찮다	to be okay	199
교수	professor; university professor	172, 173, 197 ,223
교통	transportation	133
교환 학생	exchange student	220
구 분	9 minutes	15
구 월	September	63
구름이 끼다	to be cloudy	85
구이	grilled meat	115
국제 관계학	International Studies	232
귀엽다	to be cute	203
그냥	just	79
그럼	if so; well, then; of course	102, 103
그럼요.	For sure; Absolutely.	125
그룹	group	163
그리스	Greece	174
그림 그리기	drawing	170
근처	neighborhood; vicinity	101, 120, 146, 264
글	writing	219
금년	this year	79

ㄴ

ㄷ

ㅇ

Appendix I : Vocabulary (English - Korean)

English	Korean	Page
1 month	1개월 [일 개월]	183
10 months	10개월 [십 개월]	183
2 months	2개월 [이 개월]	183
6 months	6개월 [육 개월]	183

A

English	Korean	Page
a lot	많이	41, 79
a week	일주일	219
a.m	오전	16
ability	능력	156
about	정도; 쯤	101, 102, 238
above zero	영상	86
Absolutely.	그럼요.	125
according to ~	-에 따르면	117
again	다시	14
age	나이; 연세	56, 57, 147
airplane	비행기	166, 219
all	다; 모두	165
Along With the Gods	신과 함께	160
already	벌써	57, 74, 102, 174
also	-도	157
although	~지만	124, 125, 130, 176
always	항상	58
American	미국 사람	112, 131, 142, 168, 176, 195
American Idol	아메리칸 아이돌	206
and	-이랑/-랑	187
anything	아무 거나 다	241
apartment	아파트	131
apartment rent	아파트 렌트	48
apple	사과	226
appointment	약속	186
April	4월; 사 월	63, 65
aromatic candle	향초	153
around	정도; 쯤	101, 102, 238
Around when	언제쯤	79
as for me	전; 저는	35
as for that place	거긴	101
as many as ~	~이나	209
at 에서	에서	25
at here	여기서	13
at one o'clock	한 시에	16
at there	거기서	101
at two (o'clock) thirty (minutes)		16
at what time	몇 시에	16
Atlanta	애틀랜타	166
August	8월; 팔 월	63, 64, 65
aunt	이모	143
automobile	자동차	187
automobile engineer	자동차 엔지니어	209, 214
awesome	굉장한	53

B

English	Korean	Page
background information		100
badminton	배드민턴	168
ball-point pen	볼펜	166, 219
Barcelona	바르셀로나	111
basketball	농구	84, 169
be refreshing	서늘하다	84
beautician	미용 관리사	247
beauty	미용	247
because	때문에	19, 21, 81, 238
become	~(해)지다; ~이 되다	94
beef	소고기	53, 166, 219
behind	뒤에	276
Beijing	베이징	86
being accepted	합격	151
belly	배	101
below zero	영하	86
bibimbap	비빔밥	134
birthday	생일; 생신	63, 124, 125, 147, 150, 262
birthday cake	생일 케이크	147
birthday party	생일 파티	139
black color	검은색	66
blind date	소개팅	174, 187, 211, 214, 251, 276
blog	블로그	219, 238, 246
book	책	141, 223, 261
bookstore gift card	서점 상품권	151
bookstore	서점; 책방	223
boss	사장	257
box	상자	226
boyfriend	남자 친구	23, 128, 174, 187, 214
break room	휴게실	124
breakfast	아침	28
brother	형; 오빠; 남동생	143
Buddha's Birthday	부처님 오신 날	65
buldak	불닭	110
bulgogi	불고기	53, 166, 260, 261
bus stop	버스 정류장	133
business card wallet	명함지갑	153
but	~지만	124, 125, 130, 131
by	-(으)로	219
by the way	참	251, 252

C

English	Korean	Page
cafeteria	카페테리아	186, 195, 250
calendar	달력	56
car	자동차; 차	166, 187
card	카드	153, 257
carrot	당근	35, 53
cell phone	핸드폰	276
cell phone case	핸드폰 케이스	125, 150
charger	충전기	138
cheap	(값이) 싼	179
chef	요리사	219, 233, 246
child	아이; 어린이	66
children	아이들; 어린이들	261

G

H

I

J

K

L

M

N

O

T

Appendix II : Words and expressions (Organized by lesson)

Lesson 11 What time is now?

1. New words & expressions in Conversation

NOUN

수업 class
저녁 (1) evening; (2) dinner

VERB

끝나다 (for something) to end
문자하다 to text
보다 to see

ADVERB

이따(가) later
인제 now; from now on

EXPRESSION

■ 나중에 later
■ 어떡하지? What should I/we do?; What do I/we do?
■ 여기서 at here [a shortened form of 여기에서]
거기서 at there [a shortened form of 거기에서]
어디서 at where [a shortened form of 어디에서]
■ (만날)까요? Shall I/we (meet)?
■ 저녁에 in the evening

2. Additional words & expressions (Section II ~VI in the textbook)

NOUN

(Place 장소)
오하이오 Ohio (p.27)
데이튼 Dayton (p.27)
베트남 Vietnam (p.27)
북한 North Korea (p.23)
광조우 Guangzhou (p.27)
동아시아 East Asia (p.23)
디즈니랜드 Disneyland (p.26)
말레이시아 Malaysia (p.27)
쿠알라룸프 Kuala Lumpur (p.27)
플로리다 Florida (p.26)
하노이 Hanoi (p.27)

(People 사람)
아빠 dad (p.23)
엄마 mom (p.23)
할머니 grandmother (p.23)
할아버지 grandfather (p.23)
여자친구 (acronym: 여친)girlfriend (p.23)
우리 언니 my sister [Literally, our sister] (p.27)
남자친구 (acronym: 남친)boyfriend (p.23)
채식주의자 vegetarian (p.22)

(Time 시간)
새벽 early morning (p.28)
낮 day (p.28)
밤 night (p.28)
오전 a.m. (p.28)
오후 p.m. (p.28)
자정 midnight (p.28)
정오 noon (p.28)
휴일 holiday (p.22)
이번 주 this week (p.24)
시계 watch (p.21)
반 half; 30 minutes (p.17)
경제 economics (p.23)
과목 course; subject (p.22)
노래 song (p.23)
맥도날드 McDonald's (p.26)
북한 문제 the North Korean issue (p.23)
샐러드 salad (p.21)
수학 math (p.21)
아르바이트 Arbeit; part time job (p.24)
지하철 subway (p.22)
한국 문화 Korean culture (p.23)

VERB

걸리다 (걸려요) to take (time) (p.25)
*(time)이/가 걸리다
비가 오다 (비가와요) to rain (p.20)
[Literally, for rain to come]
감기에 걸리다 (감기에 걸려요) to catch a cold (p.22)
등산 가다 to go hiking; to go mountain climbing (p.22)
가르치다 (가르쳐요) to teach (p.26)

다니다 (다녀요) to attend (p.27)

ADJECTIVE

늦다 (늦어요) to be late (p.20)
아프다 (아파요) to be sick (p.20)
배가 부르다 (배가 불러요) to be full (p.20) [Literally, for stomach to be full]
미안하다 (미안해요) to be sorry (p.22)
편하다 (편해요) to be convenient (p.22)

ADVERB

곧 soon (p.14)
또 once again (p.14)

EXPRESSION

■ 몇 과목 들어요? How many classes do you take? (p.22)
■ 배가 불러서 because (I) am full (p.22)
■ ~ 에 관심이 있다 to be interested in~ (p.23)
■ 세일이다 to be on sale (p.22)

Lesson 12 Please have some gimbap.

1. New words & expressions in Conversation

NOUN

고기 meat
고추장 gochujang (red pepper paste)
김밥 gimbap (seaweed rice roll)
떡볶이 ttokboggi (stir-fried rice cakes)
마트 mart; supermarket
맛 taste
밥 cooked rice
설탕 sugar
시금치 spinach
양파 onion
인터넷 Internet
전 as for me [shortened form of 저는]

VERB

드시다 (1) to eat; (2) to drink
*[honorific form of 들다,먹다, 마시다]
들어가다 to go in; enter
만들다 to make
맛(을) 보다 to taste; try something's taste
배우다 to learn

ADJECTIVE

대단하다 to be great; tremendous; incredible

MARKER

-에서 from ~ (e.g., 한국마트에서)

EXPRESSION

■ 아침에 in the morning

2. Additional Words & Expressions (II ~VI in the textbook)

NOUN

간장 soy sauce (p.49)
계란 egg (p.54)
김 seaweed (p.53)
나물 cooked vegetables (p.54)
당면 glass noodles (p.53)
된장 soybean paste (p.54)
두부 tofu (p.54)
밀가루 flour (p.54)
소고기 beef (p.54)
순두부 soft tofu (p.54)
아파트 렌트 apartment rent (p.48)
온라인 게임 online game (p.41)
잡채 clear noodle with soy sauce, shredded vegetables and meats (p.49)
파 scallion (p.54)
한복 traditional Korean clothing (p.48)
해물 seafood (p.54)
해물 파전 seafood scallion pancake (p.54)
호박 zucchini (p.54)
후라이 fries (p.54)
고추 chile (pepper)

VERB

자다 to sleep (p.41)
*주무시다 [honorific form of 자다]

ADJECTIVE

피곤하다to be tired (p.41)

ADVERB

가끔occasionally (p.42)

EXPRESSION

- 멋있다 (멋있어요) to be awesome, cool (p.48)
- 수업을 듣다(들어요) to take a class (p.45)
- 엄마한테서 from my mom (p.53)
- 책에서 from a book (p.53)
- 친구를 사귀다 (사귀어요, 사귀었어요) to make friends (p.41)
- 한국말로 얘기하다 (얘기해요) to talk in Korean (p.41)

Lesson 13 I am now becoming 25 years old.

1. New words & expressions in Conversation

NOUN

고등학생	high school student
나이	age
목요일	Thursday
비밀	secret
수요일	Wednesday
시간	time *[시간이 가다 for time to pass]

ADJECTIVE

맞다 to be correct; to be right

ADVERB

벌써	already
빨리	fast; quickly
아직	still; (not) yet
정말	really
참	really; very

EXPRESSION

- 그러게요. Yeah, I know.
- 에이 ~Oh, please!; Come on ~
- (저는 스물 다섯)이 돼요. (I) become (25 years old).

2. Additional Words & Expressions (II ~VI in the textbook)

NOUN

검은색	black color (p.66)
회색	grey color (p.66)
기분	feelings; mood (p.69)
연세	age [honorific word of 나이] (p.62)
생신	birthday [honorific word of 생일] (p.76)
세	age counter [honorific word of 살] (p.61)
동갑	same age (p.62) *~하고 동갑이다 to be the same age as~
직장인	businessman; businesswoman (p.67)
이십대	one's twenties (p.66)
삼십대	one's thirties (p.66)
사십대	one's forties (p.67)
오십대	one's fifties (p.67)
초등학생	elementary school student (p.67)
중학생	middle school student (p.67)
대학생	college student (p.67)
여자 아이	girl (p.67) [Literally, 여자 (woman) + 아이 (child)]
남자 아이	boy (p.67) [Literally, 남자 (man) + 아이 (child)]

VERB

보이다 to be seen (p.57)

ADJECTIVE

슬프다	to be sad (p.68)
젊다	to be young (p.76)
화나다	to be upset (p.68)

ADVERB

항상 always (p.58)

EXPRESSION

- 어떻게 되세요? (how old) are you?; How is it~? (p.61)

■ 저희 형 our older brother (spoken by a man) (p.62) [Literally, our older brother] *저희 is the humble form of 우리
■ 우리 오빠 my older brother (spoken by a woman) (p.62)[Literally, our older brother]
■ 몇 월 며칠이에요? What day is it? (p.63)
■ 김 사장님 president Kim (p.67)
■ 무슨 색 which color (p.66)
■ 농담하지 마세요! Don't make fun of me! (p.75)
■ (보고서를 끝내)야 되다 to have to (finish the report) (p.56)
■ 어려워 보이다 to look difficult (p.68)

Lesson 14 It is really cold today.

1. New words & expressions in Conversation

NOUN

여름 summer
올해 this year
가을 fall
표현 expression

VERB

죽다 to die

ADJECTIVE

(날씨 weather)
따뜻하다 (따뜻해요) to be warm
따뜻해지다 (따뜻해**져**요) to become warm
춥다 (추**워**요) to be cold (used for weather)

ADVERB

그냥 just
더 more
원래 originally [pronounced as 월래]
유난히 unusually; particularly

EXPRESSION

■ 14도 fourteen degrees
■ 네? What?
■ 뭐라구요? What did you say? *뭐라고요? is also used.
■ 언제쯤…? Around when …?
■ 이렇게 like this

2. Additional Words & Expressions (II ~VI in the textbook)

NOUN

집값 house price (p.88)
판 counter for pizza (p.80)
경기 economic conditions (p.88)
농구 basketball (p.84)
리포트 report, homework (p.81)
무료 free of charge (p.82)
수영장 swimming pool (p.83)
직원 employee (p.89)
서비스 service (p.89)
음식값 food price (p.89)
온라인 게임 online game (p.84)

(Time 세월)
금년 this year (p.79) * Sino-Korean word of the native Korean word 올해 [Literally, 올 this + 해 year]
내년 next year (p.79)
(Seasons 계절)
봄 spring (p.84)
겨울 winter (p.84)

올 봄 this spring [Literally, 올 this +봄 spring] (p.95)
올 여름 this summer [Literally, 올 this +여름 winter] (p.95)
올 가을 this fall[Literally, 올 this +fall] (p.95)
올 겨울 this winter [Literally, 올 this +봄 winter] (p.95)

(Weather 날씨)
기온 temperature (p.85)
낮기온 daytime temperature (p.85)
섭씨 Celsius (p.85)
화씨 Fahrenheit (p.85)
영상 above zero (p.86)
영하 below zero (p.86)

(Place 장소)
런던 London (p.86)
모스크바 Moscow (p.86)

베이징 Beijing (p.86)
밴쿠버 Vancouver (p.86)
부산 Busan(a port city in Korea) (p.86)

VERB

타다 to ride (p.83)
KTX를 타다 to take KTX (Korea Train Express) (p.83)
내려가다 to go down (p.98)
올라가다 to go up (p.98)
등산가다 to go hiking (p.82)
문자하다 to send a text message (p.82)

ADJECTIVE

(Weather 날씨)
서늘하다 to be cool; refreshing (p.84)
시원하다 to be cool (p.84)
덥다 (더워요) to be hot (p.84)
흐리다 (흐려요) to be cloudy (p.85)
맑다 to be clear (p.85)
쌀쌀하다 to be chilly (p.85)

깨끗하다 to be clean (p.89)
멀다 (멀어요) to be far (p.88)
부럽다 (부러워요) to be envious (p.88)
친해지다 to become close (p.88)
필요하다 to be necessary (p.80)

ADVERB

더 more (than ~) (p.95)

MARKER

-의Used to express possession
* LA의 봄 (spring of LA), 교실의 문 (the door of a classroom) * 에이미의 친구(Amy's friend), 선생님의 책 (teacher's book)

EXPRESSION

■ 이렇게 like this (p.78)
■ 구름이 끼다 to be cloudy (p.85)
■ 기온이 낮다 for temperature to be low (p.85)
■ 기온이 높다 for temperature to be high (p.85)
■ 바람이 불다 to be windy [Lit., for wind to blow] (p.85)
■ 눈이 오다 It snows. [Lit., for snow to come] (p.85)
■ 비가 오다 to rain [Lit., for rain to come] (p.83)
■ 시간이 걸리다 to take time [Lit., for time to take] (p.83)
■ 얼마 동안 for how long (p.87)
■ 놀러 오세요. Come and visit and have fun.(p.96)

■ 춥고 더워요. It is cold and hot.
[verb/adjective base + 고] (p.98)
덥고 추워요/추워져요
눈이 오고 기온이 낮아요/낮아져요
눈이 오고 흐려요/흐려져요
맑고 흐려요/흐려져요
비가 오고 바람이 불어요.

■ 겨울하고 여름 winter and summer[NOUN+ 하고 (and)] (p.98)
■ 날씨와 계절 weather and season[vowel-ending NOUN + 와 (and)] (p.98)
■ 겨울과 여름 winter and summer[consonant-ending NOUN + 과 (and)] (p.98)

■ 고향이 시카고지요? Your hometown is Chicago, isn't it?
*~지요/(reduced form) 죠 is used to seek for confirmation from the listener (Exercise 6, p.87)

Lesson 15 Let's go to eat lunch.

1. New words & expressions in Conversation

NOUN

근처 neighborhood; vicinity [e.g., 이 근처: nearby]
배 stomach; belly
불닭 spicy chicken [Literally, fire chicken]
순두부(국) soft tofu (soup)
점심 (1) lunch; (2) lunch time
정도 about ~; around ~ [Literally, degree]

PRONOUN

거기 there; that place [e.g., 거기서: at there]
우리 we (our, us)

ADJECTIVE

배고프다 to be hungry *배가 (안) 고프다 not to be hungry [Literally, for stomach to be hungry]

비싸다 to be expensive

ADVERB

아직 yet; still

EXPRESSION

■ 거긴 as for that place [shortened form of 거기는]

■ (코리아 하우스) 말이에요? Do you mean (Korean House)?

2. Additional Words & Expressions (II ~VI in the textbook)

NOUN

생선 fish (p.114)

가격 price (p.104)

대전 Daejeon (a city in Korea) (p.109)

체육관 gym (p.107)

유럽 Europe (p.111)

가수 singer (p.113)

썬글라스 sunglasses (p.114)

프레젠테이션 presentation (p.113)

한국 문화 Korean culture (p.109)

한국 역사 Korean history (p.109)

VERB

추천하다 to recommend (p.122)

시작하다 to start; begin (p.113)

여행하다 to travel (p.111)

취소되다 (취소되 + 어요→ 취소돼요) to be cancelled (p.106)

하다 to cost [Literally, to do]
*12불 하다 : It costs $12. (p.102)

EXPRESSION

■ ~도 하고 ~도 하다 to do~ and also do~ (p.109)

■ 어디 어디 where and where (p.111)

■ 요가를 배우다 to learn yoga (p.113)

■ 창문을 닫다 to close a window (p.113)

■ 연습(을) 하다 to practice (p.113)

Lesson 16 Happy birthday!

1. New words & expressions in Conversation

NOUN

생일 birthday

핸드폰 케이스 cell phone case

VERB

고르다 to choose

듣다 to hear; to listen to

쓰다 (1) to write; (2) to use

알다 to know

열다 to open

축하하다 to congratulate; to celebrate

ADVERB

마침 just in time

MARKER

~지만 ~but; although ~

-한테/-에게 to [person]

-한테(서) from [person]

-께 to [a person] [honorific word for -한테/-에게]

EXPRESSION

· 그럼요. for sure; Absolutely.

· ~기(가) 힘들다 to be hard/difficult to do ~

· 별 거 아니지만 ... It is nothing special but …

· 생일 축하해요! Happy birthday!

2. Additional Words & Expressions (II ~VI in the textbook)

NOUN

소식 news (p.128)

약국 pharmacy (p.129)

수학 문제 math problem (p.129)

화장실 bathroom (p.133)
피트니스 센터 fitness center (p.133)
사우나 sauna (p.133)
레스토랑 restaurant (p.133)

지하철 역 subway station (p.133)
교통 transportation (p.133)
버스 정류장 bus stop (p.133)

스피킹 콘테스트 speaking contest (p.136)
자켓 jacket (p.139)

대학입학 university matriculation; college admission (p.153)
졸업 graduation (p.153)
합격 passing (an exam); being accepted (p.151)
승진 promotion (p.151)
서점 상품권 book store gift card (p.151)
커피 상품권 coffee gift card (p.151)

VERB
구경하다 to look at; to go sightseeing (p.135)
드리다 (드려요) to give (something) to an older person (p.127)
*드리다 is the humble form of 주다
*주시다 is the subject honorific form of 주다
고치다 (고쳐요) to repair; to fix (p.136)
나오다 (나와요) to come out (p.139)
갔다오다 (갔다와요) to go and come back (p.140)
물어 보다 (물어 봐요) to ask (a thing) (for a person) (p.136) *(a thing)을 (a person)한테/에게 물어보다

ADJECTIVE
불편하다 to be inconvenient; to be uncomfortable (p.133)
넓다 to be wide; to be spacious (p.133)
오래되다 (for something) to be old (p.133)
고장나다 to break down; to become out of order (p.136)

EXPRESSION
■ 이야기를 하다 to tell; to tell a story (p.129)
■ ~가까이에 close to ~ (p.133)
■ 친구를 사귀다 to make a friend (p.135)
■ 장학금을 신청하다 to apply for a scholarship (p.136)
■ ~아도/~어도 돼요? Is it okay to ~?; Can I ~? (p.137)
■ 새 음악 new music (p.139)
■ 생일 선물로 for/as a birthday present (p.125)
■ ~을/를 사면서 in buying/choosing ~
■ 마음에 들다 to be one's liking (p.151)
■ ~고 싶다 to want to ~ (p.136)
■ -에 참가하다 to participate in ~ (p.136)
■ 오래간만(에) a long time since; for the first time in many days[years] (p.129)
■ ~아야/~어야 되다 (~아야/~어야 돼요) have to ~; should (p.138)

Lesson 17 You speak Korean very well.

1. New words & expressions in Conversation

NOUN
기자 journalist; reporter
동안 during~; for~
영어 English
한국말 the Korean language

VERB
다니다 to attend
알다 to know
전공하다 to major in (at a university)
졸업하다 to graduate

ADVERB
더 more

MARKER
-도 (1) also, too; (2) even ~

EXPRESSION
■ ~을/를 잘 못해요. (I) am not that good at ~.

■ 한국말(을) 참 잘하시네요! Oh, (you) speak Korean really well!
■ 한국말로 기자죠? Is (it) gija in Korean, right?

2. Additional Words & Expressions (II ~VI in the textbook)

NOUN

한국말 the Korean language (p.157)
한국어 중급반 intermediate level of Korean (p.161)
러시아어 Russian language (p.162)
러시아어를 하다 to speak Russian (p.162)
외국어 foreign language (p.162)

개월 counter for a number of months (p.183)
1개월 [일 개월] 1 month (p.183)
2개월 [이 개월] 2 months (p.183)
6개월 [육 개월] 6 months (p.183)
10개월 [십 개월] 10 months (p.183)

인기 popularity (p.160)
원작 original work (p.160)
여행 travel (p.161)
좋은 직장 good job (p.161)
계획 plan (p.162)
피구 dodgeball (p.162)
요가 yoga (p.162)
요리 cooking (p.170)
예매 reservation (p.160)
그림 그리기 painting; drawing (p.170)
포토샵 Photoshop (p.170)
프로그래밍 programming (p.170)
엑셀 Excel (p.170)
아르바이트 part-time job (p.174)
극장 movie theater (p.160)
학원 a private academy (p.173)

발표 presentation (p.176)
교수 professor (p.173)
연구 논문 research paper (p.173)
사무실 office (p.164)
히터 heater (p.164)
국제 관계학 international studies (p.167)

VERB

(히터를) 틀다 to turn on (a heater) (p.164)
떨리다 (떨려요) to feel nervous (p.177)
졸리다 (졸려요) to feel sleepy (p.177)

ADVERB

천천히 slowly (p.163)
열심히 diligently (p.173)

MARKER

-으로/-로 by/in/with [instrument/means] (p.162)
-부터 from [time] (p.162)

EXPRESSION

■ 프로그래머를 하다 to work as a programmer (p.162)
■ 자격증을 따다 to get a license/certificate (p.173)
■ 배가 고프다 to be hungry (p.176)
■ 약을 먹다 to take medicine (p.178)
■ 연습(을) 하다 to practice (p.172)
■ 인기(가) 있다/없다 to be popular/ not to be popular (p.176)
■ 인기(가) 많다 to be very popular (p.160)
■ 추위를 잘 타다 to be very sensitive to cold (p.164)
■ 기억이 나다 to remember [Literally, for a memory to come up]

Lesson 18 Would you like to go on a blind date?

1. New words & expressions in Conversation

NOUN

남자 친구 boyfriend
베트남계 미국인 Vietnamese American
사진 photo
소개팅 blind date
엔지니어 engineer
자동차 car; automobile

PRE-NOUN

무슨 what kind of ~; what ~ (e.g., 무슨 일)

ADVERB

되게 really; very (colloquial)

진짜(로) really

MARKER

-이랑/-랑(1) with ~; (2) ~ and [colloquial form of -하고/-와/과]

EXPRESSION

■ 소개팅(을) 하실래요? Would (you) like a blind date?

■ 잘나가다 to be successful; to be in high demand

■ 잘생기다 to be handsome; good-looking

2. Additional words & expressions (II ~VI in the textbook)

NOUN

제주도 Jeju Island (p.191)
워싱턴 Washington (p.191)
건물 building (p.197)
시장 market (p.209)
동네 neighborhood (p.195)

VERB

다운 받다 to download (p.191)
지내다 to spend (time); to live with (someone) (p.191)
소개하다 to introduce (p.187)

ADJECTIVE

키가 크다 (키가 커요) to be tall [Lit. height is big] (p.203)
키가 보통이다 to be of average height [Lit. height is average] (p.203)
키가 작다 to be short [Lit. height is small] (p.203)
뚱뚱하다 to be fat (p.203)
통통하다 to be chubby (p.203)
날씬하다 to be thin (p.203)
마르다 (말라요) to be skinny (p.203)
아름답다 (아름다워요) to be beautiful (p.203)
잘생기다 (잘생겼어요) to be handsome; good-looking (p.203)
*The past tense form (잘생겼어요) is used to describe one's present appearance!
못생기다 (못생겼어요) to be ugly (p.203)
*The past tense form (못생겼어요) is used to describe one's present appearance!
귀엽다 (귀여워요) to be cute (p.203)
머리가 짧다 (for one's hair) to be short (p.203)
머리가 길다 (for one's hair) to be long (p.203)
유명하다 to be famous (p.202)
인기가 많다 to be popular (p.209)

ADVERB

가장 most/best (p.195)
제일 best (p.192)

EXPRESSION

■ (직장을 찾을) 수 있다 to be able to (get/look for a good job) (p.210)

■ 잘 지내다 to be doing well (p.191)

■ 요즘 어떻게 지내세요? How are you doing these days? (p.191)

■ 그동안 어떻게 지내셨어요? How have you been doing? (p.191)

■ (날씨가 좋)을 것 같다 It seems that (the weather would be good.(p.199)
*~을/ㄹ 것 같다: It seems that ~

■ (핫도그를) 사 드릴게요. I'll buy a hotdog for you. (Exercise 14, p.208)

Lesson 19 What do you usually do when you have time?

1. New words & expressions in Conversation

NOUN

글 writing
레시피 recipe
블로그 blog
사람들 people [사람 person + 들 plural marker]
스트레스 stress
요리 cooking
요리사 cook; chef

일주일 a week; one week
취미 hobby
파워 블로거 influencer
해물 파전 seafood pancake

EXPRESSION
■ 스트레스도 풀고 relieving (my) stress
■ 요리사 해도 되겠어요! (You) should become a chef!; You can become a chef!
■ 취미로 해요. (I) do (it) as a hobby.

2. Additional words & expressions (II ~VI in the textbook)

NOUN
교환학생 exchange student (p.220)
지하철 subway (p.223)
마라톤 marathon (p.225)
달리기 running (p.225)
돼지 불고기 Korean spicy pork stir-fry (p.225)
수영 선수 swimming athlete (p.236)
화장실 bathroom; restroom (p.236)
이틀 two days (p.236)
정도 or so (e.g., 한 번 정도 once or so) (p.238)
설거지 dishwashing (p.241)
*설거지를 하다 to do dishwashing (p.241)
빨래 laundry (p.241)
*빨래를 하다to do laundry (p241)
미용 beauty (p.247)
미용실 hairdresser's; beauty salon (p.238)
스타크래프트 Starcraft (online game) (p.247)
영양사 nutritionist (p.247)
미용관리사 beautician (p.247)
연구 research (p.247)
비행기 airplane (p.219)
독서/책읽기 reading (as a hobby) (p.243)
드라마 감상 watching dramas (as a hobby) (p.243)
등산(을 하다) (to go) hiking (p.248)

PRE-NOUN
그런 such; that kind/sort of (e.g., 그런 남자 such man) (p.228)

VERB
미끄러지다 to slip (p.236)
놀다 to have fun (p.236); to hang out

ADJECTIVE
싫어하다 to hate; dislike (p.223)
외식하다 to eat outside (p.238)

MARKER
쯤 about; around (p.237)

EXPRESSION
■ 고등학생 때 at the time when I was a high school student (p.236)
■ 잠을 자다 to sleep (p.236)
■ 출장 가다 to go on a business trip (p.236)
■ 여러 가지 various things (p.241)
■ 이것 저것 this (thing) and that (thing) (p.248)
■ 아무거나 다 anything [아무 거나 anything; 다 all] (p.241)
■ 늦게까지 until late (p.234)

Lesson 20 How was the blind date last time?

1. New words & expressions in Conversation

NOUN
베트남 Vietnam
별 star
별카페 Star Cafe
서로 each other
소개팅 blind date

VERB
기다리다 to wait
망가지다 to break down; to be out of order; to be destroyed
망하다 to be messed up

ADJECTIVE
아쉽다 to be a shame; be sorry; feel sad

ADVERB

참 (1) by the way; (2) really, very

EXPRESSION

- ~말이에요 I mean ~
- 어땠어요? How was (it)?
- 연락을 하다 to contact [someone]; to contact [some place]
- 지난번 last time

2. Additional words & expressions (II ~VI in the textbook)

NOUN

학기 school/academic term (e.g., semester; quarter) (p.269)
*가을 학기 (Fall term), 겨울 학기 (Winter term), 봄학기 (Spring term), 여름 학기 (Summer term)

PRONOUN

다들 everybody; everyone (p.272)

VERB

갖다 주다 to bring (thing) to (person) (p.264)
망치다 to have something messed up; screw something up (p.277)

걱정(을) 하다 to worry (p.268)
걱정(을) 하다 to worry (p.268)
기대(를) 하다 to expect (p.268)
시작(을) 하다 to start (something) (p.268)
사용(을) 하다 to use (p.268)
완성(을) 하다 to complete (p.268)
이해(를) 하다 to understand (p.268)
연락(을) 하다 to contact (p.268)
준비(를) 하다 to prepare (p.268)
해결(을) 하다 to solve (p.268)

걱정(이) 되다 to be worried (p.268)
기대(가) 되다 to be expected (p.268)
시작(이) 되다 (for something) to be started (p.268)
사용(이) 되다 to be used (p.268)
완성(이) 되다 to be completed (p.268)
이해(가) 되다 to be understood (p.268)
연락(이) 되다 to be contacted (p.268)
준비(가) 되다 to be prepared (p.268)
해결(이) 되다 to be solved (p.268)

ADVERB

바로 immediately; right away (p.264)

EXPRESSION

- (선물을 사)야 되다 to have to (buy a gift) (p.267)
  *~아야/~어야 되다 "have to ~"

Appendix Ⅲ: Grammar (organized by lesson)

BEGINNING 1

Lesson 1 Hi!

(1) NOUN이에요/예요. "am/are/is NOUN"
(2) NOUN이요/요. "(It is) NOUN"
(3) 성함이 어떻게 되세요? "May I have your name?"
(4) 뭐예요? "What is this?"

Lesson 2 I am an American.

(1) A은/는 B이에요/예요 "A is B"
(2) Name + 씨 "Mr. ... ; Mrs. ... ; Miss ..."
(3) NOUN은요?/는요? "What about ~?; How about ~?"
(4) Questions in Korean

Lesson 3 Are you a college student?

(1) A은/는 NOUN이/가 아니에요. "am/are/is not NOUN"
(2) 몇 학년이에요?" "What year are you in school?"
(3) 저도 ~ 이에요/예요. "I am also ~."

Lesson 4 What are you doing?

(1) Verbs and adjectives
(2) Conjugating verbs and adjectives
(3) Verb/Adjective + 아요/어요. sentence ending
(4) 안 + verb/adjective "not ~"
(5) "Subject-Object-Verb" (SOV) word order

Lesson 5 What do you do?

(1) Verb/Adjective + 으세요/세요. sentence ending
(2) 무슨 + NOUN "What ~; What kind of ~"
(3) Make a request or suggestion using ~으세요/~세요.
(4) … 잘하시겠어요. "You must be good at ..."

Lesson 6 How is your dorm?

(1) place name + -에 "in/on/at/to + place name"
(2) NOUN은/는/이/가 있어요 & 없어요.
(3) 근데 "but"
(4) NOUN은/는/이/가 + 어때요? "How is NOUN?"

Lesson 7 May I have your phone number?

(1) The subject-focus marker -이/-가
(2) The topic/contrast marker -은/-는
(3) Reading phone numbers
(4) Verb base + 을게요/ㄹ게요. "I will ~"
(5) NOUN은/는/이/가 어떻게 되세요? "What is~?"
(6) Expressing possession

Lesson 8 I'll buy it today.

(1) Verb base + 을래요?/래요? "Would you like to ~?; Do you want to~?"
(2) Korean numerals for the numbers: 1~10
(3) 그럼, ~ "if so ~; Well, then ~"
(4) NOUN + 하고 "~ and ; with ~"

Lesson 9 Do you have any siblings?

(1) Verb/Adjective + 잖아요. "You know"
(2) 여기; 거기; 저기 "here; there; over there"
(3) 있으세요 and 계세요.
(4) 혹시 "I wonder ~; Do you happen to ~?"
(5) 좀 verb base + 으세요/세요. "Please do ~."
(6) 잠시만요. "Just a second, please."

Lesson 10 How many people are coming?

(1) Native-Korean and Sino-Korean numerals beyond 10
(2) Using native Korean numerals
(3) Using Sino-Korean numerals
(4) Verb/Adjective + 을까요?/ㄹ까요? "Shall I/we ~?; Do you think ~?
(5) 그렇게 ~? "that (much) ~?"

BEGINNING 2

Lesson 11 What time is it now?

(1) Telling time in Korean (Korean numerals)
(2) Verb/Adjective base + 아서요/어서요. "It is because ..."
(3) NOUN에 vs. NOUN에서 "at/on/in/from/to ~"

Lesson 12 Please have some *gimbap.*

(1) Past tense: Verb/Adjective base + 았어요/었어요.
(2) Object marker : -을/-를
(3) Who ... What ... Verb/Adjective.
(4) ~네요 : Expressing the speaker's spontaneous reaction or realization

Lesson 13 I am now becoming 25 years old.

(1) Talking about one's age (Korean numerals)
(2) Expressing a date
(3) Noun + 으로 보여요/로 보여요. "to look like ~"
(4) Adjective + 아/어 보여요. "to look ~"

Lesson 14 It is really cold today.

(1) ~이면/~면, ~으면/~면 "if ~; when ~"
(2) Weather expressions
(3) ~아 지다/~어 지다. "to become ~"
(4) ~아 죽다/~어 죽다. "~ to death"

Lesson 15 Let's go to eat lunch

(1) Responding to a negative question : 안 ~; ~ 지 않
(2) Verb base + 으러 가다/러 가다. "to go for the purpose of ~"
(3) Verb base + 아 봤다/어 봤다. "to have done ~"
(4) Verb/Adjective + ~는데, ~은/~ㄴ데, ~인데 : Giving background information

Lesson 16 Happy birthday!

(1) NOUN한테; NOUN한테서 "to [person]; from [person]"
(2) Verb/Adjective + 지만 " ... but; although ..."
(3) Verb base + 아/어 보세요. "Please try doing ~."
(4) Verb base + 아/어 봐도 돼요? "Is it okay to try to~ ?; May I try to~ ?"
(5) Non-honorific speech level : The ~아 speech style

Lesson 17 You speak Korean very well!

(1) Verb/Adjective +을/ㄹ 거예요. "will ~ [prediction; volition]"
(2) Verb/Adjective + 지요?/죠? : Seeking the listener's agreement
(3) NOUN+으로/로 "by~; in ~; with ~" [Instrument/means]
(4) 잘해요; 못해요; 잘 못해요. : Expressing one's ability
(5) Verb base + 으려고/려고 하다 "intend to ~"
Verb base + 으려고/려고 "intending to ~"
(6) Verb/Adjective base + 는데도, 은/ㄴ데도, 인데도 "even though ~; even if ~"

Lesson 18 Would you like to go on a blind date?

(1) NOUN + 동안; Verb base + 는 동안 "during/for ~; while ~ing"
(2) Noun-modifying forms of verbs
(3) Noun-modifying forms of adjectives
(4) Describing people's appearances
(5) 이; 그; 저 "this; that; that over there"
(6) ~거든요. "It is because ···; ··· , you see."

Lesson 19 What do you usually do when you have time?

(1) Verb/Adjective + 다가 : Depicting transition from one event to another
(2) 어떤 + NOUN "which ~/what kind of ~; some/any ~"
(3) The honorific speech level : The ~습니다 speech style
(4) Verb/Adjective + 겠 ~ "must ~"
(5) Frequency expressions
(6) [NOUN 1]도 Verb/Adjective고 [NOUN 2]도 Verb/Adjective고 : "to do NOUN 1 and to do NOUN 2 as well"

Lesson20 How was the blind date last time?

(1) 주다, 주시다, 드리다. "to give [verbs of giving]"
(2) ~아 주다/~어 주다. "to do (something) for (someone)"
~아 주시다/~어 주시다.
~아 드리다/~어 드리다.
(3) ~기로 하다. "to decide to ~"
(4) -을/-를 하다. "(for someone) to do (something)"
-이/-가 되다. "for something) to be done"
(5) 지난/이번/다음 + NOUN "last/this/next ~"

Appendix Ⅳ: Speech levels, styles, and types

The table shows two speech levels (Honorific vs. Non-honorific), four speech styles, and four speech types under each style. For rules, refer to Lesson 4 (Beginning Korean 1), Lesson 16 & 19 (Beginning Korean 2) and Lesson 1 (Intermediate Korean 1).

<table>
<tr><th rowspan="4">Sentence types</th><th colspan="4">Speech levels</th></tr>
<tr><th colspan="2">Honorific</th><th colspan="2">Non-honorific</th></tr>
<tr><th colspan="2">More Formal ⟪——⟫ More Informal</th><th colspan="2">More Formal ⟪——⟫ More Informal</th></tr>
<tr><th>"~습니다" style
[Lesson 19]</th><th>"~아요" style
[Lesson 4]</th><th>"~는다" style
[Intermediate, L2]</th><th>"~아" style
[Lesson 16]</th></tr>
<tr><td rowspan="2">Statement (with falling intonation)</td><td>~습니다/~ㅂ니다.</td><td>~아요/~어요.</td><td>~는다/~ㄴ다/~다.</td><td>~아/~어.</td></tr>
<tr><td>1. 책을 읽습니다.
2. 친구를 만납니다.
I read a book.
I meet a friend.</td><td>1. 친구를 만나요.
2. 책을 읽어요.
I meet a friend.
I read a book.</td><td>1. 친구를 만난다.
2. 책을 읽는다.
3. 한국어가 좋다.
I meet a friend.
I read a book.
Korean is good.</td><td>1. 친구를 만나.
2. 책을 읽어.
I meet a friend.
I read a book.</td></tr>
<tr><td rowspan="2">Question (with rising intonation)</td><td>~습니까?/~ㅂ니까?</td><td>~아요/~어요?</td><td>~니? or ~냐?</td><td>~아/~어?</td></tr>
<tr><td>1. 책을 읽습니까?
2. 친구를 만납니까?
Do you read a book?
Do you meet a friend?</td><td>1. 친구를 만나요?
2. 책을 읽어요?
Do you meet a friend?
Do you read a book?</td><td>1. 친구를 만나니?
2. 책을 읽니?
Do you meet a friend?
Do you read a book?</td><td>1. 친구를 만나?
2. 책을 읽어?
Do you meet a friend?
Do you read a book?</td></tr>
<tr><td rowspan="2">Proposal</td><td>-읍시다/~ㅂ시다.</td><td>~아요/~어요.</td><td>~자.</td><td>~아/~어.</td></tr>
<tr><td>1. 책을 읽읍시다.
2. 친구를 만납시다.
Let us read a book.
Let us meet a friend.</td><td>1. 친구를 만나요.
2. 책을 읽어요.
Let us meet a friend.
Let us read a book.</td><td>1. 친구를 만나자.
2. 책을 읽자.
Let us meet a friend.
Let us read a book.</td><td>1. 친구를 만나.
2. 책을 읽어.
Let us meet a friend.
Let us read a book.</td></tr>
<tr><td rowspan="2">Command</td><td>~으십시오/~십시오.
* ~으시오/~시오.</td><td>~아요/~어요.</td><td>~아라/~어라.</td><td>~아/~어.</td></tr>
<tr><td>1. 책을 읽으십시오.
2. 친구를 만나십시오.
Read a book.
Meet a friend.</td><td>1. 친구를 만나요.
2. 책을 읽어요.
Meet a friend.
Read a book.</td><td>1. 친구를 만나라.
2. 책을 읽어라.
Meet a friend.
Read a book.</td><td>1. 친구를 만나.
2. 책을 읽어.
Meet a friend.
Read a book.</td></tr>
</table>

* ~으시오/~시오 in commands is rarely used in daily conversation. It is usually used on sign boards for the public or in written (formal) documents.

Appendix Ⅴ: Irregular verbs and adjectives

1. "ㄷ" irregular verbs: ㄷ changes to ㄹ when followed by a vowel.

걷다 (to walk) : 걷 → 걸 + 어요 → 걸어요
걷 → 걸 + 으세요 → 걸으세요
걷 → 걸 + 었어요 → 걸었어요
걷 → 걸 + 을 거예요 → 걸을 거예요
걷 → 걸 + 으니까 → 걸으니까
걷 → 걸 + 으면 → 걸으면

Exceptions: *받다 (to receive) → 받아요
*쏟다 (to pour) → 쏟아요
*닫다 (to close) → 닫아요

Verb/Adj	ㅂ니다/습니다	아요/어요	(으)세요	았어요/었어요	(으)ㄹ 거예요	(으)니까	(으)면
걷다 (to walk)	걷습니다	걸어요	걸으세요	걸었어요	걸을 거예요	걸으니까	걸으면
듣다 (to listen)	듣습니다	들어요	들으세요	들었어요	들을 거예요	들으니까	들으면
묻다 (to ask)	묻습니다	물어요	물으세요	물었어요	물을 거예요	물으니까	물으면
싣다 (to load)	싣습니다	실어요	실으세요	실었어요	실을 거예요	실으니까	실으면

2. "ㄹ" irregular verbs/adjectives: ㄹ in the base drops when followed by ㄴ, ㅂ, and ㅅ.

놀다: (to hang out) 놀 → 놀 + 는 → 노는
놀 → 놀 + ㅂ니다 → 놉니다
놀 → 놀 + 세요 → 노세요

Verb/Adj	ㅂ니다/습니다	아요/어요	았어요/었어요	(으)ㄹ 거예요	(으)니까	(으)면	는군요	(으)세요
놀다 (to hang out)	놉니다	놀아요	놀았어요	놀 거예요	노니까	놀면	노는군요	노세요
들다 (to carry)	듭니다	들어요	들었어요	들 거예요	드니까	들면	드는군요	드세요
만들다 (to make)	만듭니다	만들어요	만들었어요	만들 거예요	만드니까	만들면	만드는군요	만드세요
멀다 (to be far)	멉니다	멀어요	멀었어요	멀 거예요	머니까	멀면	멀군요	
살다 (to live)	삽니다	살아요	살았어요	살 거예요	사니까	살면	사는군요	사세요
알다 (to know)	압니다	알아요	알았어요	알 거예요	아니까	알면	아는군요	아세요
열다 (to open, unlock)	엽니다	열어요	열었어요	열 거예요	여니까	열면	여는군요	여세요
팔다 (to sell)	팝니다	팔아요	팔았어요	팔 거예요	파니까	팔면	파는군요	파세요
힘들다 (to be difficult, tiring)	힘듭니다	힘들어요	힘들었어요	힘들 거예요	힘드니까	힘들면	힘들군요	

3. "ㅂ" irregular verbs/adjectives: ㅂ in the base changes to 우 (or *오 for a few words) when followed by a vowel.

Vowel contraction

쉽다 (to be easy) : 쉽 → 쉬 + 우 + 어요 → 쉬워요

쉽 → 쉬 + 우 + 세요 → 쉬우세요

쉽 → 쉬 + 우 + 었어요 → 쉬웠어요

쉽 → 쉬 + 우 + ㄹ 거예요 → 쉬울 거예요

쉽 → 쉬 + 우 + 니까 → 쉬우니까

쉽 → 쉬 + 우 + 면 → 쉬우면

*Exceptions: 집다 (to hold) → 집어요

씹다 (to chew) → 씹어요

Verb/Adj	습니다	아요/어요	았어요/었어요	을 거예요	으니까	아서/어서	으면	지만
가볍다 (to be light)	가볍습니다	가벼워요	가벼웠어요	가벼울 거예요	가벼우니까	가벼워서	가벼우면	가볍지만
고맙다 (to be thankful)	고맙습니다	고마워요	고마웠어요	고마울 거예요	고마우니까	고마워서	고마우면	고맙지만
귀엽다 (to be cute)	귀엽습니다	귀여워요	귀여웠어요	귀여울 거예요	귀여우니까	귀여워서	귀여우면	귀엽지만
눕다 (to lie down)	눕습니다	누워요	누웠어요	누울 거예요	누우니까	누워서	누우면	눕지만
더럽다 (to be dirty)	더럽습니다	더러워요	더러웠어요	더러울 거예요	더러우니까	더러워서	더러우면	더럽지만
덥다 (to be hot) (weather)	덥습니다	더워요	더웠어요	더울 거예요	더우니까	더워서	더우면	덥지만
뜨겁다 (to be hot) (temperature)	뜨겁습니다	뜨거워요	뜨거웠어요	뜨거울 거예요	뜨거우니까	뜨거워서	뜨거우면	뜨겁지만
무겁다 (to be heavy)	무겁습니다	무거워요	무거웠어요	무거울 거예요	무거우니까	무거워서	무거우면	무겁지만
맵다 (to be spicy)	맵습니다	매워요	매웠어요	매울 거예요	매우니까	매워서	매우면	맵지만
밉다 (to be hateful)	밉습니다	미워요	미웠어요	미울 거예요	미우니까	미워서	미우면	밉지만
쉽다 (to be easy)	쉽습니다	쉬워요	쉬웠어요	쉬울 거예요	쉬우니까	쉬워서	쉬우면	쉽지만
어렵다 (to be difficult)	어렵습니다	어려워요	어려웠어요	어려울 거예요	어려우니까	어려워서	어려우면	어렵지만
차갑다 (to be cold) (temperature)	차갑습니다	차가워요	차가웠어요	차가울 거예요	차가우니까	차가워서	차가우면	차갑지만
춥다 (to be cold) (weather)	춥습니다	추워요	추웠어요	추울 거예요	추우니까	추워서	추우면	춥지만
*곱다 (to be pretty)	곱습니다	고와요	고왔어요	고울 거예요	고우니까	고와서	고우면	곱지만
*돕다 (to help)	돕습니다	도와요	도왔어요	도울 거예요	도우니까	도와서	도우면	돕지만

4. "ㅅ" irregular verbs/adjectives: ㅅ in the base drops when followed by a vowel.

낫다 (to get better) : 낫 → 낫 + 아요 → 나아요
낫 → 낫 + 았어요 → 나았어요
낫 → 낫 + 을 거예요 → 나을 거예요
낫 → 낫 + 으면 → 나으면

Verb/Adj	ㅂ니다/습니다	아요/어요	았어요/었어요	(으)ㄹ 거예요	(으)면	고	지만
낫다 (to get better)	낫습니다	나아요	나았어요	나을 거예요	나으면	낫고	낫지만
잇다 (to connect)	잇습니다	이어요	이었어요	이을 거예요	이으면	잇고	잇지만
짓다 (to build)	짓습니다	지어요	지었어요	지을 거예요	지으면	짓고	짓지만
붓다 (to pour; to swell)	붓습니다	부어요	부었어요	부을 거예요	부으면	붓고	붓지만

5. "ㅎ" irregular adjectives: ㅎ in the base drops when followed by a vowel.

Vowel contraction

노랗다 (to be yellow): 노랗 → 노랗 + 아요 → 노래요
노랗 → 노랗 + 았어요 → 노랬어요
노랗 → 노랗 + 아서 → 노래서

Verb/Adj	ㅂ니다/습니다	아요/어요	았어요/었어요	어서/아서	고	지만
까맣다 (be black)	까맣습니다	까매요	까맸어요	까매서	까맣고	까맣지만
하얗다 (be white)	하얗습니다	하얘요	하얬어요	하얘서	하얗고	하얗지만
그렇다 (be so; be that way)	그렇습니다	그래요	그랬어요	그래서	그렇고	그렇지만
이렇다 (be this way)	이렇습니다	이래요	이랬어요	이래서	이렇고	이렇지만
어떻다 (be how)	어떻습니까?	어때요?	어땠어요?	어때서?	어떻고?	--

6. "르" irregular verbs/adjectives: — in 르 in the base drops and additional ㄹ is added, when followed by a vowel.

모르다 (to not know) : 모르 → 모르 + 아요 → 몰ㄹ + 아요 → 몰라요 (contraction)
모르 → 모르 + 았어요 → 몰ㄹ + 았어요 → 몰랐어요
모르 → 모르 + 아서 → 몰ㄹ + 아서 → 몰라서

Verb/Adj	ㅂ니다/습니다	아요/어요	었어요/았어요	(으)ㄹ 거예요	(으)니까	어서/-아서	(으)면	지만
고르다 (to choose)	고릅니다	골라요	골라요	고를 거예요	고르니까	골라서	고르면	고르지만
누르다 (to press)	누릅니다	눌러요	눌렀어요	누를 거예요	누르니까	눌러서	누르면	누르지만
다르다 (be different)	다릅니다	달라요	달랐어요	다를 거예요	다르니까	달라서	다르면	다르지만
모르다 (to not know)	모릅니다	몰라요	몰랐어요	모를 거예요	모르니까	몰라서	모르면	모르지만
배(가) 부르다 (to be full)	배부릅니다	배불러요	배불렀어요	배부를 거예요	배부르니까	배불러서	배부르면	배부르지만
부르다 (to call; to sing)	부릅니다	불러요	불렀어요	부를 거예요	부르니까	불러서	부르면	부르지만
빠르다 (be fast)	빠릅니다	빨라요	빨랐어요	빠를 거예요	빠르니까	빨라서	빠르면	빠르지만

7. "ㅡ" irregular verbs/adjectives: ㅡ in the base drops when followed by a vowel.

바쁘다 (to be busy) : 바쁘 → 바쁘 + 아요 → 바ㅃ + 아요 → 바빠요 (contraction)
바쁘 → 바쁘 + 았어요 → 바ㅃ + 았어요 → 바빴어요
바쁘 → 바쁘 + 아서 → 바ㅃ + 아서 → 바빠서

Verb/Adj	ㅂ니다/습니다	아요/어요	았어요/었어요	(으)ㄹ 거예요	(으)면	고	지만
나쁘다 (to be bad)	나쁩니다	나빠요	나빴어요	나쁠 거예요	나쁘면	나쁘고	나쁘지만
배(가) 고프다 (to be hungry)	배고픕니다	배고파요	배고팠어요	배고플 거예요	배고프면	배고프고	배고프지만
바쁘다 (to be busy)	바쁩니다	바빠요	바빴어요	바쁠 거예요	바쁘면	바쁘고	바쁘지만
크다 (to be big)	큽니다	커요	컸어요	클 거예요	크면	크고	크지만
슬프다 (to be sad)	슬픕니다	슬퍼요	슬펐어요	슬플 거예요	슬프면	슬프고	슬프지만
쓰다 (to write; to use)	씁니다	써요	썼어요	쓸 거예요	쓰면	쓰고	쓰지만
아프다 (to be sick)	아픕니다	아파요	아팠어요	아플 거예요	아프면	아프고	아프지만
예쁘다 (to be pretty)	예쁩니다	예뻐요	예뻤어요	예쁠 거예요	예쁘면	예쁘고	예쁘지만

Appendix Ⅵ: Noun-modifying forms

The following show the noun-modifying forms of verbs and adjectives. For more details, refer to Lesson 18 in Beginning 2.

1. NOUN-MODIFYING FORMS OF VERBS

Dictionary form	Past tense form	Present tense form	Future tense form
Verb base + 다	Verb base + 은/ㄴ+ NOUN	Verb base + 는 + NOUN	Verb base +을/ㄹ+ NOUN
Verb base (ending in a consonant): 먹다	먹은 음식	먹는 음식	먹을 음식
Verb base (ending in a vowel): 가다	간 식당	가는 식당	갈 식당

▶Note 1: The following table shows noun-modifying verb forms according to tenses.

Dictionary form	Past tense form	Present tense form	Future tense form
Verb base + 다	Verb base + 은/ㄴ	Verb base + 는	Verb base + 을/ㄹ
읽다 (to reda) 보다 (to see) 가다 (to go) 사다 (to buy) 주문하다 (to order) 먹다 (to eat) 드시다 (to eat) 가르치다 (to teach) 만나다 (to meet) 시작하다 (to begin) 일어나다 (to get up) 끝나다 (to end) 공부하다 (to study)	읽은 본 간 산 주문한 먹은 드신 가르친 만난 시작한 일어난 끝난 공부한	읽는 보는 가는 사는 주문하는 먹는 드시는 가르치는 만나는 시작하는 일어나는 끝나는 공부하는	읽을 볼 갈 살 주문할 먹을 드실 가르칠 만날 시작할 일어날 끝날 공부할

▶Note 2: For the noun-modifying form of a "ㄹ" irregular verb, follow the rules, as shown in the table below.

Dictionary form	Past tense form	Present tense form	Future tense form
Verb base + 다	Verb base + ㄴ	Verb base + 는	Verb base + ㄹ
살다 (to live) 만들다 (to make) 팔다 (to sell)	(살 → 살+ㄴ) 산 (만들 → 만들+ ㄴ)만 든 (팔 → 팔+ㄴ) 판	(살 → 살 + 는) 사는 (만들 → 만들 + 는) 만드는 (팔 → 팔 + 는) 파는	(살 → 살 + ㄹ) 살 (만들 → 만들 + ㄹ) 만들 (팔 → 팔 + ㄹ) 팔

▶Note 3: The noun-modifying forms of ㄷ irregular verbs are:

Dictionary form	Past tense form	Present tense form	Future tense form
Verb base + 다	Verb base + 은	Verb base + 는	Verb base + 을
듣다 (to hear) 걷다 (to walk) 묻다 (to ask)	(듣 → 들 + 은) 들은 (걷 → 걸 + 은) 걸은 (묻 → 물 + 은) 물은 Rule: 1) ㄷ changes to ㄹ 2) 은 is attached	듣는 걷는 묻는	(듣 → 들 + 을) 들을 (걷 → 걸 + 을) 걸을 (묻 → 물 + 을) 물을 Rule: 1) ㄷ changes to ㄹ 2) 을 is attached

▶**Note 3:** The following table shows the noun-modifying forms of the 이다 verbs.

Dictionary form	Past tense form	Present tense form	Future tense form
Noun이다 **Noun다**	**Noun이 + 던 /Noun이었+던** **Noun + 던 /Noun였+던**	**Noun이 + ㄴ** **Noun이 + ㄴ**	**Noun이 + ㄹ** **Noun이 + ㄹ**
학생이다 (to be) 가수다 (to be)	학생이던/학생이었던 가수던/가수였던	학생인 가수인	학생일 가수일

2. NOUN-MODIFYING FORMS OF ADJECTIVES

Dictionary form	Past tense form	Present tense form	Future tense form
Adjective base + 다	**Adjective base + 던**	**Adjective base + 은/ㄴ**	**Adjective base + 을/ㄹ**
Adjective base (ending in a consonant): 좋다	좋던 음식	좋은 음식	좋을 것
Adjective base (ending in a vowel):비싸다	비싸던 식당	비싼 식당	비쌀 것

▶**Note 1:** The following table shows noun-modifying adjective forms according to tenses.

Dictionary form	Past tense form	Present tense form	Future tense form
Adjective base + 다	**Adjective base + 던**	**Adjective base + 은/ㄴ**	**Adjective base + 을/ㄹ**
좋다 (to be good;nice)	좋던	좋은	좋을
괜찮다 (to be okay)	괜찮던	괜찮은	괜찮을
많다 (to be many)	많던	많은	많을
예쁘다 (to be pretty)	예쁘던	예쁜	예쁠
싸다 (to be cheap)	싸던	싼	쌀
비싸다 (to be expensive)	비싸던	비싼	비쌀
바쁘다 (to be busy)	바쁘던	바쁜	바쁠
크다 (to be big)	크던	큰	클
유명하다 (to be famous)	유명하던	유명한	유명할
편하다 (to be convenient)	편하던	편한	편할
대단하다 (to be incredible)	대단하던	대단한	대단할

▶**Note 2:** The table below shows the noun-modifying forms of "ㅂ" irregular adjectives.

Dictionary form	Past tense form	Present tense form	Future tense form
Adjective base + 다	Adjective base + 던	Adjective base + ㄴ	Adjective base + ㄹ
쉽다 (to be easy) 어렵다 (to be difficult) 춥다 (to be cold) 덥다 (to be hot) 반갑다 (to be glad) 맵다 (to be spicy)	쉽던 어렵던 춥던 덥던 반갑던 맵던	(쉽 → 쉬우 + ㄴ) 쉬운 어려운 추운 더운 반가운 매운 Rule: 1) ㅂ changes 우 2) ㄴ is attached	(쉽 → 쉬우 + ㄹ) 쉬울 어려울 추울 더울 반가울 매울 Rule: 1) ㅂ changes 우 2) ㄹ is attached

▶**Note 3:** For the noun-modifying forms of ㄹ irregular adjectives, follow the rules, as shown in the table below.

Dictionary form	Past tense form	Present tense form	Future tense form
Adjective base + 다	Adjective base + 던	Adjective base + ㄴ	Adjective base + ㄹ
멀다 (to be far) 길다 (to be long)	멀던 길던	(멀 → 멀 + ㄴ) 먼 (길 → 길 + ㄴ) 긴 Rule: 1) Drop ㄹ 2) ㄴ is attached	(멀 → 멀 + ㄹ) 멀 (길 → 길 + ㄹ) 길 Rule: Drop the second ㄹ

▶**Note 4:** The noun-modifying forms of adjectives ending ~있다/~없다 are shown below:

Dictionary form	Past tense form	Present tense form	Future tense form
Adjective base + 다	Adjective base + 던	Adjective base + 는	Adjective base + 을
재미있다 재미없다 맛있다 맛없다	재미있던 재미없던 맛있던 맛없던	재미있는 재미없는 맛있는 맛없는	재미있을 재미없을 맛있을 맛없을